The Making of the Queen Elizabeth Olympic Park

The Making of the Queen Elizabeth Olympic Park

John Hopkins and Peter Neal

Foreword by Sir Nicholas Serota
Afterword by Professor James Corner

A John Wiley and Sons, Ltd, Publication

ISBN 978-1-118-48727-3 (hardback)
ISBN 978-1-118-49467-7 (ebk)
ISBN 978-1-118-49470-7 (ebk)

Executive Commissioning Editor: Helen Castle
Project Editor: Miriam Swift
Assistant Editor: Calver Lezama

Cover design, page design and layouts by Jeremy Tilston
Printed in Italy by Printer Trento
Front cover image © Peter Neal
Background back cover and flap image © LOCOG/Anthony Charlton
Three back cover inset images © ODA/Anthony Charlton

JOHN HOPKINS

DEDICATION

*To Rosie and Jack in the hope that
the one planet will be conserved in
their lifetimes.*

*To family and friends too numerous
to mention. You know who you are.*

To LW 143.

ACKNOWLEDGEMENTS

Being project sponsor for the parklands and public realm on behalf of the Olympic Delivery Authority (ODA) was an honour, a privilege and a joy. Chairman Sir John Armitt, the board, Chief Executive Sir David Higgins, directors, fellow project sponsors and all staff deserve the highest accolades for their sheer excellence, dedication and teamwork. It was a unique convergence of some of the best and most creative minds in sustainable development. Especial thanks go to Alison Nimmo, Simon Wright, Jerome Frost, Selina Mason and Phil Askew all of the ODA who supported me throughout. Accolades are also due to the whole CLM team without whom the Park would not have become what it is, particularly Programme Director Ian Galloway and my successive project managers Matt Heal, Sam Stevens and Jackie Roe and their teams. The vast array of stakeholders also deserve much credit for listening carefully and then reacting swiftly, critically and supportively in most cases. Consultants, contractors and suppliers also stepped up to the plate, responding to extraordinary demands and circumstances with skill, expertise, commitment and good grace. Of particular note are Jason Prior and Bill Hanway of EDAW (now AECOM) who led the masterplanning team, and George Hargreaves, Andrew Harland and Neil Mattinson of LDA Design • Hargreaves Associates who led the landscape architect team.

Peter Neal, as the former Head of Public Space at the Commission for Architecture and the Built Environment (CABE), was an advisor to the ODA from its earliest days. But for co-authoring this book, he would be one of the many unsung heroes who worked quietly and extremely effectively in the background. Suffice to say that throughout the trials and tribulations of writing, collating, editing and finalising the book we remain the best of friends and colleagues. The idea for the book was ours, but without the support of Dennis Hone who took over as Chief Executive of the ODA from Sir David Higgins, and of Simon Wright it would not have been written and published. Nor would it have been possible without the time, space and excellent research facilities offered by Professor James Corner, Chair of Landscape Architecture and Dean Marilyn Jordan Taylor at the University of Pennsylvania's School of Design.

Helen Castle, our commissioning editor, was always clear, concise and correct with her invaluable criticism and advice as the manuscript emerged – the book is all the better for it. Simon Wright, Simon Knowles and Andrew Shields checked the manuscript but any errors are those of the authors.

PETER NEAL

DEDICATION

*To Elizabeth and Rosanna with
thanks for your encouragement,
patience and good humour, may
we enjoy parks together for many
years to come.*

ACKNOWLEDGEMENTS

It is a rare opportunity to be involved in creating a new park, and for one the size and stature of the Queen Elizabeth Olympic Park it has been a unique and privileged experience. This has been a project of intense and open collaboration across many teams and individuals. In preparing the interviews for this book, it is clear all have enjoyed and learnt much along this journey.

John Hopkins has acknowledged many who have been central to making this Park what it now is; more are named in the text and there are many others who have played their dedicated part – be it through designing the fine detail, project-managing construction, sourcing plants, planting trees, mixing seeds or cutting the grass – it is a very long list. I am particularly grateful to my colleagues at CABE who gave me the time to be involved at the outset and the CABE Space enablers who shared their expertise in the early stages. I would also like to acknowledge the photographers Anthony Palmer, who enthusiastically and tirelessly shot the Park in all weathers to record its progress, and Edward Denison along with Paul Jennings at the London Organising Committee of the Olympic Games and Paralympic Games (LOCOG) who provided many additional images to tell this story. And finally, thanks to John for his eclectic humour, understanding of the big picture and enthusiasm to share it.

Contents

View from the top of Orbit taken in June 2012 looking north along the City Mill river and the main concourse with patterned paving and halo lights with vertical wind turbines.

FOREWORD

The Making of the Queen Elizabeth Olympic Park

The attraction and, at worst, tolerability of life in urban conglomerates is fundamentally conditioned by the nature of the public realm. In the 19th century, the character of a growing London was established in part by the presence of tree-filled squares and the conversion of Royal Parks into public spaces. The density of New York – that is of Manhattan – is alleviated by Frederick Law Olmsted's creation of a 'natural' Central Park. In Munich, what is described as the largest urban park in the world bears the name 'Englischer Garten'. Each of these cities had the opportunity to preserve space as the city grew, often a hard task achieved only by determined campaigns. However, the creation of new public space within the fabric of an existing city is a much rarer challenge. Short-term economic considerations and existing property values make it difficult even in cities, such as Liverpool, which are shrinking and leaving 'holes' in the urban fabric that would benefit the city and the value of the surrounding land if they were transformed into public open space rather than again built over.

The creation of a new urban park, and especially of a park the size of the Queen Elizabeth Olympic Park in east London, is an opportunity that occurs only once in a generation or even only once in a century. The decision to make the Park, with some major public venues within and on its fringes, the centrepiece of a major urban regeneration project is therefore a bold strategic choice. It has the potential to transform the lives of millions who live in the east of the city and make a dramatic impact on the economy of a part of London that has traditionally served as an entrepôt, a source of labour or a dumping ground for the more wealthy city to the west.

The enormous challenge may be compared with the task facing urban planners and politicians in the period of post-war reconstruction. However, the challenge is heightened because it has come at a moment when public faith in strategic planning has almost evaporated. The creation of the Park has been a £6 billion project involving the removal of power lines, complex negotiations with private and public authorities and a massive construction project. Success demonstrates that the chance could only be seized because there were very clear goals and a determination and rigour in the development of ideas. It was also made possible because strategic decisions about the nature of development in east London had been taken years earlier through work on the Thames Gateway, the Lea Valley, the regeneration of the docks and major infrastructure improvements such as the Jubilee Line. Such long-term strategic thinking is even more vital during periods of economic recession. As we know from the experience of post-war new towns, public investment of this kind is more than repaid by long-term economic, cultural and social return.

That the design and delivery of the Park and the venues was achieved within budget and ahead of time is due in part to this early planning. It is also due to the exceptional work by the team at the Olympic Delivery Authority (ODA) with their consultants, led by David Higgins and John Armitt, setting clear goals and lines of responsibility at the outset, pursuing them with unwavering consistency, but with necessary flexibility when market conditions changed. The completion of a Park in time for the Games and in a form that promises sustainability for the future is a major achievement.

Sir Nicholas Serota

Sir Nicholas Serota has been Director of the Tate since 1988, where he has frequently worked with architects in the creation of new buildings, including Herzog & de Meuron at Tate Modern and currently Caruso St John at Tate Britain and Jamie Fobert at Tate St Ives. A founding commissioner at the Commission for Architecture and the Built Environment, he has been a board member and design champion at the Olympic Delivery Authority since 2006.

The main concourse in the middle of the Park looking towards the Olympic Stadium during the Games in July 2012.

INTRODUCTION

INTRODUCTION

The Power of the Games

The tension was palpable. On 6 July 2005, Jacques Rogge, the President of the International Olympic Committee (IOC), stood in front of the hushed IOC General Assembly in Singapore and slowly opened the envelope. When he declared 'the Games of the 30th Olympiad in 2012 are awarded to the city of ... London', the London 2012 delegation went wild, as did 30,000 people gathered on the other side of the world in front of giant screens in Trafalgar Square, and at similar events across the country. London had hosted the Games twice before – in 1908 and 1948 – but it had never before had to bid. And while the two previous London Games had been staged in west London, this time, support for the bid by Tony Blair and Ken Livingstone, the then Prime Minister and Mayor of London respectively, was predicated on the Games being centred on a new Olympic Park in east London. The power of the Games would be the trigger for investment and regeneration of a neglected part of the city on an epic scale. Ken Livingstone promised to 'deliver a compact and sustainable Olympic Park, which will transform one of London's most neglected areas and re-connect it to the rest of London and to Europe. This will kick-start regeneration in east London, while bringing all parts of the city together to celebrate the unifying force of Olympism.'[1]

Havana, Istanbul, Leipzig, London, Madrid, Moscow, New York City, Paris and Rio de Janeiro had all submitted bids by the 15 July 2003 deadline. On 18 May 2004, following technical evaluations, the IOC reduced this list to just five: London, Madrid, Moscow, New York City and Paris. By 19 November 2004, each city had submitted their candidate files. London's 550-page candidate file – the 'Bible' of the bid – set out how the Games would be delivered, the location of the venues, the political and economic structure, environment, finances, transport, security and detailed plans for the new Park. An IOC inspection team visited each candidate city during February and March 2005, publishing technical evaluations on 6 June 2005. Although these reports did not contain any scores or rankings, Paris was considered the best followed closely by London, but with New York City and Madrid also receiving positive evaluations. Led by Olympian Lord Coe, chairman of the bid company, London went head to head with Paris for the final vote in Singapore, narrowly winning by 54 votes to 50.

The euphoria of the bid team quickly evaporated, however, as they returned from Singapore to the horror of the 7 July central London bombings. The bombings set a very

Celebrations on 6 July 2005 in Trafalgar Square, London as the vast crowd went wild on hearing that London had won the bid to host the Games of the 30th Olympiad.

Greater London with its centre and Canary Wharf coloured yellow (left and right respectively) and Lee Valley Regional Park stretching north in green. (Lee is used when referring to the Regional Park Authority and Lee Navigation; Lea is used when referring to the valley and the river.)

0   5   10km

difficult, challenging and emotional backdrop to the early and urgent preparations in 2005 that were needed to get on with the job of planning and delivering the Games. The overwhelming response of politicians, the bid team and the truly diverse communities of London was to reject violence, and redouble efforts in offering a sincere and warm welcome to all those throughout the world who wished to celebrate sports, arts and culture at a safe, secure and inclusive Games.

London's response to winning the bid was swift and decisive. The London Organising Committee of the Olympic Games and Paralympic Games (LOCOG) was established in October 2005 as a private company owned by the UK Government. LOCOG held the contract with the International Olympic Committee (IOC), and was responsible for preparing and staging the Games. Its funding of £2 billion came mainly from private-sector sources including sponsorship, broadcasting rights, ticket sales and selling merchandise. The Olympic Delivery Authority (ODA) was established in March 2006 as a public body with responsibility to deliver the venues and infrastructure for the Games and their use afterwards, particularly the Park. The ODA's budget was set at £9.3 billion in March 2007.

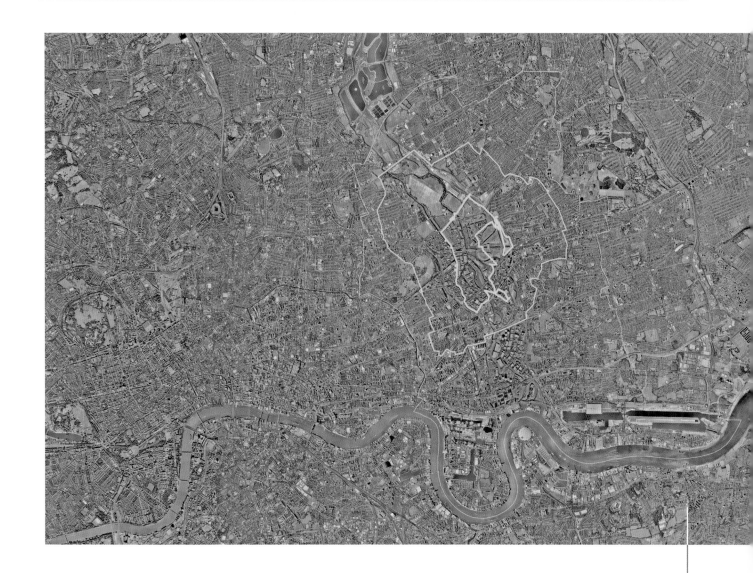

Significantly, 75 pence in every pound it spent would be on permanent venues and infrastructure. In 2009 the Government and the Mayor of London established the Olympic Park Legacy Company (OPLC) – now the London Legacy Development Corporation (LLDC) – with responsibility for continuing the long-term planning, development, management and maintenance of this transformative, sustainable Park and its facilities after the Games.[2] On 7 October 2010, it was announced that Her Majesty The Queen, the British Olympic Association (BOA) and the IOC had given their permission for the Park to be renamed the Queen Elizabeth Olympic Park after the Games. On reopening, east London was to have the unique endorsement of a new Royal Park of international significance to match, among others, Greenwich Park south of the river Thames. For the first time, the legacy of an Olympic and Paralympic Games was secured well before they were held.

London had promised to deliver not only a great Games but also a sustainable legacy. It would use the power of the Games to trigger massive investment in east London creating

The strategic location of the Olympic Park in east London (inner yellow outline) and its inner and outer impact areas within the Lower Lea Valley (middle and outer yellow lines) at the southern end of the Lee Valley Regional Park of which it is a part. The Olympic Park has made a significant contribution to addressing the imbalance of open space on the eastern side of the capital.

Looking north up the Lea Valley over the Olympic Park site before the start of construction. The green area at the centre top of the image is Thornton's Field railway sidings, which became the main concourse of the Olympic Park, with the Olympic Stadium to its left and the Aquatics Centre to its right.

nothing less than a new piece of city. West London had its legacy of royal parks, palaces, playgrounds and accessible rivers. East London, always the workhouse of London with intermingled docks, industry and worker housing, now needed public patronage on a grand scale to shift the city's centre of gravity forever eastward. The vision was extraordinary. The Park would be almost as big as Hyde Park and Kensington Gardens combined, but unlike those preserved tracts of land, it would be created from the largely derelict and contaminated land left from well over a century of industrial use. The site chosen for the Park was in the Lower Lea Valley – the cradle of the industrial revolution in London. The valley had been home, variously, to a gin distillery, tanneries and chemical works. Petrol was invented there, as was the first plastic. The Park would emulate Victoria Park, just a short distance from the site. As one of the world's first public parks, opened in 1845, over time it improved the environment and the health of the predominantly working poor of the area, created the context for development, enhanced land and property values, and provided for recreation and education.

The Park would do all this and more. It would be socially and economically sustainable – providing both private and affordable housing, improving the education and training of local people, their health and well-being, and increasing job opportunities. It would be environmentally sustainable, minimising waste and the use of energy, materials and potable water. It would have a wonderful green and blue heart of restored rivers and waterways, wetlands, woodlands, lawns and innovative meadows surrounded by sports venues, a school, shops, a transport hub and the entire infrastructure required for 10,000 homes – all as a legacy of the Games. It would rekindle the great British traditions for integrating public park, landscape, city design and engineering. It would be the largest construction project in Europe, twice the size of Heathrow's Terminal Five, the UK's last biggest construction project, and be built in half the time. It would demonstrate how to design and build while limiting negative impacts on people and the environment, and at the same time promoting economic activity, training and job opportunities for all members of the community. This was not to be an island-like Canary Wharf, just five kilometres (three miles) to the south of the Park, that benefited the financial few, but an integrated piece of city woven into the existing social and economic fabric.

Our unsustainable lifestyles have meant that for many decades we have been eating into the Earth's capital rather than living off its interest. Although patterns of consumption vary significantly in different parts of the world, if everyone lived as Europeans do, we would need the resources of three planets to survive – in the United States it is five planets. To ensure that the Games and their legacy would be sustainable, the One Planet Living organisations, WWF and BioRegional, helped to draw up commitments that would become a central driver for planning and designing the Games.[3] WWF works worldwide to stop the degradation of the planet's natural environment. BioRegional is an entrepreneurial charity that initiates and delivers practical solutions to help communities live within their fair share of the Earth's resources. They work on a range of practical projects, including BedZed, a sustainable, mixed-use development in south London designed and built in conjunction with Peabody, a social housing landlord; and Middlesbrough and Sutton, which have been accredited by BioRegional as 'One Planet Regions'.

A One Planet approach supported the aspirations of the IOC's Sport for Sustainable Development and the Olympic Games Global Impact initiative, which provides an objective analysis after each Games.[4] It would not only help the IOC move towards sustainable Games, but also articulate and define in practical terms London's sustainability objectives for the Games and their legacy.

The unique power of the Games draws together hundreds of thousands of athletes, spectators and officials, and over four billion television viewers worldwide to celebrate sports, arts and culture. It is one of those rare occasions when we can have a visceral sense of being part of a global community that, with all the rights and responsibilities this entails, will be crucial if 9.22 billion people – the United Nations predicted peak population by 2075 – are to learn to live together equitably on our one, finite planet. The power of the Games, with the Park as an exemplar of sustainable development, is to move us a step closer to understanding our place within the global community. The Park demonstrates a step on the way to delivering sustainable development, and the consequential social, economic and environmental security this should bring.

This book tells the story of how the Park was planned, designed and delivered by the ODA, along with a multitude of designers and contractors, up to the Games and the subsequent transformation of the Park immediately following the Games ready for development in legacy. It focuses on the Park itself, the landscape – the parklands and public realm at the heart of the Games.[5] It describes how the Park evolves one of Britain's perhaps greatest contributions to world culture: the public park. How the Park draws together Britain's equally influential traditions for planning and for infrastructure, city, landscape and garden design. And how these were all brought together in an utterly unique way to deliver an exemplary sustainable development. It is about the making of a new piece of city that, through aligned political and design visions, delivered global and local priorities.

It describes how One Planet Living principles were embedded throughout the masterplanning, design and construction of the Park, how targets were set, and how performance was independently monitored. It is a story that celebrates the successes of the ODA, notes the challenges and difficulties, logs the lessons learned and defines new standards for sustainable development. It is a story that, like those of the great Olympians and Paralympians, should resonate with people and professionals across the world who seek to find new ways to create and convert communities capable of living equitably within the resources of one planet.

The story is set out chronologically, starting with the bid and concluding with 'A Walk in the Park' and the lessons learned. Chapter One, 'Start with the Park', describes how strategic planning on an epic scale for the Thames Gateway and east London supported a similarly epic vision for the Park, underpinned by legacy objectives and One Planet Living principles. Chapter Two, 'Delivering the Park', describes the strategies, policies, targets and governance arrangements that were critical to the successful planning, design, management and monitoring of the delivery of the Park – which was completed in just five years, on time, within budget, a year ahead of the Games, under the watchful eyes of Government, the press, the public and the IOC. Chapter Three, 'Planning and Designing the Park', describes the refinement of the masterplan and the finalisation of design briefs written in conjunction with multiple stakeholders, including local communities. It then describes how the utilities, roads, bridges, structures, venues and parklands were designed, often concurrently, requiring sophisticated computer modelling and an extraordinary level of cooperation and coordination by designers and contractors. Chapter Four, 'Constructing the Park', describes how the site was secured, habitats and species translocated, noxious weeds eradicated, buildings demolished and tunnels excavated for undergrounding the overhead power lines. It goes on to describe how contaminated ground was remediated, and a completely new infrastructure of utilities, roads, bridges, parklands, temporary and permanent venues, and the Olympic and Paralympic Village was constructed. Chapter Five, 'A Walk in the Park', describes the Park during the Games and how it will be transformed ready for legacy. Recognising that the Park provides a new model and step on the way towards achieving sustainable development, lessons learned are highlighted for future development and regeneration programmes.

In 2005, when London won the right to host the Games, the world economy was thriving. The unforeseen global market crash of 2008 caused significant additional financial challenges for the project, and deep soul-searching on the priorities for public investment. The ODA had to seek government approval to use some of its contingency to take on the funding of the Olympic and Paralympic Village, which was originally intended to be a public-private partnership. Recognising that large-scale city planning programmes such as the Park need to ride out not one, but several economic cycles, Alexander Garvin in his seminal book *The American City: what works, what doesn't* defined successful city planning as 'public action that generates a desirable, widespread, and sustained private market reaction'.[6] The Park is a classic example of public investment in infrastructure intended to trigger private market reaction sustained over time. The lesson of public investment in the British New Towns of the 20th century is apposite: all public borrowings required to fund them were repaid by 1999.[7] Time will tell if the Park is able to achieve a similar return to the public purse, as well as fully meeting its social, economic and environmental goals, particularly in changing economic circumstances.

The wetland bowl on the river Lea in the north east of the Park with the Velodrome in the background during the Games in July 2012.

CHAPTER ONE

CHAPTER ONE

Start with the Park

It was no accident that a new kind of park lay at the heart of London's bid for the Games in 2012, or that it was located in a largely underdeveloped and contaminated part of east London. A park based on One Planet Living principles of sustainable development would help to achieve many of London's long-term strategic planning and national policy objectives. It would also justify significant public investment in permanent venues and infrastructure to provide a lasting legacy for existing and future generations. Furthermore, it would contribute to the policy objective of the International Olympic Committee (IOC) to move towards sustainable Games.

Olympic and Paralympic Games can provide Host Cities with a rare opportunity to invest in large-scale infrastructure. More often than not this involves the creation of some form of Olympic Park. Beijing 2008 created a monumental campus, a park bound within it. Athens 2004 had architect Santiago Calatrava revamp an existing sports campus comprising major venues and other sports facilities. Sydney 2000 expanded Bicentennial Park through the conversion of an industrial wasteland into a connected sequence of wetlands, wildlife corridors and shoreline as the setting for its Olympic Park. Centennial Olympic Park is credited with the revitalisation of the surrounding urban area following Atlanta 1996. Barcelona 1992 – recognised as one of the most successful urban regeneration projects of the late 20th century – renewed Montjuïc as its Olympic Park, but more importantly reconnected to its waterfront through the development of the Olympic and Paralympic Village, new beaches, a promenade and a port. Munich 1972 converted a redundant airfield into its Olympic Park with a dramatic new topography and lake providing a contrasting setting for architect Frei Otto's venues, many of which were retained and continue to serve the city's citizens. Key members of the Olympic Delivery Authority (ODA) and its

The Olympic Park in Munich, Germany, built for the 1972 Games. It took five years to construct and is a classic example of a unified and homogeneous architectural and landscape design. It has become a popular and heavily used park, but at 85 hectares is much smaller than London's 250ha Olympic Park, reflecting the growth in scale of the Games since then.

The Olympic Park in Sydney, Australia, built for the 2000 Games. The entire parklands total over 450ha and are one of Australia's largest urban parklands, including existing regional and national parks and former industrial and military sites that were remediated for the Games.

consultant teams visited many of these past examples. They wanted to understand the lineage not only of Olympic Parks, but also of the great British tradition of public parks, and for combining city, engineering, architectural, landscape and garden design. The ODA commissioned landscape historian David Lambert to tell the fascinating story of the emergence of the public park in Britain, and the role and importance of landscape in the planning and design of British towns and cities, and what this might mean for the planning and design of a new kind of park for the 21st century – what was to become the Queen Elizabeth Olympic Park.[1]

A GREAT BRITISH TRADITION

The first parks in the world designed specifically for public use were in England. They were designed in response to unprecedented industrialisation and urbanisation, the public health crisis that ensued, and a pressing need for recreational facilities. They were also designed to create the context for development and enhance land values. Derby Arboretum was the first, opened in 1840. London's Victoria Park, opened in 1845, is just

a 15-minute walk from the London 2012 Olympic Park, and was specifically intended to halt migration to west and north London following the recent construction of railways. It succeeded over time, becoming an exemplary neighbourhood park, and underwent a major refurbishment ready for 2012. Birkenhead Park, Liverpool, was opened in 1847, and is often cited as the inspiration for New York's Central Park that was opened a decade later.

Hyde Park, Regent's Park, St James's, Greenwich and London's other great Royal Parks characterise the city. All but Regent's Park are conserved royal hunting grounds with public uses added over time. Parks are common ground, accessible to all, where people can meet, greet, volunteer, hold fairs and festivals and create their sense of community. They can have quiet places for contemplation, active areas for recreation, and can give a place a sense of identity by linking it to its culture and history. They can be an educational resource for both adults and children, providing inspiration for art, or an outdoor laboratory for the study of the environment and natural sciences. They can be havens for wildlife, providing a link between the urban and abstract, the environmental and natural. Parks also improve health and well-being, offering recreational facilities for the use of communities. One of the arguments for Victoria Park made in 1839 by the Registrar of Births, Deaths and

Victoria Park in east London was first opened in 1845. It was one of the world's first public parks, embracing social, health and amenity objectives that are similar to those for all public parks of today, including the Olympic Park. One major difference is the overarching sustainability objectives that are embedded within the plans for London 2012.

Marriages for Bethnal Green was that 'a park in the East End of London would probably diminish the annual deaths by several thousands ... and add several years to the lives of the entire population.'[2] Natural England, the Government's adviser, documented the role of the natural environment in maintaining healthy lifestyles in its 2009 publication *Our Natural Health Service*. It noted that people who 'lived furthest from public parks were 27 per cent more likely to be overweight or obese'; and that 'children able to play in natural green space gained 2.5 kilos less per year than children who didn't have such opportunities'. They estimated that 'for every £1 spend on establishing healthy walking schemes, the NHS could save £7.18 in the cost of treating conditions such as heart disease, stroke and diabetes'; and that 'if every household in England were provided with good access to quality green space it could save an estimated £2.1 billion in healthcare costs.'[3]

Parks are also economic assets, creating attractive areas for people to move to and businesses to invest in, uplifting property values in the process. For example, within 15 years of New York's Central Park being completed, property values within two and a half blocks increased nine times while in the rest of New York City they only doubled.[4] Another North American example is Chattanooga, Tennessee, where, since the early 1980s,

Hyde Park in central London was first opened to the public in the 1630s. It was one of the earliest Royal Parks and was originally a hunting ground for Henry VIII before being established by Charles II as a forum for military reviews and fashionable promenading.

US$356 million has been invested by the public and private sectors in redeveloping the town's riverfront. In the eight years between 1988 and 1996 the number of businesses and full-time jobs in the district more than doubled, and assessed property values went up 127 per cent. Over the same period, the annual combined city and county property tax revenues went up US$592,000, an increase of 99 per cent.[5]

In response to continuing urban squalor and overcrowding caused by industrialisation at the beginning of the 20th century, Ebenezer Howard published *Garden Cities of Tomorrow*. Garden cities were intended to be self-sustaining communities that provided energy, food, work and civic activities, and were connected by public transport – the first conceptualisation of 'a balanced ecological town'.[6] Public parks, open spaces and the public realm were the 'formative structure' of the garden cities, the most notable example of which is Letchworth, designed by Parker and Unwin, the leading architects of the movement. Small-scale communal space, pedestrian routes, street planting, a green belt and a coherent green network inspired town planning around the world. The evolution of town and country planning continued in the first half of the 20th century and led to what landscape architect Hal Moggridge termed 'landscape without boundaries'.[7] Examples include Sir Patrick Abercrombie's proposals for a connected park system in Sheffield, and his similar scheme for the County of London, which proposed connecting the Thames to the green belt. The latter laid the foundation for London's Green Grid to which the Park contributes. Later in the 20th century, at Harlow New Town, Sir Frederick Gibberd based his town plan on open spaces running from the rural edge to its centre. This led to the idea of what landscape architect Sir Geoffrey Jellicoe memorably termed 'the city as total landscape', probably best seen in the new town of Milton Keynes.[8]

With the growing ecological awareness of the last 40 years, the role of strategic thinking to support individual parks has been recognised as critical, and this has led to a greater understanding of parks as part of greenspace systems and ecological processes. The vision for the South Essex Green Grid was 'an environmental infrastructure that promotes the establishment and management of appropriate character settings and provides the context for development over the next 100 years ... a living system threading through the urban and rural landscape providing clean and healthy air, food, water, energy, minerals and materials and beautiful places to escape, relax, learn and enjoy for existing and future communities and investors.' It recognised that this was 'a major and radical vision which placed landscape at the heart of the development process, and environmental process at the heart of sustainable development and the economy.'[9] The Government appointed both architect Sir Terry Farrell and the Commission for Architecture and the Built Environment (CABE) to develop this vision, drawing together all the Green Grids into a framework for the Thames Gateway, a national government priority for regeneration stretching 70 kilometres (40 miles) from Tower Bridge to the mouth of the estuary. The Thames Gateway Parklands is an ambitious vision of a multi-functional 'working landscape'.[10]

While the Park will be measured against the timeless objectives of public park, city and landscape design, there were two other overarching objectives: sustainability and legacy. This would be the first Olympic Park where sustainability and legacy underpinned everything – location, funding, masterplan and the design of the venues and infrastructure. It would be the first that was masterplanned 'backwards' from a vision of the Park some 25 years hence where vibrant, mixed communities would live, work, play and stay. Using One Planet Living principles to drive sustainability, it would be a Park where the consumption of energy and water and the generation of waste were all minimised not only in its use, but in its construction as well. All the homes would be super-efficient, light and airy, and with a high proportion made available to people of all income levels. There would be an academy catering for children from kindergarten to sixth form available from day one. Public transport would connect neighbourhoods as easily to Europe as to the rest of London. World-class sports venues for swimming, cycling, hockey, tennis, athletics and more would be on the doorstep. Walking or cycling to and through new and existing neighbourhoods – and beautiful parklands and gardens with woodlands, wetlands and meadows teeming with wildlife – would be easy and natural. Parkland cafes would serve coffee and cakes,

Old Ford Lock at the southern edge of the Park on the river Lee Navigation. Named after a natural ford that originally crossed the uncanalised river Lea, the lock was at the heart of a key transport corridor that served the industrial expansion of the area, proving an important commercial network linking the Thames to Hertfordshire and Essex.

boating and kayaking would take place on the waterways. There would be festivals, fairs and events put on to suit all ages, tastes and interests. Allotments and community gardens would provide locally grown food. This new 21st-century, sustainable Park at the heart of the Games would see investment in city-scale design and infrastructure, developing those great British traditions not only for public parks and town planning, but also for engineering as exemplified by, among others, Thomas Telford, Isambard Kingdom Brunel and Joseph Bazalgette who respectively built fully functional infrastructure to connect and serve local communities of the time.

WHY EAST LONDON?

The Romans sailed up the river Thames and founded Londinium around AD 50. It grew and prospered, overtaking Colchester as the capital of Roman Britain. Since then, the Thames has powered London's economy and global outreach. The 'East End' extends from the walls of the City of London, built by the Romans around AD 200, to the river Lea which the Park straddles. 'East London' is not the same as the 'East End': it is the broader area extending now almost to the M25 motorway that girdles the greater London metropolis. Before the 19th century the eastern walls of the City of London were dotted with a series of hamlets – hence the borough of 'Tower Hamlets' that borders both the City of London and the Park.[11] Powered by industrialisation, the City of London began to develop rapidly, and in the late 19th century overcrowding became a serious problem. St Katharine Docks, designed by Thomas Telford and opened in 1828, were the first to be built on the Thames. Their construction displaced more than 11,000 inhabitants and, alongside construction of the railways, exacerbated overcrowding in the city leading to further expansion eastwards.

As trade increased exponentially, and ships grew in size, successive docks were built eastwards to accommodate them. Wapping, followed by Limehouse, East and West India, Millwall, Surrey and the Royal Docks were built and all required labour. The need was for casual labour only, which was also poorly paid and, as a consequence, crowded slums arose without sanitation or water. Charles Dickens wrote of the desperate and destitute in *Oliver Twist*, *Our Mutual Friend* and other novels, based on his experiences of the East End where his father had a sail-making shop. The Peabody Trust, the modern-day partner with BioRegional for the BedZed One Planet Living development in south London, was founded by the eponymous American philanthropist in 1862 to clear the slums and provide housing for the poor. The arrival of Huguenot weavers at the end of the 17th century presaged successive waves of Irish, Jewish, Russian and, most recently, Bangladeshi and other immigrants to east London. Each wave contributed to the rich cultural melange – one cannot now fully experience the East End without a visit to Brick Lane's curry houses, tellingly portrayed in Monica Ali's novel named after the much-visited street. East London continues its historic role of accepting immigrants from far and near. It has one of the most diverse populations anywhere in the world, with more than 160

languages spoken within the boroughs surrounding the Park. Just under eight per cent of the UK's population is from non-white ethnic groups, compared to around 30 per cent of London's, and 40 per cent of the population of the boroughs surrounding the Park. Walking east London can feel like walking the world.

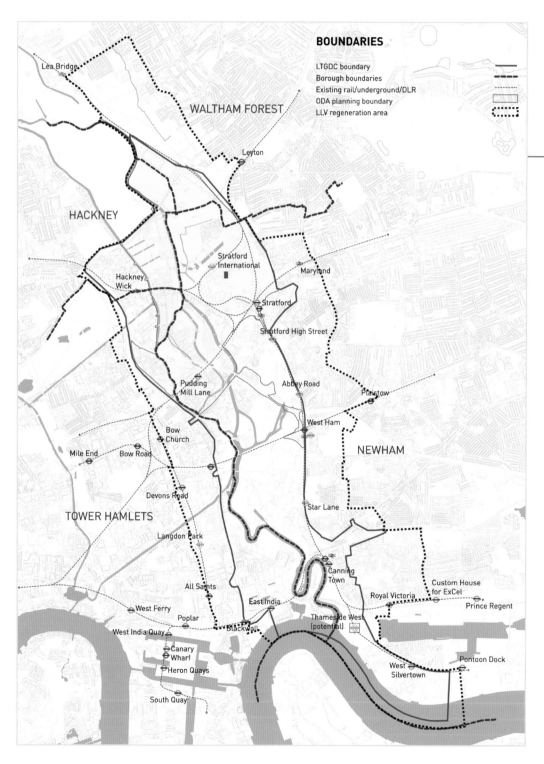

BOUNDARIES

LTGDC boundary
Borough boundaries
Existing rail/underground/DLR
ODA planning boundary
LLV regeneration area

The Park located within the Lower Lea Valley Opportunity Area Planning Framework (LLV OAPF) area, published in January 2007. The designated site for the Park is at the intersection of four London Boroughs: Hackney and Tower Hamlets to the west and Waltham Forest and Newham to the east.

Poverty and overcrowding remained problems into the 20th century, which the London County Council tried to address through the construction of large estates of council housing. During the Second World War the docks, railways and industry in the area were a constant target for aerial bombardments, devastating large sections. The Royal Docks were the last to be closed within London in 1980, ceding to Tilbury Docks 18 kilometres (11 miles) downstream of the City of London. The construction of the London Gateway port 40km (25 miles) east of the City began in 2010. One of the biggest in the world, capable of handling the largest container ships, it reinforces the importance of the Thames, its estuary and London's pre-eminent role in the national economy. The continuing social, economic and environmental problems of the area saw the establishment of a succession of Government-funded public corporations intended to regenerate east London and its docklands: the London Docklands Development Corporation in 1981, wound up in 1998, and the London Thames Gateway Development Corporation (LTGDC), founded in 2005, and whose functions were being transferred to the London Legacy Development Corporation and to the boroughs by the coalition Government from 2011.

The Park sits at the junction of the boroughs of Tower Hamlets, Newham, Hackney and Waltham Forest. At the time of the bid, the first three of these boroughs were in the most deprived five per cent in the country. Nearly 30 per cent of all households in these boroughs were workless, compared to 18 per cent of all households in England, and nearly 20 per cent in London. Each had only about 55 per cent of their population of working age in employment. There was a continuing housing shortage and the quality of the stock was poor, with a higher than average number of homes being rented social housing. The link between poor-quality jobs, casual labour and poor housing continued more than 100 years after the publication of Dickens's novels and Peabody's philanthropy. More than 60 per cent of the households within the area were flats, maisonettes or apartments, and therefore less likely to have access to their own private garden. A quarter of the land within the area of the Park had poor access to parkland and nature.[12] Education standards were significantly lower than the UK average. Crime rates were higher, 'postcode wars' prevalent. Fewer than 10 per cent of the population was aged over 65 in three of the boroughs, compared to a national average of 16 per cent. But there was a high proportion of young people, 39 per cent of the people aged less than 35 years, compared to a national average of 31 per cent. The high numbers of young people compounded and concentrated the impact of high youth unemployment, creating a sometimes febrile atmosphere, evidenced by the summer 2011 riots in parts of the area and in similar communities around London and the UK. The general deprivation of the area had a stark impact on people's health, illustrated by a shocking statistic: in 2005, an eight-stop journey east on the Jubilee line from Westminster represented a seven-year drop in average male life expectancy; in Westminster it was 77.7 years, in Canning Town it was 70.7 years.[13]

In 1858 the river Thames was little more than an open sewer. In response to the 'great stink' of that year, which caused the closure of the Houses of Parliament, an act was passed and Bazalgette was commissioned to design and implement a completely new sewer network for the metropolis. It was one of the great engineering wonders of the world comprising 1,800km (1,100 miles) of underground brick sewers, and a similar length of street sewers. Abbey Mills pumping station adjacent to the Park was one of four across London that were veritable palaces of elaborate, decorative ironwork. The whole system still functions today, and the Great Northern Outfall Sewer crosses the Park and its waterways. On top of Bazalgette's brick-lined Great Northern Outfall Sewer tunnel is the Greenway, a

This aggregate works on the river Lea close to the Park reflects much of the area's heavy industrial past that made a significant contribution to defining the environmental character and identity of the town and riverscape of east London.

Fly-tipping on a vacant site within the Park boundary prior to construction. At the start of the project many sites were blighted by the impact of high-voltage power lines and pylons along with significant levels of pollution, contamination and illegally dumped waste.

A light industrial building supplies site adjacent to the river Lea in 2003. Located south of the Park site, such land uses have typified the industrial and commercial activities in the Lower Lea Valley for many decades.

The infamous 'fridge mountain' within the Park site in 2003. Located adjacent to the Waterworks river, the site is now home to the Aquatics Centre.

The Manor Garden Allotments located in the middle of the Park site, photographed in May 2007. The idyllic site was established over 100 years ago, and its removal was one of the most difficult and controversial decisions London 2012 had to make. The ODA worked closely with the Manor Gardening Society on the design of the new allotments that will be relocated within the Park.

footpath and cyclepath connecting Victoria Park to Beckton and the Thames. Upgrading part of the Greenway was a key project for the Park. Bazalgette's system is a great example of multifunctional infrastructure that the Victorians were so good at – another is the Embankment, which provides a promenade and road adjacent to the Thames, an underground railway and a utilities corridor. The Park emulates this multifunctional focus on long-term legacy –with a 21st-century sustainability sensibility.

The Lower Lea Valley, within which the Park sits, was a cradle of the industrial revolution in London. The legacy of over 150 years of use and misuse was post-industrial dereliction, and inaccessible waterways. Power lines, under-used railway sidings, abandoned buildings and waterways characterised the area. The infamous 'fridge mountain' – thousands of

(continued on page 38)

THE BID AS CATALYST FOR REGENERATION

Alison Nimmo CBE

Director of Design and Regeneration, Olympic Delivery Authority, 2006-2011

For the bid, the then Mayor of London Ken Livingstone had a clear vision to use the London 2012 Olympic Games and Paralympic Games to achieve a radical transformation of east London and the Lower Lea Valley. There had been numerous plans and good ideas over many years, but none had come to fruition. We needed a big-scale masterplanning approach and the Games could provide the catalyst, generating the expertise, money and focus to compress more than 25 years of work into just seven, accelerating this transformation. There was strong support from the Prime Minister, Tony Blair, alongside Gordon Brown, the Chancellor of the Exchequer, who committed to financially underwrite the bid on behalf of the Treasury.

The bid was carefully and professionally orchestrated with an ambition that placed sustainability and long-term legacy at its heart. Taking young local students to Singapore for the final round of voting and playing the next-generation card was a compelling illustration that contributed to winning the argument. We wanted to promote an image of hosting the 'Games in the Park'. While capitalising on London's and Britain's great tradition of urban parks, with the triathlon in Hyde Park and equestrian events in Greenwich Park, we never intended to follow a Victorian or Royal Park model for the main Olympic Park site. We wanted to reinvent a park for a modern context that would work on many different levels. Designed for 100 years, yet capable of accommodating around 250,000 visitors per day during the Games, it would be fun and intensive, but also a relaxing environment. The bid projected an image of a landscape that would be of a different

East London school children with the athlete Daley Thompson celebrating London's winning bid in Singapore on 6 July 2005.

Looking south over the Olympic Stadium 'island site' towards Canary Wharf in April 2007 just as demolition and clearance commenced. The Aquatics Centre on the left of the image was the first to start on site.

Construction of the new Three Mills Lock on the Prescott Channel in September 2008. It enabled around-the-clock access to the Park for construction barges.

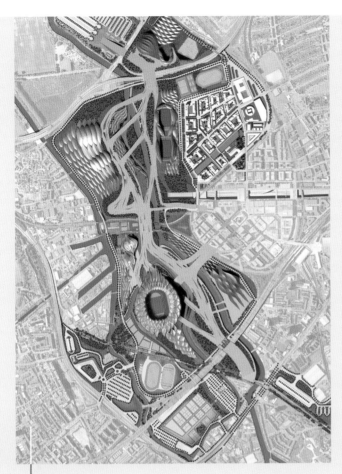

Illustrative masterplan for the Games pre-bid planning application prepared by the EDAW Consortium in 2004.

muscular character – that was a strong concept from day one – and that would leave a new park as a gift to London after the Games.

On joining the bid team in December 2003, my first job was to review the draft masterplan for the planning application ensuring the viability of the bid proposals. The London Development Agency (LDA) did a huge amount of work in the early years in pulling together the masterplans, assembling the site and undertaking the initial stages of remediation. Probably not enough credit has been given to that immense task. But the LDA was not the vehicle to deliver the regeneration and development programme for the Games and legacy. Most Games have been delivered in quite a formulaic way using the Organising Committees of the Olympic Games (OCOGs) which liaise directly

with the International Olympic Committee, and steer the operational phase at Games time. London needed a separate vehicle to build the venues and drive the complex regeneration of the site, and so the London Olympics Bill established the Olympic Delivery Authority (ODA) in April 2006 to lead this work. After the Games, the site and the legacy programme would then pass on to the Olympic Park Legacy Company (renamed the London Legacy Development Corporation). It is the first time that a legacy vehicle has been set up pre-Games. We have been able to maintain continuity between the organisations by seconding and transferring LDA and ODA staff and expertise across to the Legacy Company.

Whilst Sydney put the environment at the heart of their Games, we took a 'total sustainability' approach for London. It was not just a matter of what we built, but how we built it. The reuse of rainwater, the procurement of timber, the use of the railhead to bring 70 per cent of materials by weight onto the site, the whole social inclusion and access agenda, climate change, biodiversity, reinstating Prescott [Three Mills] Lock with British Waterways to turn the river from tidal to locked, improvements in public transport, and the investment in wider connectivity with new bridges and refurbished towpaths to encourage walking and cycling – the key has been the total approach.

The geography was complex with a mosaic of mixed uses, waterways and lost landscapes of allotments and cycle tracks. The site straddled four local authority boundaries and had become everyone's backyard and dumping ground. So there was a lot of heavy lifting during the early stages of the programme, removing the blight of the power lines by placing them underground, clearing away the scrapyards and the infamous 'fridge mountain'. Many people haven't really got their head around the scale of the transformation. But the Games have provided the mechanism to mend, restore and reconnect the site, creating a new heart and a new piece of the city in east London.

discarded fridges piled high – was here. Noxious and invasive weeds had taken hold. There were only three roads connecting neighbourhoods either side of the valley, which was a tear in the fabric of east London. Despite the many unappealing features of this landscape, it was not without some charm and a sense of post-industrial melancholy. Also, the Manor Gardening Society allotments that lay in the middle of the future Park were idyllic. Accessed only by a narrow bridge across the river Lea, they were a wonderfully eclectic community haven in the middle of a chaotic landscape. A largely utilitarian and polluted land within sight and sound of the City of London, and in the shadow of the towers of Canary Wharf, where the average annual salary was £100,000[14] compared to Stratford's £24,000.[15] High worklessness, poor housing, lack of jobs, education, health and access to parks, but with availability of land, and a continuing national and metropolitan priority for regeneration: this is why east London, and Stratford in particular, was chosen as the location for the Park.

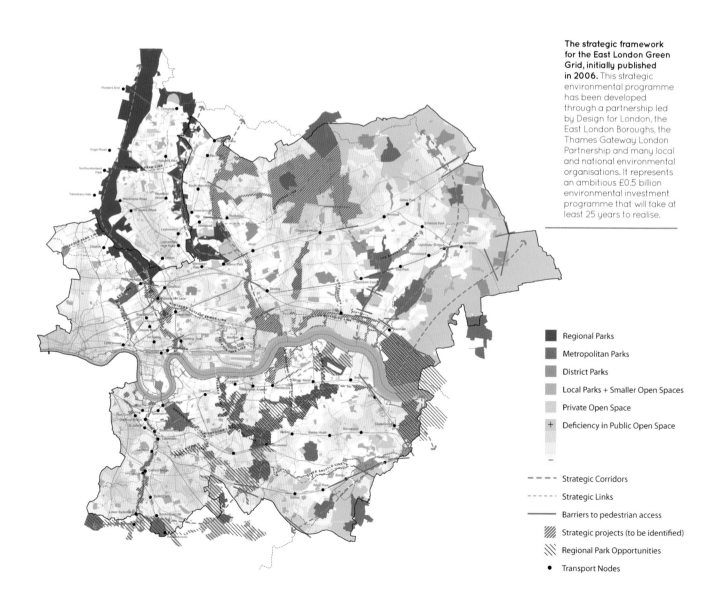

The strategic framework for the East London Green Grid, initially published in 2006. This strategic environmental programme has been developed through a partnership led by Design for London, the East London Boroughs, the Thames Gateway London Partnership and many local and national environmental organisations. It represents an ambitious £0.5 billion environmental investment programme that will take at least 25 years to realise.

■ Regional Parks

■ Metropolitan Parks

■ District Parks

Local Parks + Smaller Open Spaces

Private Open Space

+ Deficiency in Public Open Space

– – – Strategic Corridors

----- Strategic Links

——— Barriers to pedestrian access

▨ Strategic projects (to be identified)

▧ Regional Park Opportunities

● Transport Nodes

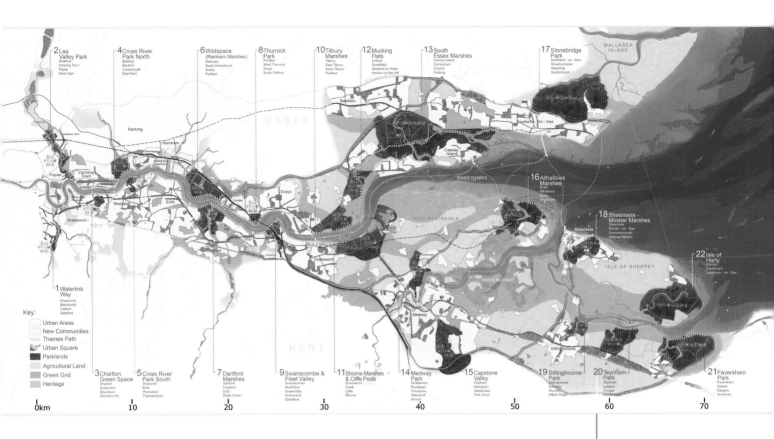

Key:
- Urban Areas
- New Communities
- Thames Path
- Urban Square
- Parklands
- Agricultural Land
- Green Grid
- Heritage

STRATEGIC PLANNING AND REGENERATION

The planning, location, design and development of the Park cannot be fully appreciated without an understanding of the UK's and London's planning system. A whole host of mutually supportive development plans, policies and guidance notes cascade from the national to the local level.[16] The Government's Sustainable Communities Plan provided the overarching context for the preparation of spatial plans by statutory planning authorities. Environmental impact assessments were required for all planning applications, and, alongside the design and quality of the built and natural environment, were assessed against a series of national Planning Policy Guidance notes and Planning Policy Statements addressing key issues such as Delivering Sustainable Development, Green Belts, Housing, Biodiversity, Geological Conservation and Development, Open Space, Sport & Recreation and Flood Risk.[17] Additionally, a number of Government agencies had statutory responsibilities for environmental protection, particularly the Environment Agency with a remit that included waste and protecting the quality of air, land and water; English Nature (now Natural England) responsible for conservation of biodiversity; and English Heritage responsible for the historic environment. The initial planning application for the Park was approved in October 2004 to underpin the validity of the bid. To ensure that legacy was embedded in the planning process, two masterplans were prepared to support the bid: one for the Games, and one for legacy. The four Host Boroughs within which the Park was located approved these applications at a joint session at City Hall. This was followed by the Mayor's approval then the Government's ratification. The potentially

Terry Farrell and Partners' proposals for the Thames Gateway Parklands, published in 2008. Centered on the corridor of the Thames Estuary and including the Olympic Park on the western boundary, the Parklands provide an environmental investment framework to create a network of accessible, high-quality and fully functional landscapes to support the Gateway's rich cultural and biodiverse assets.

fissile approvals process was hard fought. Inevitably there were vested interests, patches to be defended, deals to be done, costs and benefits calculated, and risks and returns weighed by all participants.

Not only would the Park be one of Europe's largest construction projects, it would also sit within Europe's largest regeneration programme, the previously mentioned Thames Gateway.[18] The M4 motorway corridor west of London is largely fully developed. Green Belt and commuter territories militate against large-scale development to the south and north. Consequently, successive governments have recognised the Gateway as the place for London to expand. With acres of post-industrial land available, and a reasonable level of transport and other infrastructure, it is primed for redevelopment over the long term. The last Government's intention was to deliver 160,000 homes and 225,000 jobs by 2016. The programme is a recognition of the importance of London and the south-east as a key driver of the UK's prosperity. Government also saw that the Park was a key development programme within the Gateway and wanted to ensure that the legacy benefits were exploited and maximised for the local and wider communities there. As noted above, environmental improvement in the Gateway is driven by a series of Green Grid plans that were consolidated in the vision for the Thames Gateway Parklands and aims 'to provide a network of accessible, high-quality and sustainable landscapes and waterways, which capitalise on existing natural, built, historic and cultural assets. It supports their conservation, enhancement and ongoing use. Parklands will boost Thames Gateway's rich biodiversity, strengthen its character and identity, and transform perceptions of the area into it being a great place to live, work and invest in. Parklands will be a key economic driver in the Gateway, encouraging investment and supporting regeneration.'[19]

The location of the Olympic Park at the southern end of the Lee Valley Regional Park that was first designated in 1967. The Regional Park stretches north for 42km (26 miles) into Hertfordshire and Essex. A key strategic role for the Olympic Park is to kick-start the extension and development of the Regional Park south to the river Thames.

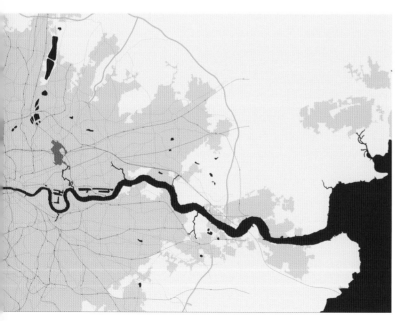

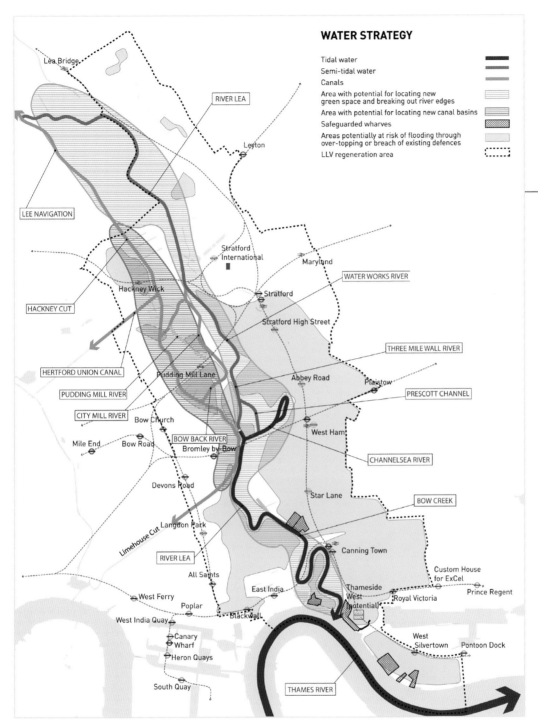

WATER STRATEGY

Tidal water	
Semi-tidal water	
Canals	
Area with potential for locating new green space and breaking out river edges	
Area with potential for locating new canal basins	
Safeguarded wharves	
Areas potentially at risk of flooding through over-topping or breach of existing defences	
LLV regeneration area	

The Water Strategy plan, published in the GLA's Lower Lea Valley Opportunity Area Planning Framework in 2007. The regeneration framework set out a vision for a 'Water City' at the heart of the regeneration including ecological enhancement and re-naturalisation of sections of the waterway system to encourage greater use for living, transportation and recreation.

The Park also sits within the Lee Valley Regional Park, first promoted by Sir Patrick Abercrombie in his Greater London Plan of 1944, which also consolidated London's green belt. Eventually created by Act of Parliament in 1967, the Regional Park is a 40,000-hectare, 42-kilometre (26-mile) long river corridor stretching from Ware in Hertfordshire down to the Thames. In 1963 the Civic Trust was invited to look into the potential for the Lee Valley Regional Park. Remarkably, its report included proposals for an open-plan 'Fun Palace'

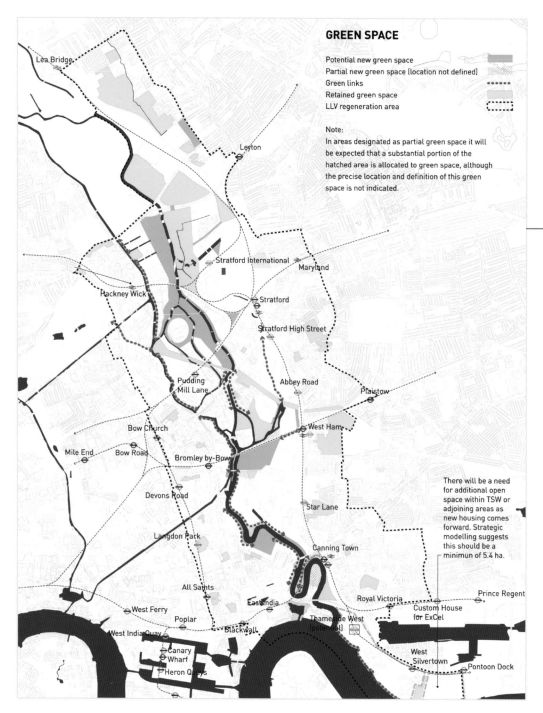

GREEN SPACE

Potential new green space
Partial new green space (location not defined)
Green links
Retained green space
LLV regeneration area

Note:
In areas designated as partial green space it will
be expected that a substantial portion of the
hatched area is allocated to green space, although
the precise location and definition of this green
space is not indicated.

There will be a need
for additional open
space within TSW or
adjoining areas as
new housing comes
forward. Strategic
modelling suggests
this should be a
minimun of 5.4 ha.

**The Green Space
plan, published in the
GLA's Lower Lea Valley
Opportunity Area Planning
Framework in 2007.** The
proposed green space
network in the OAPF
focused on the provision
of at least 130ha of new
public open spaces in
areas of deficiency. The
Olympic Park would
begin the establishment
of a multifunctional
ecological corridor along
the waterways linking the
upper Lee Valley Regional
Park to the Thames and the
East London Green Grid.

where 'people of all ages and interests will find space to enjoy their leisure, to relax or be active, at any time, day or night'. The Park was located on the very site proposed for the 'Fun Palace' envisioned some 50 years earlier![20] The Lee Valley Regional Park Authority owns one third of the Park and it will run and operate the legacy hockey and tennis centre at Eton Manor, the VeloPark, as well as the White Water Centre just to the north of the Park.

The regeneration of east London was a priority of the Mayor's spatial development framework for the metropolis adopted in 2004. The London Plan promoted staging the

Games as a 'major catalyst for change and regeneration in east London, especially the Lea Valley, levering resources, spurring timely completion of already programmed infrastructure investment and leaving a legacy to be valued by future generations'. The Plan recognised that without the Games change would still happen but it would be 'slower, more incremental and less ambitious from a sporting, cultural and environmental perspective'.[21] In other words, the Games would fast-forward regeneration. The Plan set out an integrated social, economic and environmental framework for a 15–20-year period, spearheading London's aim to become an exemplary sustainable world city. It was underpinned by a series of interrelated strategies published between 2001 and 2004 that addressed transport, economic development, biodiversity, air quality, municipal waste management, energy, ambient noise and culture. It noted that the plan for the Park would release the necessary development land for a successful sustainable Games, assure improvements to the open space and network of waterways in the Park and surrounding areas, and require that special attention be paid to long-term flood risk and improving public access for local communities to Lee Valley Regional Park. The East London Green Grid was and remains a unifying green infrastructure framework, a network of interlinked and high-quality open and green spaces, guiding strategic environmental investment intended 'to promote healthy living and community spirit through access to recreational and cultural opportunities, while at the same time promoting biodiversity and acting as a "green lung" for east London'. As part of the wider Thames Gateway Parklands vision, it will result in a connected ecological infrastructure for east London and the estuary.

The final piece in this complicated jigsaw puzzle of planning and environmental policies underpinning the masterplanning and design of the Park was the Lower Lea Valley Opportunity Area Planning Framework (OAPF). It was the key supporting document setting the planning framework for the Park that was developed in parallel with the bid. The decision to bid for the Games focused attention on what could be achieved in the Lower Lea Valley and addressed the capacity of the area for change, identifying the optimum scale of development and confirming the location of the Park. The OAPF took national and London Plan policies as a starting point, and concluded that there was capacity for 50,000 new jobs in the Lower Lea Valley, between 30,000 and 40,000 new homes (at least 44 per cent family housing), 10,000 of which would be in the Park. The overall vision was to create 'a vibrant, high-quality and sustainable mixed-use city district, that is fully integrated into the urban fabric of London and is set within an unrivalled landscape that contains new high-quality parkland and a unique network of waterways'.[22]

TOWARDS ONE PLANET LIVING

There is no doubt that the UK and London's unique planning system provided an unrivalled and comprehensive foundation for the planning, location, design, development and legacy of the Park for the bid. Winning the Games would indeed 'kick-start' the regeneration of an area of London that needed it, and had been planned and acted on for decades. However, the bid needed a sharper focus and credibility on sustainability. The legislative framework for delivering sustainable developments, and the setting and monitoring of targets, have developed at an ever-increasing rate. Despite the publication of *The Limits to Growth* in 1972,[23] the Brundtland Commission report *Our Common Future* in 1987,[24] and the 1992 Earth Summit in Rio de Janeiro, Brazil, many remain increasingly alarmed at the continuing, exponential depletion of finite natural capital resources, and the consequent degradation and pollution of the environment. Rio+20 did little to alleviate that alarm.

One Planet Living elegantly and simply states the obvious: we have to live within the capacity of one planet. It is an initiative developed by the WWF and BioRegional.[25] It recognises that present levels of consumption and waste production in the developed world are outstripping the productive and absorptive capacity of the planet. Europeans use three planets' worth of resources, North Americans use five planets' worth to sustain their lifestyles. One Planet Living promotes the development of sustainable communities that provide a high quality of life but use only their fair share of the Earth's resources. It

Zero carbon		making buildings more energy efficient and delivering all energy with renewable technologies
Zero waste		reducing waste, reusing where possible, and ultimately sending zero waste to landfill
Sustainable transport		encouraging low-carbon modes of transport to reduce emissions, reducing the need to travel
Sustainable materials		using sustainable and healthy products, such as those with low embodied energy, sourced locally, made from renewable or waste resources
Local and sustainable food		choosing low-impact, local, seasonal and organic diets and reducing food waste
Sustainable water		using water more efficiently in buildings and in the products we buy, tackling local flooding and water-course pollution
Land use and wildlife		protecting and restoring existing biodiversity and natural habitats through appropriate land use and integration into the built environment
Culture and community		reviving local identity and wisdom; supporting and participating in the arts
Equity and local economy		creating bioregional economies that support fair employment, inclusive communities and international fair trade
Health and happiness		encouraging active, sociable, meaningful lives to promote good health and well-being

The One Planet Living Action Plan developed by WWF and BioRegional. This provides a practical framework for individuals, businesses and government organisations to operate, work and live within a fair share of the Earth's resources. It focuses on 10 integrated environmental, social and economic elements that underpin sustainable living.

Theme	Proposed actions	Benefits
Low-carbon Games		
Transport and air quality	100% public transport for spectators Promotion and maximum use of Channel Tunnel Rail Link to reduce air travel Low-emission zone for Olympic Park and Olympic fleet of low/no-emission vehicles Active spectator programme for walking and cycling Carbon-offset programme for all Olympic travel	Significant reduction of CO_2 emissions Improvement to air quality Powerful link to health agenda Innovative, comprehensive and durable low-carbon strategy – benchmark for future Olympic Games
Resources	Olympic Park powered by mix of tri-generation (combined cooling, heat and power), locally generated and off-site renewable energy Sustainable water management	An exemplar model for sustainable cities tackling the core issues of integrated resource management, and reducing CO_2 emissions
Sustainable construction	Build to highest sustainable construction standards consistent with the principles of One Planet Living	High-quality built environment – reduced CO_2, proofed against climate change and respecting local heritage
Zero-waste Games		
Waste management	Closed-loop system for zero-waste Games	Diverting waste from landfill Boost to recycling market
Procurement	Sustainable procurement policy applied to materials, services, food and merchandise	Healthy products and materials Resource efficient, reducing waste at source
Conserving biodiversity		
Enhancing urban green space	Integrated restoration strategy for Lower Lea Valley Creation of large new urban park Olympic Biodiversity Action Plan	Major gain in quality green space Valuing biodiversity as an integral component of the built environment Bringing nature and people closer together
Promoting environmental awareness and partnerships		
Community engagement	Community-based Sustainable Sport Programme Annual 'clean-up' projects	Raised public awareness and participation in environmental and community initiatives Legacy for future events
International	Exchange programmes, scholarships, technology transfers and capacity-building projects for developing countries	Building global sustainability networks through sport

The environmental key-point action plan system included in London's bid document prepared in 2004. This set out a suite of sustainable development actions and benefits including those for conserving biodiversity, preparing an Olympic Biodiversity Action Plan and enhancing urban green space.

acknowledges the diversity and fragility of the planet and the importance of the global community in defining a common future for all current and future generations. The 10 One Planet themes cut across the entire agenda of sustainability, providing a holistic model that ensures every aspect, not just the environmental objectives for resource efficiency, is considered. It also addresses the 'softer' community objectives for local and sustainable food, culture and heritage, equity and the local economy, and health and happiness. One Planet Living complemented the second of the Olympic Movement's Fundamental Principles, which is 'to place sport at the service of the harmonious development of humankind'.[26] It also supported the aspirations of the IOC's Sport for Sustainable Development and the Olympic Games Global Impact initiative, which provides an objective analysis of the impact of each Games.

Towards a One Planet 2012, published with the bid in 2005, set out the aspirations.[27] Objectives and priorities that were particularly important to the Park included commitments to a low-carbon Games that would showcase responses to the impacts of a changing climate. Minimising waste and maximising reuse and recycling eventually drove some remarkable progress, particularly in the construction of the Park.

(continued on page 50)

MASTERPLANNING THE ECOLOGICAL SUPERSTRUCTURE

Jason Prior
Chief Executive of Planning, Design and Development, AECOM

Bill Hanway
Executive Director of Operations, Europe, AECOM

Our very first steps en route to the Games began in August 2003 when we were asked to prepare a regeneration framework for the Lower Lea Valley. Looking at the area from Hackney Marshes south to the Thames, we focused on the environmental and ecological integrity of the corridor and early in the process the idea for a park began to crystallise. This took in the wider social, environmental and economic objectives that would become the Opportunity Area Planning Framework (OAPF). As momentum built around proposals for a bid, the discussions became increasingly intense. We could see that while the strategic regeneration objectives could be delivered without the Games, the catalyst provided by the Games would accelerate the process and provide a focus for the area. The Mayor of London, Ken Livingstone, saw this as the key way to attract investment from central government.

Many thought that London was not a strong contender to host the Games and at that stage was at least 18 months behind Paris in its preparations. The reputation of our protracted planning system did little to build confidence that London was a realistic option. Following an extensive planning process, the failure to fund a venue for the World Athletics Championships at Pickett's Lock, just to the north of the site, only compounded the perception that London couldn't deliver on time. So we were working to an extremely tight deadline to produce a credible bid that would also satisfy considerable planning requirements. In addition, the sequencing of applications which is unique to English planning law meant that the OAPF had to be developed and adopted in parallel to the Games plans. This was because it was not possible to secure planning permission for the Games without a planning framework to work within. Furthermore, to complete the land assembly, a Compulsory Purchase Order (CPO) could not be submitted without establishing the long-term regeneration objectives for the valley. So this was a regeneration framework that featured the Games as a major investment opportunity on the way to securing the economically, socially and environmentally sustainable long-term future for the Lower Lea Valley.

The goal of this legacy became a practical and political tool to deliver the regeneration needs of east London. While housing, employment and transport demands were great, it was the idea of the Park and new public open space in the area that attracted the greatest political support from the local communities,

The first masterplans for the pre-bid planning application set within the Lower Lea Valley Opportunity Area Planning Framework prepared by EDAW in 2004. The plan for the Games is on the left and that for legacy is on the right.

mayors and leaders. The Games, and the key element of the Park, then became the structure around which we were able to discuss other issues of social need. Winning the bid meant that delivering the Park and its attendant benefits would be achieved with the greatest possible speed. From those early days, whenever we produced a plan for the Park as it would look during the Games, we also showed how it would look in legacy. The concept of the Games with an integrated legacy plan was at the heart of London's bid and it is significant that the IOC now uses legacy as a key criterion for a winning city.

Having won the bid, much to the surprise of many people, the challenge rapidly turned to designing the masterplan to respond to the requirements of the Games. Through our work on the OAPF we

Aerial photograph indicating the boundaries of the Park (in blue) as illustrated in the Lower Lea Valley Opportunity Area Planning Framework (outlined in white), which covered an area stretching from Hackney Marshes in the north to the river Thames in the south.

had a thorough understanding of the Park site, its opportunities and its challenges. During our research we had built up multiple layers of social, economic and environmental geographic information system (GIS) data and evaluations for the site. This included road and rail capacities, wider transport requirements alongside natural and man-made waterways, historic artefacts and key built assets. It was important to understand the constraints of the site, the power lines, rail lines and sewers, while developing a strong design response that struck a balance between exposing the inherent beauty of the site and retaining its key urban qualities.

Although the site was extremely complex, at a strategic level we got to the answer very quickly. We realised that a robust approach was required to create the development platforms for the venues and other elements needed for the Games, to rejuvenate the waterways and land and to integrate the site with its surrounding communities and the rest of London. We swiftly developed the armature, or framework, and then spent time refining the masterplan and exploring the many and varied options. By overlaying the natural and man-made constraints of the rail and waterways, these started to define the south area of the Park. Locations for the Olympic Stadium and Aquatics Centre were quickly fixed. The Olympic Stadium needed to be set some distance from the transport hubs to help facilitate the management of crowd movement and volumes, while the Aquatics Centre needed to have direct and easy access to transportation and local communities to maximise the ease of regular use in the future.

Meanwhile, the north area of the Park was more open in character, providing more flexibility in its planning and use. We placed the Velodrome in the north-east corner of the site because we knew that,

with Britain's enthusiastic cycling community and strength in cycling events, this was likely to be a big powerful building, an architectural icon, anchoring the north end of the Park. The locations of smaller venues, temporary and permanent, were kept fairly flexible, but the most powerful fix from day one was the Park itself. The Park became a totally dependable asset. All the boroughs supported the idea of a new Park and it was especially well defended when it came to the CPO enquiry.

The power of the sustainability objectives were there at the outset. The earliest images were of a strong flowing landscape and ground plane interwoven with venues and buildings, and it was clear to us that this project would become a model for sustainability in regeneration projects. To have sustainability embedded in all aspects of the project, you have to always be mindful of the need to incorporate all factors into the planning conditions. We took every opportunity to try to ensure the sustainability outcomes were written into the planning agreements. You also have to push hard to incorporate it into the briefs – which was a challenge with the Aquatics Centre because the design was commissioned before the detailed sustainability targets were set. The need for fixed targets for sustainability was as important as the need to retain flexibility for the legacy of the site. Finding this balance was essential so that the density of the future urban development could not be set too high or too low to allow different responses to the demands of a fluctuating market. The ultimate urban structure had to be driven by an exacting and high-quality street pattern and public realm. The Park, with its integration of landscape, ecology and riverscape, was always the central ecological superstructure for the entire project.

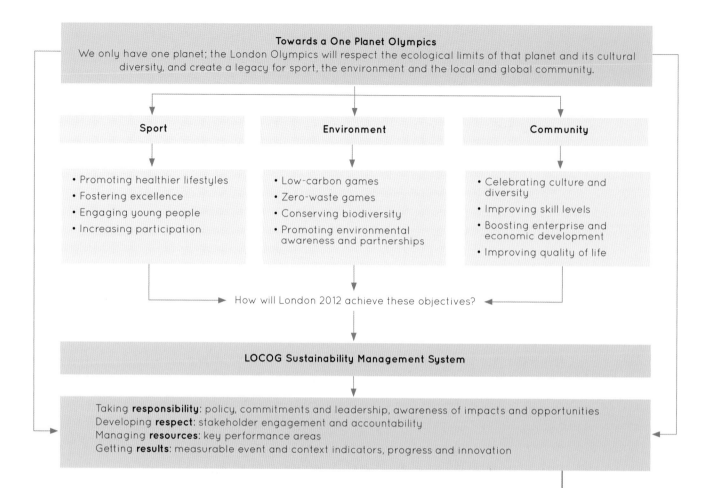

Towards a One Planet Olympics
We only have one planet; the London Olympics will respect the ecological limits of that planet and its cultural diversity, and create a legacy for sport, the environment and the local and global community.

Sport	Environment	Community
• Promoting healthier lifestyles • Fostering excellence • Engaging young people • Increasing participation	• Low-carbon games • Zero-waste games • Conserving biodiversity • Promoting environmental awareness and partnerships	• Celebrating culture and diversity • Improving skill levels • Boosting enterprise and economic development • Improving quality of life

How will London 2012 achieve these objectives?

LOCOG Sustainability Management System

Taking **responsibility**: policy, commitments and leadership, awareness of impacts and opportunities
Developing **respect**: stakeholder engagement and accountability
Managing **resources**: key performance areas
Getting **results**: measurable event and context indicators, progress and innovation

Conserving biodiversity, enhancing green spaces and bringing nature closer to people, similarly encouraged progress. Creating the Park as a new piece of city in east London offered a high-profile opportunity to demonstrate how sustainable developments could be delivered within an urban context. The elegance and simplicity of the One Planet Living message, supported by the credibility of WWF and BioRegional, made it an effective model that drove sustainability, not only in the bid, but also throughout the whole of the Games and the Park.

The environmental management system included in London's bid document prepared in 2004. This established a set of sustainable development goals described as *Towards a One Planet 2012* that took an integrated approach to sustainable consumption, production and use of natural resources, including the management of water, energy, materials and waste.

THE LONDON 2012 BID

With the principle of the Park established, its location in east London agreed, the planning and design framework already in place, and One Planet Living themes underpinning the drivers of the sustainability agenda, London's Candidate File for the 30th Olympiad was finalised and submitted in November 2004. The bid document formed the basis of the Host City Contract that was underwritten by the British Government following the award of the Games in 2005.[28] Its 550 pages set out how the Games would be delivered, the location of the venues, legacy, political and economic structure, environment, finances, transport and security. It promised to deliver 'the experience of a lifetime for athletes', leaving 'a legacy for sport in Britain' and supporting 'the IOC and the Olympic Movement'.

But more important for the Park was the commitment to benefit 'the community through regeneration'. In addition to the sporting legacy of the Games, investment in a new permanent, sustainable infrastructure would leave the lasting social, economic and environmental legacy east London so badly needed. The Games and legacy masterplans set out how the utilities and infrastructure for the Park would be sized to serve the Games and a legacy community of around 10,000 homes with minimal conversion. Where required, the permanent venues would have additional temporary seating for the Games. Bridges and concourses that had to accommodate up to 250,000 spectators during the Games would have substantial additional temporary sections that would be removed following the Games – for example, a 40-metre-wide bridge required for the Games would be reduced to 4m for a permanent legacy footpath and cycle-path connection.

Business plans determined which venues would be viable in legacy, ensuring that only those that had a reasonable chance of a workable future were built as permanent structures. All others would be temporary. At the time of the bid, there was no need for a major new stadium in London. Wembley Stadium had only recently been completed and there was no interest from Premiership football clubs who could fill such a large stadium regularly. Additionally, the bid committed London to retaining athletics track and field facilities within the stadium. Athletics could only sustain crowds of up to 25,000 periodically. Consequently, and for the first time, it was proposed that the Olympic Stadium would be converted from an 80,000 capacity for the Games to a 25,000-capacity multi-purpose venue with athletics at its core. It was to become a 'house of sport with training facilities, offices and sports science and sports medicine facilities'.[29]

Before the Games, London did not have an Olympic-sized swimming pool; the proposed Aquatics Centre would have two 50m pools, a 25m diving pool, and a fitness centre to accommodate elite, local club and community users. It would accommodate 17,500 spectators during the Games, which would be reduced to a permanent capacity of 3,500 for legacy. The proposed Velodrome would be at the heart of the best urban VeloPark anywhere in the world. It would have a 6,000 capacity for the Games and in legacy, a one-mile road track replacing the original track previously located on the site, competition and recreational BMX tracks, and a mountain-biking course for use by all levels of bikers. After the Games, Eton Manor would become a sporting hub for the local community with facilities for hockey and tennis and 5-a-side football. A multi-use indoor sports centre with flexible seating for 6,500 spectators was proposed, which would host Handball, Goalball and the fencing element of the Modern Pentathlon during the Games, and in legacy be converted into a training and competition venue for a range of indoor sports and other cultural events. Other temporary venues would include the Water Polo Arena and Basketball Arena. This innovative approach of assuring the use of permanent venues and infrastructure in legacy, and embracing the temporary on such a scale, had never been adopted at a Games before.

Parc olympique
Olympic Park

Ⓐ **Stade olympique**
Olympic Stadium
Athlétisme/Athletics

Ⓑ **Arènes sportives**
Sports Arenas
Basketball/Basketball
Escrime/Fencing
Handball/Handball
Pentathlon moderne (Tir/Escrime)
Modern Pentathlon (Shooting/Fencing)
Volleyball/Volleyball

Ⓒ **Vélodrome**/Velodrome
Cyclisme (BMX)/Cycling (BMX)
Cyclisme (Piste)/Cycling (Track)

Ⓓ **Centre de hockey**
Hockey Centre
Hockey/Hockey

Ⓔ **Centre aquatique**
Aquatics Centre
Natation/Swimming
Natation synchronisée
Synchronised Swimming
Pentathlon moderne (Natation)
Modern Pentathlon (Swimming)
Plongeon/Diving
Water-polo/Water Polo

Zone de la Tamise
River Zone

Ⓕ **Le Dôme**/The Dome
Basketball/Basketball
Gymnastique (artistique)
Gymnastics (Artistic)
Gymnastique (Trampoline)
Gymnastics (Trampoline)

Ⓖ **ExCeL**
Boxe/Boxing
Haltérophilie/Weightlifting
Judo/Judo
Lutte/Wrestling
Taekwondo/Taekwondo
Tennis de table/Table Tennis

Ⓗ **UEL Docklands**
Water-polo/Water Polo

Ⓘ **The Royal Artillery Barracks**
Tir/Shooting

Ⓙ **Arène de Greenwich**
Greenwich Arena
Badminton/Badminton
Gymnastique (rythmique)
Gymnastics (Rhythmic)

Ⓚ **Greenwich Park**
Pentathlon moderne (Équitation/Course à pied)
Modern Pentathlon (Riding/Running)
Sports équestres/Equestrian

Zone centrale
Central Zone

Ⓛ **Lord's Cricket Ground**
Tir à l'arc/Archery

Ⓜ **Regent's Park**
Baseball/Baseball
Cyclisme (Route)/Cycling (Road)
Softball/Softball

Ⓝ **Horse Guards Parade**
Volleyball de plage/Beach Volleyball

Ⓞ **Hyde Park**
Triathlon/Triathlon

Ⓟ **Wembley**
Football/Football

Ⓠ **Wimbledon**
Tennis/Tennis

Autres sites
Other venues

Ⓡ **Broxbourne Canoe Slalom Course**
Canoë-kayak (Slalom)
Canoe/Kayak (Slalom)

Ⓢ **Weald Country Park**
Cyclisme (VTT)/Cycling (Mountain Bike)

Ⓣ **Eton Dorney**
Aviron/Rowing
Canoë-kayak (Eaux calmes)
Canoe/Kayak (Flatwater)

Ⓤ **Weymouth and Portland**
Voile/Sailing

Ⓥ **Hampden Park/St James's Park/Villa Park/Old Trafford/Millennium Stadium**
Football/Football

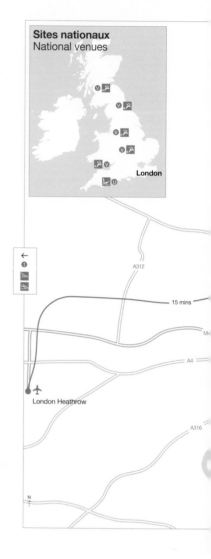

Sites nationaux
National venues

London

London Heathrow

A312

15 mins

A4

A316

Légende/Key

● **Stations de métro et gares ferroviaires**
Tube and train stations

⇌ **Gare ferroviaire**/National Rail

⊖ **Station de métro**
Underground station

⇌ **Eurostar**

— **Routes nationales**/Main roads

— **Itinéraire olympique principal**
Olympic main route

— **Lignes de trains principales**
Main rail lines

⊗ **Sites de compétition**
Competition venues

◼ **Hébergement CIO**
IOC accommodation

⬚ **Sites de compétition par sport**
Competition venues by sport

Lieux touristiques :
Places of interest:

❶ **Palais de Westminster**
Palace of Westminster

❷ **British Airways London Eye**

❸ **Tower Bridge**

❹ **Le Dôme**/The Dome

❺ **Quartier maritime de Greenwich**
Maritime Greenwich

❻ **Wimbledon**

❼ **Jardin botanique royal, Kew**
Royal Botanic Gardens, Kew

◎ **Sites du patrimoine mondial**
World Heritage sites

Importantly, the Olympic and Paralympic Village would become a new, sustainable residential community with 3,600 new homes – including a mix of affordable tenures and housing for sale and rent – along with a new school, community health centre, shops and open spaces.[30] The apartments would be energy efficient, light and airy. The blocks would be set on tree-lined streets, with footpaths and cycle paths connecting them to public transport, shops, the school and surrounding neighbourhoods. It would have its own open-space network culminating in a beautiful wetland landscape that collected and cleansed water from the site, and cascaded down to the core, river parklands in the north of the Park.

For the first time, the masterplans for an Olympic Park integrated planning and design strategies for land use, transport, waterways, landscape, ecology and socio-economic conditions for all temporary and permanent infrastructure for the Games and legacy. The masterplans set out a vision for revitalising the river ecosystem, increasing

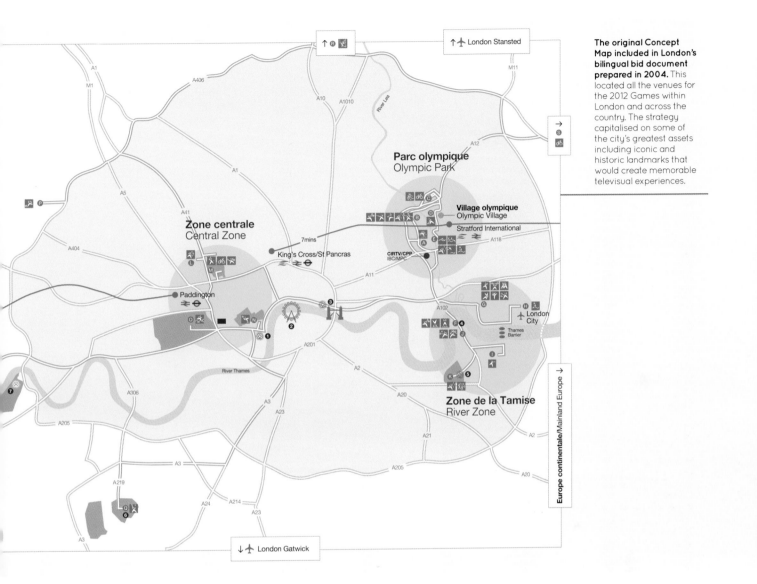

The original Concept Map included in London's bilingual bid document prepared in 2004. This located all the venues for the 2012 Games within London and across the country. The strategy capitalised on some of the city's greatest assets including iconic and historic landmarks that would create memorable televisual experiences.

biodiversity and enhancing the quality of urban green space. With sustainability in mind, a high degree of self-sufficiency in energy, water supply and waste would be built in from day one. Detailed environmental surveys for ecology, hydrology, water quality, air quality, noise, contaminated land, built heritage and archaeology had already been undertaken. These would form the baseline for detailed planning, soil remediation, development, monitoring and environmental management of the new Park and its environs. Noxious and invasive alien plants including Japanese knotweed, Himalayan balsam and giant hogweed would all be eradicated within the Park. A Biodiversity Action Plan Framework was prepared in partnership with local communities, statutory and other environmental organisations and accompanied the 2004 planning application. It set out a strategy for increasing and enhancing target species and habitats, and committed to prepare a more detailed Biodiversity Action Plan that would formally drive implementation across the Park. The rivers and waterways would be restored along with

8.3 Plan des zones de sites et infrastructure de transport
Venue and transport infrastructure zone maps

Parc olympique
Olympic Park

Ⓐ **Stade olympique**
Olympic Stadium
Athlétisme/Athletics

Ⓑ **Arènes sportives**
Sports Arenas
Basketball/Basketball
Escrime/Fencing
Handball/Handball
**Pentathlon moderne
(Tir/Escrime)**
Modern Pentathlon
(Shooting/Fencing)
Volleyball/Volleyball

Ⓒ **Vélodrome/**Velodrome
Cyclisme (BMX)/Cycling (BMX)
Cyclisme (Piste)/Cycling (Track)

Ⓓ **Centre de hockey**
Hockey Centre
Hockey/Hockey

Ⓔ **Centre aquatique**
Aquatics Centre
Natation/Swimming
Natation synchronisée
Synchronised Swimming
Pentathlon moderne (Natation)
Modern Pentathlon (Swimming)
Plongeon/Diving
Water-polo/Water Polo

Légende/Key

Métro et trains/Tube and Trains:

‖ **Lignes de métro et de trains
existantes/**Existing tube and
train lines

‖ **Améliorations prévues aux lignes
de métro et de train**
Planned improvements to tube
and train lines

═ **Service de navette supplémentaire
Olympic Javelin/**Additional *Olympic
Javelin* Service

㉘ **Principaux échangeurs ferroviaires
et de métro existants/**Existing tube
and train major interchanges

㊶ **Améliorations prévues sur les
principaux échangeurs ferroviaires
et de métro/**Planned improvements
to tube and train major interchanges

● **Stations de métro et gares de
trains existantes/**Existing tube
and train stations

● **Améliorations prévues sur les
stations de métro et les gares
de trains/** Planned improvements
to tube and train stations

⁻₆⁻ **Nᵒˢ de lignes de métro et de train.
Voir table 14.1/**Tube and train line
numbers refer to table 14.1

Roads/Roads:

─ **Routes principales/**Main roads

─ **Itinéraire olympique principal**
Olympic main route

─ **Voie circulaire du parc olympique**
Olympic Park loop road

⋯ **Promenade**
Footpath

⋯⋯ **Piste cyclable**
Cycle path

**Sites de compétition et
hébergement/**Competition
venues and accommodation:

Ⓧ **Sites de compétition**
Competition venues

▨ **Sites de compétition par disciplines**
Competition venues by sport

■ **Hébergement CIO**
IOC accommodation

Parc olympique
Olympic Park

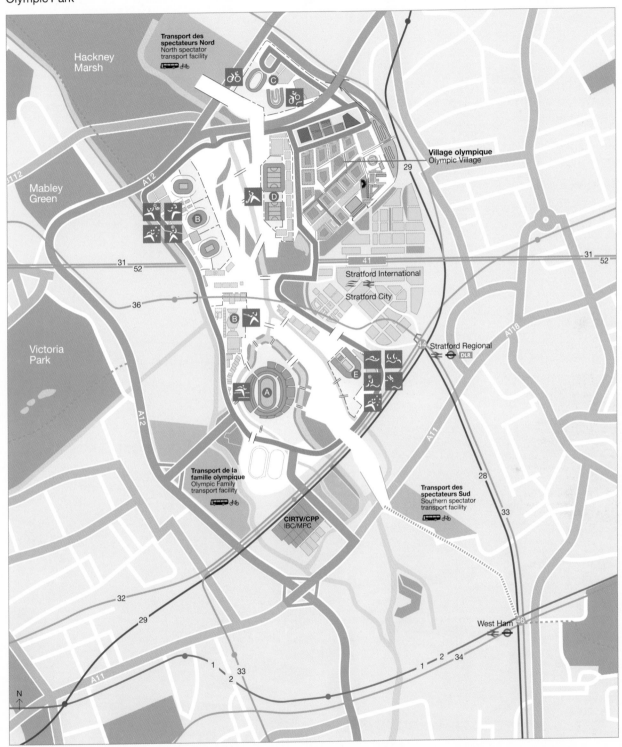

The initial framework for the Park included in London's bilingual bid document prepared in 2004. Proposals for a compact Park concentrated infrastructure, parklands, venues and the Olympic and Paralympic Village in one location. As importantly, 75 per cent of this investment would be in permanent infrastructure to accelerate development in line with the already established, wider regeneration objectives for east London.

a wetland bowl and a sustainable urban drainage system. Vegetation on roofs and walls, and a large number of wildlife installations from bird and bat boxes, would all be designed to encourage biodiversity. But the Park would not just be for plants and wildlife – it would also be a safe, inclusive and accessible place for people.

Sustainable public transport was integral to the bid. It focused on minimising carbon emissions produced by Games-related travel and legacy communities. 100 per cent of Games spectators would get to the Park by foot, bicycle or public transport, another first for a Games, and with special provisions for people with disabilities. £10 million would be invested in nine new, permanent strategic footpath and cycle routes leading to and from the Park from surrounding neighbourhoods, one of which would be the Greenway. Once complete, the Park would be served by two national rail lines, one London Overground line, two London Underground lines, the High Speed 1 and Eurostar lines, the Docklands Light Railway and a multitude of bus routes. Even the delivery of construction materials to the Park would, as far as possible, be by rail and water, rather than by road, saving tonnes of carbon emissions. This exceeded the ODA's target of over 50 per cent by weight.

'Lean, green and mean' was the 'energy mantra' for Games and legacy. Buildings and facilities would be designed and constructed to minimise energy demand by including well-designed building envelopes, passive solar design, natural ventilation, efficient

A plan of the waterways and green spaces of London included in London's bilingual bid document prepared in 2004. The bid highlighted the many sites of environmental and cultural importance that London offered, including the river Thames itself. The bid had to demonstrate that staging the Games would not cause any harm to these assets and would contribute to a major environmental enhancement of the Lower Lea Valley.

The visualisation for the Park included in London's bid document prepared by the EDAW Consortium in 2004. This illustrated a unified landscape and architectural design of interconnected waterways and green spaces. The proposed Park would also contribute socio-economic benefits to enhance the legacy value of the site including improved air and water quality and providing recreational and amenity value.

Parc olympique/Olympic Park

River Thames

River Thames

Thames Barrier

Zone à risque d'inondation/Flood extent

Périmètre des terres inondables de la basse vallée de la Lea en crue centennale/1 in 100 years flood contour for Lower Lea Valley

Légende/Key

Tamise sujette aux marées/Tidal Thames

Classe chimique/Chemical class
Classe A – Très bon/Class A – Very good
Classe B – Bon/Class B – Good
Classe C – Assez bon/Class C – Fairly good
Classe D – Moyen/Class D – Fair
Classe E – Médiocre/Class E – Poor

Réservoirs/Reservoirs
Ceinture verte et terrains découverts de métropole londonienne (total = 50 000 ha, 31,5 % de la superficie du Grand Londres)/Greenbelt and Metropolitan Open Land (total = 50,000 ha, 31.5% of Greater London area)

An image of the proposed Park prepared by the EDAW Consortium in 2004. The parklands were a strong element of the bid that would enhance the delivery of the Games through environmental excellence. It provided a key part of demonstrating that sustainability would be embedded in all planning and implementation stages through regeneration of both east London communities and their environment.

lighting and appliances, smart metering to help to manage energy consumption, and green roofs to reduce energy usage by cooling naturally in summer and insulating in winter. Some 20 per cent of the Park's electricity requirements would be met by a new combined heat, power and cooling plant powered by natural gas and biomass with an 82 per cent average efficiency, compared with 45 per cent efficiency for electricity from the National Grid. Photovoltaic panels and small-scale wind turbines would be used where possible. An integrated approach to water management would be adopted. Demand for potable water would be significantly reduced, and a blackwater (recycled effluent) main would be installed. Surface water would be collected where possible, retained and recycled through a system of sustainable drainage, including permeable pavements, green roofs, retention ponds and reed beds, improving water quality in the river Lea and the river Thames.

The biggest economic legacy of the Games would be wider employment opportunities and improvements in the education, skills and knowledge of the local labour force. The nature and range of those skills would enable existing and new residents to have a stake in the economic development of their area, and begin to reduce the deprivation. It was estimated that up to 7,000 full-time equivalent jobs in the construction industry would be created, and around 12,000 permanent jobs as a result of the legacy development of the Park and surrounding areas.[31]

ON YOUR MARKS GET SET, GO!

Winning the bid triggered the start of one of Europe's largest regeneration projects within the United Kingdom's largest regional regeneration programme, the Thames Gateway. In just five years, the Olympic Delivery Authority had to be established, and complete the design and delivery of the 2.5-square-kilometre Olympic Park, ensuring that it would be ready for testing one year ahead of the Games. Not only that, it had to build the teams, develop strategies and policies, and put in place the programme and project management systems that would deliver on the design, development and sustainability targets that had been set in the bid. To put it mildly, there was a more than healthy scepticism that this would be successfully achieved. The UK was not perceived to have a great track record of delivering major projects on time and on budget, never mind against such taxing sustainability targets, and under the baleful eye of the politicians, public and press. Following Jacques Rogge's announcement on 6 July 2005, it really was time to start with the Park.

The 'Fantasticology' annual meadows planted along the south-eastern banks of the City Mill river in peak flower at the start of the Games in July 2012.

CHAPTER TWO

CHAPTER TWO

Delivering the Park

From scratch and in six years, the Olympic Delivery Authority (ODA) had to be established and deliver a programme that included the flagship Olympic Park. The complexities of the bid commitments on Games, legacy and sustainability required a series of detailed policies, strategies, timelines and targets against which the ODA could report to a sceptical press, public and political establishment. It is a textbook example of how large, complex projects can be achieved successfully to exacting standards.

The announcement of London's winning bid on 6 July 2005 pressed the trigger of the starting gun for a hectic seven years of activity. First off the blocks was the Mayor's economic development and regeneration arm, the London Development Agency (LDA), which had led the masterplanning of the Lower Lea Valley Opportunity Area Planning Framework (OAPF) and of what has become the Queen Elizabeth Olympic Park. It continued its pivotal role by establishing a separate directorate, effectively an Interim Olympic Delivery Authority, to progress the masterplanning, acquire the land, procure design teams and let contracts for moving the high-voltage overhead power lines that crossed the site underground, demolition, land clearance and decontamination.[1] With the OAPF and Park masterplans having already received outline planning permission and the bid won, bringing the land under single ownership was the first critical hurdle. Much of the land had to be bought through time-consuming and complicated compulsory purchase order procedures.[2] The LDA submitted the Lower Lea Valley, Olympic and Legacy Compulsory Purchase Order (CPO) on 17 November 2005. A Public Inquiry was held between 9 May and 4 August 2006. The Inspector at the Public Inquiry agreed that the case for the CPO was a compelling one and the Secretary of State for Trade and

Dismantling one of 52 pylons in October 2008. These pylons ran across the entire Park and were removed at the start of the construction works once the power lines had been moved into two underground tunnels.

The 'muncher' demolishing two disused University of East London tower blocks in October 2007 to make way for the start of construction of the Olympic and Paralympic Village.

Industry confirmed it on 18 December 2006. The LDA spent nearly £700 million on land acquisition. It was one of the largest and most complex compulsory purchase orders ever undertaken in the UK, covering around 2,220 different land interests across the site, and not without controversy.

'The first major contests of the 2012 Olympics are taking place not in one of the new stadiums but in the Royal Courts of Justice,' trumpeted the *Guardian*.[3] Several businesses fought relocation, but perhaps most controversial were the Manor Gardening Society Allotments, which were in what is now the north of the Park. Captain Arthur Villiers, an Old Etonian and a director of Barings Bank, founded The Manor Charitable Trust (now the Villiers Park Educational Trust) in 1924. Eton College had been running a mission and a club for disadvantaged boys in Hackney Wick, which was expanded to include the Eton Manor Boys' Club and the allotments.[4] 'Manor Garden Allotments,' wrote Cleve West in the *Independent* on 27 August 2005, 'having occupied this unique spot in the Lea Valley for almost a century, may soon be bulldozed to make way for the London Olympics in 2012.' And in a thinly veiled reference to the designers of the Park, 'areas such as these are organic, unique in their local distinctiveness and a far cry from the manicured landscapes conceived on the drawing board.'[5] The allotments sat right in the middle of the north of the Park and could not be preserved. Through a sometimes fractious process, the allotment holders were relocated temporarily to a new site nearby. Planning approval for their permanent relocation within the Park was achieved in 2010 and they will move back into the Park following its transformation after the Games.

Yet, despite a total of 400 objections, the LDA met and exceeded its statutory responsibilities throughout the compulsory purchase process by assisting businesses, residents, travellers, allotment holders and cycle-track users to find satisfactory alternative locations. Some 98

Initial sorting of soils on the Velodrome site prior to remediation in April 2008. Over 1.4 million cubic metres of soil were remediated and reused across the Park, minimising the cost of removing it off-site to landfill.

per cent of the jobs that had been on the site were protected and several companies – including Forman & Field, a salmon processing company, and Bowater and Newsfax, a paper processing and newspaper company – used the move to consolidate and expand their business operations. A full six years after London won the right to stage the Games the LDA was still locked in compensation negotiations with 93 cases, an indication of just how difficult and time-consuming the compulsory purchase order process was. Nonetheless, on schedule, the LDA handed over the site to the ODA on 26 July 2007.

THE SCALE OF THE PARK

At twice the size of Heathrow's Terminal 5, one of the UK's largest infrastructure projects that preceded the Games, the Park had to be delivered in half the time. The scope of the ODA's programme of works was daunting. It would oversee one of the largest construction sites in Europe, creating thousands of new jobs with a peak site workforce of more than 10,000. An area roughly equivalent to Hyde Park and Kensington Gardens combined, 2.5 square kilometres (1 square mile) of brownfield land was remediated. Some 102 hectares of new parklands was created with nearly half of that designated as wildlife habitat. More than 30 new bridges and 20km (12 miles) of roads were constructed and 8km (5 miles) of waterways refurbished and revitalised. The International Broadcast Centre provides 80,000 square metres of employment space in legacy and is able to accommodate five jumbo jets parked wing-tip to wing-tip. Along with the Main Press Centre, it housed 20,000 TV and print journalists during the Games. In November 2007, the ODA provided even more clarity and detail on what it was delivering, alongside timescales and the risks it faced, in a 500-page Programme Baseline Report which it updated in 2009.[6] Everyone, from the Government to local residents, had absolute clarity on the ODA's mission. (See table on page 70.)

(continued on page 70)

SQUARING THE CIRCLE BETWEEN LOCAL AND NATIONAL INTEREST

Sir David Higgins
Chief Executive, Olympic Delivery Authority, 2005–2011

The Olympic Park was always the heart of the London 2012 vision. There were huge expectations, but also huge responsibilities. We had to honour commitments to local users, such as the Eastway cycle group, local allotment owners, and people who valued the right of free access through the old industrial site.

Local users gave the area its authenticity, its own brand of east London; but alongside this we needed to create a Park owned by the country and the nation, of which we could all be proud and in which we all had a stake. Therefore, it was important to us to make the most of our wide group of stakeholders, using the planning process to square local, national, commercial, sport and leisure demands.

Openness and transparency was central to our process. Sometimes it felt like performing open-heart surgery with everyone watching on, but there were huge benefits of having everyone involved and talking the whole time. We held our design reviews in our open-plan offices with people able to walk by and see how decisions were made, and we didn't value hierarchy – if you had an idea with integrity and intellectual value, we'd take it.

One of the big things that make this Park different is the river running through it. However, the river brought us no shortage of issues to deal with. One of the challenges was how to manage the bridges through the Park – the 60m-wide concourses needed to move up to 250,000 people each day during the Games. In legacy the undercroft spaces of the bridges would have been unattractive and impacted the river. Our solution was to cut the number of bridges and split them into permanent and temporary bridge structures, so what remained would be more in scale for the Park in legacy.

A community art event hosted by the ODA on the Greenway in July 2009. The View Tube was a very popular venue for local residents and visitors. As the View Tube was outside the Park's secure boundary, anyone could just turn up and see progress of construction on the Park.

The character of the north-eastern section of the future Park looking west towards Canary Wharf in April 2007. Early clearance of the land for the Olympic and Paralympic Village was underway, although the power lines were yet to be dismantled.

The first of five bridges to be installed around the Stadium 'island site' in July 2008. As with the majority of bridges in the Park, there are both permanent and temporary sections that can be clearly seen here. The temporary section on the right is to be removed during the transformation of the Park after the Games.

Having got the geographic boundary of the Park fixed, our next challenge was the topography of the site. The Park had a real grade change in it, and while it was an interesting site it didn't really have a diversity of plant life or interesting corridors. While this was a challenge, it presented us with an opportunity to create something really special as a lasting legacy. We brought in LDA Design and George Hargreaves to work with us on this. George's insight was exceptional – he saw straight away how the grade in the Park hid the river from view in many parts. So he suggested corridors, avenues, swales and wetlands. 'This is how we bring the river to life, he said, 'and we bring it into the rest of the Park.' We were all convinced, but we had already got planning approved, flood modelling done and we were already on site building the platform. Changes needed to be made in real time, and it was

now or never. We all took a deep breath and agreed to change the design.

Now, the undulation in the Park, the planting and the wetlands really bring the Park to life. We had nesting swans and kingfishers on site throughout construction. I first saw them when I used to walk down the old avenues in 2006, and they are there now.

Before I took on the job at the ODA, I knew sustainability was key to the London 2012 Games. But it wasn't until the expectations on outputs landed on my desk that I realised how great a challenge this would be to deliver. Our rule was to do fewer things that would be extraordinary. They needed to be authentic, and copied by the industry. So we did low-energy concrete in a way that the rest of the industry could copy, and we recycled commercially by setting up recycling and treatment plants for all the waste so that we could prove it was cheaper than 'dig and dump'.

I never believed in tokenism, and health and safety wasn't a stick-on or gimmick. Having occupational health for our workforce was vital to getting the job done competitively. We had a lot of requirements for the Park. It had to do things – for example, it had to clean water, provide recreation and education and ideally create energy. I have deeply ingrained values in these areas, whether it be for health and safety or environmental sustainability. On site I wanted to see and understand the steps our staff were taking. I wanted to see proof that we were listening to the community and I never wanted us to fall behind in our duties to local people.

On a site like this, community was always going to be the key. I remember having a big debate about the Greenway, which was supposed to remain shut during construction because it was unsafe and considered a security breach. But if the community owned it they would keep it safe, they would be the security, because it is their Park. And although it seems such a trivial thing, it was such a highlight for me: once the 'View Tube' was in place I'd just sit there and watch visiting community groups and schools. They would never have to get any approval, and the teachers would start talking about their Park, explaining to their kids what was going on. That's real ownership of the Park.

The wetland bowl in the north of the Park looking west in February 2011. The sculptural landform and large areas of wetland planting are key elements of the Park's character and identity.

Venues, Infrastructure and Programme Support
• Power lines undergrounding
• Utilities
• Enabling works
• Structures, bridges and highways
• Prescott Lock
• Parklands and public realm
• Olympic Stadium (80,000 capacity for Games, 25,000 capacity for legacy)
• Site preparation and Warm-up Track (temporary)
• Aquatics Centre (17,500 capacity for Games, 2,500 for legacy)
• Handball, renamed the Copper Box (conversion to a multi-use sports venue in legacy)
• VeloPark (Comprising cycling track and BMX for Games and a one-mile road circuit and mountain-bike trails for legacy)
• Hockey Centre, renamed the Riverbank Arena (primarily delivered by LOCOG with site platform preparation by the ODA)
• Basketball Arena (temporary arena with capacity for 12,000 seats made available for relocation via Sport England after the Games)
• Eton Manor (Wheelchair Tennis and Paralympic Archery venue for Games; hockey, tennis and 5-a-side football facility in legacy)
• Training venues (temporary Olympic training facilities for Swimming)
• International Broadcast Centre and Main Press Centre (broadcasting and print media, providing support and facilities for the duration of the Olympic and Paralympic Games)
• Logistics (provided a series of services to manage people and material logistics during construction across the whole Olympic Park)
• International Broadcast Centre (permanent)
• Main Press Centre (permanent)
• Multi-storey car park (for the International Broadcast and Main Press Centres)
• Olympic and Paralympic Village
• Security
o Venues and infrastructure support
o Capital projects
o Operations
• Programme (ODA staff and consultancy, delivery Partner, ODA facilities and other management costs)
• Programme contingency
Transport
• Stratford station (a capacity enhancement for the legacy needs of passengers, as well as additional temporary measures to meet the specific needs of the Games)
• Thornton's Field relocation (relocation of carriage sidings depot)
• Surface transport (Enhancements to surface transport for the Games, including cycling, walking, river transport, buses, shuttle buses, and specialist vehicles)
• Heavy rail (delivery of four heavy rail infrastructure schemes)
• Docklands Light Railway (financial assistance to improve DLR capacity and infrastructure)
• London Underground (enhancement of West Ham Station)
• North London Line (upgrade the North London Line over the busiest section of the railway to enable more frequent services to meet Games-time and legacy requirements)
• Javelin® Services (the Javelin® service was a major contributor to Games-time transport, delivering a capacity of up to 25,000 people an hour to Stratford)

Summary of the ODA's scope and programme of works published in the Programme Baseline Report, November 2007.

SETTING UP AND FUNDING DELIVERY

While the LDA kept the London 2012 project rolling immediately after winning the bid, the Government Olympic Executive (GOE), a unit within the Department for Culture, Media and Sport, was set up with responsibility for overseeing and coordinating the Games. The London Organising Committee of the London Olympic and Paralympic Games (LOCOG) was incorporated as a government-owned, private company in October 2005 to stage the Games. The ODA was set up as a single-purpose, single-focus non-departmental public body by act of parliament in March 2006. It was empowered to

Summary of the delivery structures for the 2012 Games

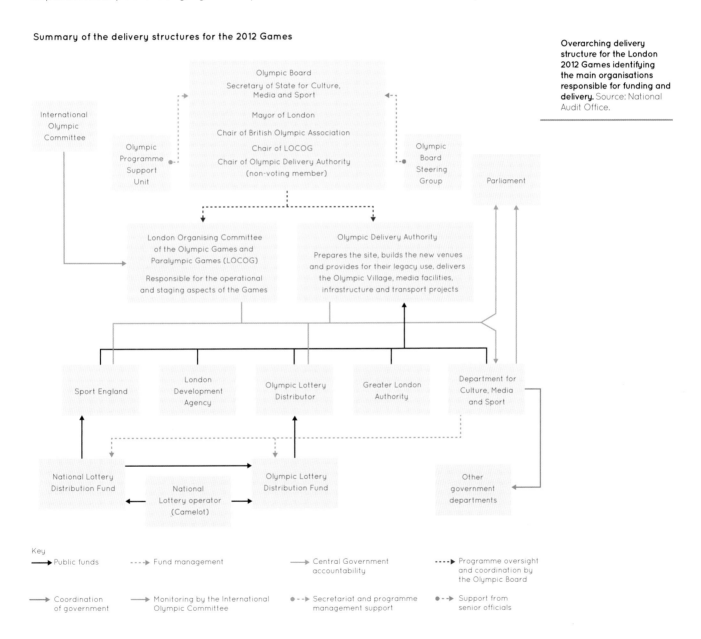

Overarching delivery structure for the London 2012 Games identifying the main organisations responsible for funding and delivery. Source: National Audit Office.

NOTES

1 The Figure shows a summary of the main organisations involved in delivering and funding the Games.

2 LOCOG also received public funding towards the costs of the Paralympic Games.

buy, sell and hold land, make arrangements for building works and develop transport and other infrastructure. It was also set up as the local town planning authority for the Park area and established an independent Planning Committee with representatives from the local boroughs supported by a Planning Decisions Team. The Olympic Park Legacy Company (OPLC) was founded in 2009 by the Mayor of London in partnership with central Government as the public-sector, not-for-profit organisation responsible for the long-term planning, development, management and maintenance of the Park and its facilities after the Games. At the start of April 2012 it became the London Legacy Development Corporation (LLDC) through powers given to the Mayor of London in the Localism Act 2011 and is accountable to Londoners through the office of the Mayor. This was the first time an organisation responsible for development following the Games had been set up so early. Delivery on London's bid promises was already taking shape.

Funding for the Games was always going to be controversial. On 15 March 2007, the Olympics Minister, Tessa Jowell, announced to Parliament a funding package for the Games of £9.325 billion. It was a substantial increase on the bid figure of £2.375 billion. The

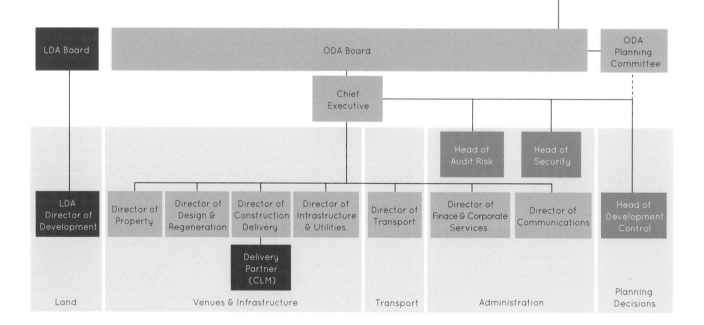

The international organisational structure of the ODA. Lifetime Corporate Plan, July 2007. Source: ODA.

Project	Detailed projects	Base cost £m	Tax £m	Gross cost £m
Site preparation and infrastructure	Undergrounding power lines	240	42	282
	Utilities	217	38	255
	Enabling works	310	54	364
	Structures, bridges, highways	706	124	830
	Prescott Lock	5	0	5
	Other infrastructure (Greenway and landscape)	175	31	206
	Total site preparation and infrastructure	**1,653**	**289**	**1,942**
Venues	Olympic Stadium	422	74	496
	Other Olympic Park venues	488	86	574
	Non-Olympic Park venues	86	15	101
	Total venues	**996**	**175**	**1,171**
Transport	Stratford regional station	114	5	119
	Contribution to DLR upgrade	86	0	86
	Thornton's Field relocation	40	7	47
	Contribution to North London Line	110	0	110
	Other transport capital projects	161	17	178
	Other transport operating expediture	328	29	357
	Total transport projects	**839**	**58**	**897**
Other Park-wide projects	Logistics for site construction	287	50	337
	Section 106 and Masterplanning	108	19	127
	Insurance	42	8	50
	Security for park construction	301	53	354
	Total other park-wide projects	**738**	**130**	**868**
IBC/MPC, Village	IBC/MPC, Village	491	1	492
Programme Delivery	Programme Delivery	580	67	647
Taxation	Corporation Tax and Net Interest	0	73	73
Total ODA budget before contingency		**5,297**	**793**	**6,090**
Contingency				**2,009**
Maximum available funding for ODA				**8,099**

increase, according to the Minister, was due to allowances for inflation, VAT, contingency, an additional allowance of £1.7 billion for the wider regeneration of the Lower Lea Valley, security and policing costs and additional elite sport and Paralympic funding. The package included amounts outside the ODA's remit, such as contributions to the operations of the Paralympic Games and wider security arrangements. The announcement followed a protracted process of pinning down cost estimates to fix the budget. Shrill headlines ran the gamut from 'Olympic costs set to double'[7] to 'Cuts could result in plasterboard Olympics'.[9] The public-sector funding package for the ODA comprised £5,975 million

ODA's overall budget consolidating projects, programme delivery, taxes and contingency in the Programme Delivery Baseline Report, January 2008. Source: ODA.[8]

from central Government, £2,175 million from the National Lottery, £925 million from the Greater London Authority (GLA) and £250 million from the LDA. The GLA's contribution came partly through a £20-per-annum precept on council tax to run from 2006 to 2017 and partly through direct LDA investment. On 24 May 2010, the new coalition Government announced that it would reduce the overall budget by £27m to £9.298 billion as part of its austerity measures. Consequently, the total funding available to the ODA was £8.099 billion: £6.09 billion for drawdown and £2.009 billion held as contingency.[10]

Without any warning, in September 2008 the financial markets collapsed worldwide. Tessa Jowell, the Olympics Minister, announced that an acceptable deal could not be reached with Lend Lease, the preferred private-sector partner for the £1bn Olympic and Paralympic Village. As a consequence and to keep the project progressing, it would be funded primarily from the public purse rather than through a public-private partnership. The ODA had already achieved savings by reducing the number of apartments from 3,600 to 2,800 and through efficiencies realised in other parts of the Park. It requested and received £324 million – £262 million from the contingency fund and £63 million from its savings – with a further £268 million invested through a deal with social housing landlord Triathlon Homes, which had agreed to buy half of the apartments to add to its affordable homes portfolio. The intention was to sell the remaining apartments and development plots within the Village when market conditions improved. The ODA did indeed sell its holdings to the Delancey and Qatari Diar joint venture in August 2011 for £557 million. The International Broadcast Centre and Main Press Centre were similarly intended to be financed by the private sector but were taken on by the ODA with the OPLC responsible for their use after the Games, along with any receipts.

The Olympic Park Delivery Programme was structured around the '2-4-1 schedule': 2 years for preparatory work including planning and design; 4 years to build the venues and infrastructure; and 1 year for 1 year for LOCOG to stage test events before the Games.

TIMESCALES FOR DELIVERY

The ODA was adept at communicating its complex delivery programme in simple terms. In July 2006, before it had published its detailed Baseline Report, it set out a straightforward '2-4-1' delivery programme: two years' planning and design, four years' construction and one year for LOCOG to stage test events. As David Higgins noted: 'This is our delivery route map to 2012. I recognise it is a bold move setting out indicative target dates that we can be measured against, but it is important that we are transparent and accountable. It is a timetable that is challenging but achievable and one that will require a relentless focus on delivery, timely decision-making and sound project management over the next six years.' During the first two years land acquisition was completed, site clean-up commenced, the masterplan and venue designs refined, necessary planning permissions achieved and essential Tier One contractors procured. In the next four years the ODA built the infrastructure and completed the venues ready for one full year of test events preceding the Games Opening Ceremony on 27 July 2012.[11] The ODA also published 'milestones' and, again, reported regularly on progress. The first 10 milestones in the Demolish, Dig,

Olympic Park Delivery Programme

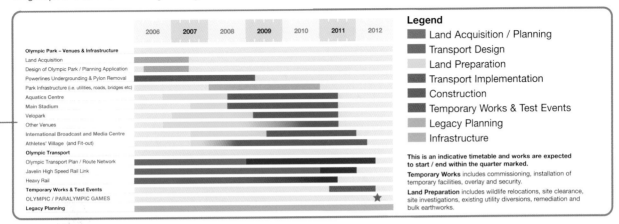

Legend

- Land Acquisition / Planning
- Transport Design
- Land Preparation
- Transport Implementation
- Construction
- Temporary Works & Test Events
- Legacy Planning
- Infrastructure

This is an indicative timetable and works are expected to start / end within the quarter marked.

Temporary Works includes commissioning, installation of temporary facilities, overlay and security.

Land Preparation includes wildlife relocations, site clearance, site investigations, existing utility diversions, remediation and bulk earthworks.

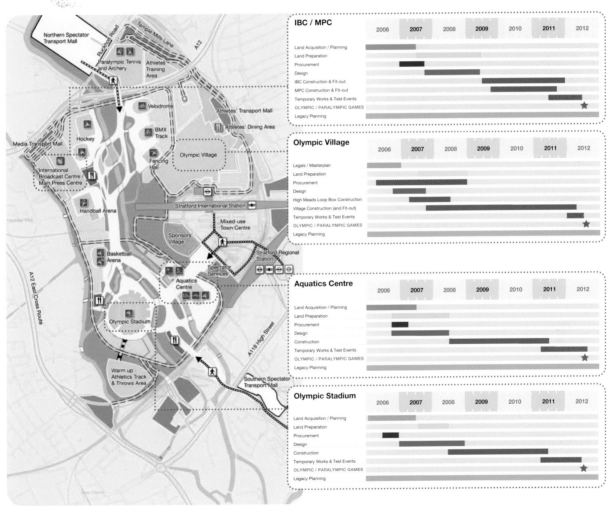

The Delivery Programme for the Olympic Park is 2-4-1 – 2 years to acquire the land, start to clean it up, secure the necessary planning permissions and do the design work and procurement; 4 years to build the venues and infrastructure which will enable test events to be staged from 1 year before the Games start on July 27, 2012. It is a timetable that is challenging but achievable. We are confident that we can deliver in partnership and leave a lasting legacy the country can be proud of.

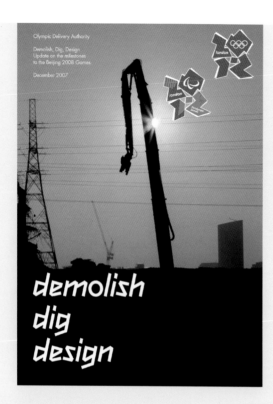

Demolish, Dig, Design – Milestones from December 2007 to the start of the Beijing Games in August 2008.

Milestone 01 The majority of the Olympic Park will be cleared and cleaned.

Milestone 02 With the tunnels and cabling complete, the power for the Olympic Park will be set to switch underground.

Milestone 03 The main temporary roads and bridges will have been built, giving access to a safe and secure construction site for the 'big build'.

Milestone 04 The installation of new water and energy systems that will serve the Olympic Park during and after the London 2012 Games will have started.

Milestone 05 The regeneration of the waterways will have started, improving the environment and access for the 'big build'.

Milestone 06 The transport enhancements that will open up east London and support the London 2012 Games will have started, with many complete.

Milestone 07 Construction will have started on the bridge that will take people over the Aquatics Centre to the Olympic Stadium. Building work on the Olympic Stadium will be about to begin.

Milestone 08 Construction on the Olympic and Paralympic Village will have started.

Milestone 09 Contracts will have been let and designs agreed for the 'big four' venues in the Olympic Park – and at venues outside London work on site will have started.

Milestone 10 The development of the Legacy Masterplan Framework (LMF) for the Olympic Park will be well advanced.

The Big Build: Foundations – Milestones from July 2008 to 27 July 2009

Milestone 01 Almost all of the Olympic Park will have been cleared and cleaned. The overhead pylons will have been removed and the erection of the new perimeter security fence will be underway.

Milestone 02 Seven bridges will be structurally complete, 10 further bridges and underpasses will be under construction and the building of the permanent roads will have started. The refurbishment of the waterways in the Olympic Park will be complete.

Milestone 03 The new Primary Substation at Kings Yard will be substantially complete, with the new equipment also in place to transmit permanent power to the Olympic Park from the wider national network. The construction of the new Energy Centre will be well underway.

Milestone 04 The foundations of the Olympic Stadium will be complete. Work on the upper seating structure and roof will be underway.

Milestone 05 The foundations of the Aquatics Centre will have been completed with work on the building's structure well underway.

Milestone 06 Work will have started on the foundations of the Velodrome and International Broadcast Centre/Main Press Centre.

Milestone 07 Contracts will have been let, designs agreed and work will be about to start on the Handball Arena (renamed the Copper Box). The design of the Basketball Arena will have been agreed, and the process of appointing construction contractors will be underway.

Milestone 08 Building work will be underway on the majority of the Olympic and Paralympic Village plots.

Milestone 09 Significant progress will have been made on the transport projects that are increasing capacity to support the Games. Of the 25 underway, 13 will be nearing completion.

Milestone 10 Outside of London the ODA works at Weymouth and Portland will have been completed and ready for use. Construction work will have also started.

Key construction milestones published annually by the ODA.

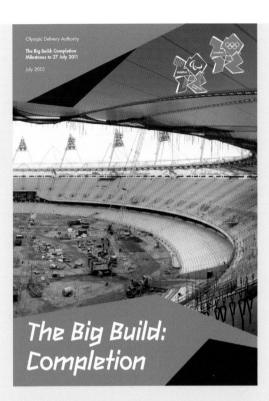

The Big Build: Structures – Milestones from July 2009 to 27 July 2010

Milestone 01 The structure of the Olympic Stadium including the roof will be complete. The first seats will be fitted and work on the field of play about to start.

Milestone 02 The Aquatics Centre's permanent structure and roof will be complete and all three swimming pools will be dug out.

Milestone 03 The Velodrome structure and roof will be complete, with work about to start on installing the timber track.

Milestone 04 The structure of the International Broadcast Centre and multi-storey car park will be finished, with roof and wall cladding well underway. The Main Press Centre's structure will be nearing completion.

Milestone 05 The Handball Arena, renamed the Copper Box, and Basketball Arena structures will be in place with internal works underway. Building work will have begun on the new Eton Manor sporting facilities.

Milestone 06 The majority of the Olympic and Paralympic Village homes will be structurally finished and internal works will have started. All the major infrastructure needed to support the development will be complete.

Milestone 07 All works will be complete at the Eton Dorney Rowing venue. The new lake and competition courses at Lee Valley White Water Centre will be finished with the facilities building almost complete. A planning application will have been submitted for the Shooting facilities at The Royal Artillery Barracks.

Milestone 08 More than half of the new bridges and underpasses will be complete and parts of the Olympic Park Loop Road in operation. Planting will have begun across the Park.

Milestone 09 The Energy Centre, Primary Substation, main sewer and deep sewer pumping station will all be operational.

Milestone 10 All major transport improvements will be in progress or complete, and the next level of detailed planning for transport operations during the Games will have been completed.

The Big Build: Completion – Milestones from July 2010 to 27 July 2011

Milestone 01 Construction of the Olympic Stadium will be complete and the venue ready to be handed over.

Milestone 02 Construction of the Aquatics Centre will be complete and the venue ready to be handed over.

Milestone 03 Construction of the Velodrome will be complete and the venue ready to be handed over.

Milestone 04 Construction of the International Broadcast Centre/Main Press Centre will be complete and ready for occupation by the Olympic Broadcasting Service and the London 2012 Organising Committee.

Milestone 05 Construction of the Handball Arena (renamed the Copper Box) and Basketball Arena will be complete and the venues ready to be handed over.

Milestone 06 Construction of the Lee Valley White Water Centre will be complete and the venue handed over to Lee Valley Regional Park Authority.

Milestone 07 Construction work on Eton Manor and The Royal Artillery Barracks will be underway and on track to be completed as planned in spring 2012.

Milestone 08 The external structure of the Olympic and Paralympic Village will be finished with the internal fit-out complete in most of the blocks.

Milestone 09 Construction of all permanent bridges will be complete. All utilities will be operational. Landscaping will be well advanced across the Park.

Milestone 10 Construction work at Stratford station will be complete, with Londoners already benefiting from hundreds of millions of pounds of additional investment across London's transport system.

Design phase focused on preparing the site for the main construction of the venues and infrastructure for the Games and the legacy beyond 2012. The second 10 milestones in The Big Build: Foundations phase focused on the first phase of construction, putting in place the foundations of the main venues and infrastructure in the Park. The third set of milestones focused on the delivery of the main venues and infrastructure – The Big Build: Structures. The final milestones – The Big Build: Completion– focused on completing the main venues and infrastructure with one year to go. As each milestone was ticked off over the six years, the ODA's credibility was enhanced. And as the venues and parklands emerged, the scepticism of politicians, press and public turned slowly to admiration and pride.

THE DELIVERY PARTNER

The ODA knew that the skills and numbers of personnel it required would change radically throughout the delivery of the Park. Consequently, it appointed CLM as Delivery Partner in August 2006. CLM was a private-sector consortium comprising a partnership of three parent companies brought together exclusively to deliver the Park – CH2M Hill, Laing O'Rourke and Mace. The consortium had extensive experience of large-scale programme management through CH2M Hill (including experience of managing prior Olympic construction programmes) and a breadth of construction project and contract management experience through Mace and Laing O'Rourke. It also brought with it turn-key tools and processes, including design management, contract management, change control and cost and programme reporting. The ODA therefore secured both the resource for each phase of the programme through planning, design, procurement, delivery to commercial close out and also the ability to tap into the expertise of these three major organisations as required. The Delivery Partner was responsible for managing the programme and delivery of all infrastructure and venues to briefs, budgets and time-scales set by the ODA. Each project had an ODA project sponsor – the budget holder responsible for driving the project forward, defining the brief, overseeing the design and planning process, securing approval of the business case and managing stakeholders – and a delivery partner project manager who was responsible for delivery of the project. The project sponsors and project managers were the hub at the centre of the wheel of every project, everything went through them, nothing happened without their knowledge and approval.

Once the ODA had committed to what it was going to deliver, at what cost and over what timescales, it resisted any changes. It did this through an internal Change Control Board, which met every month to debate and agree any changes to the project. Attended by directors, project sponsors, project managers and others, they were heady sessions where critical decisions were made. 'Is it nice to have, or essential?' was the pointed question behind every decision to increase or change what was being delivered. It was also where savings on projects were announced and celebrated. More often than not, changes that were accepted were driven by previously unforeseen factors – such as the discovery of underground contamination – and covered by contingency funds, or by enhancements that would benefit legacy.

DELIVERING SUSTAINABILITY

Sydney 2000 was the first Games to put the environment on the agenda explicitly. Like London 2012, it restored a heavily contaminated site for its Olympic Park, implemented a water management system supplying both potable and non-potable water, restored waterways for people and wildlife, and provided some renewable energy particularly through the use of photovoltaics in its Village. Greenpeace helped to develop environmental guidelines and also did a review following the Games, scoring them 7 out of 10. However, it wasn't until well after the Games that Sydney drew up its legacy masterplan. It was several years before the venues and infrastructure were deemed relatively successful. The big lessons from Sydney 2000 were that legacy must be planned from the start, and sustainability targets must be set up front, and then managed and monitored throughout design and delivery.

The well-documented problems of Athens 2004 to meet its programme meant that sustainability was not seriously considered. WWF scored the environmental component only 0.77 out of 4. It did improve transport infrastructure, but paid only lip service to water and waste management and embodied carbon. It was also criticised for lack of protection for fragile environmental and cultural assets. The lessons were to plan and design early, including for legacy, use existing venues wherever possible, only build permanent venues that had a legacy use, embrace the temporary and sustainability.

The United Nations Environment Programme advised Beijing 2008 on how to deliver a more sustainable Games and set 20 ambitious environmental goals addressing air quality, transport, sewage treatment and a target of 20 per cent of energy to come from renewables. Beijing's overriding goal, however, was to establish itself on the world stage. The symbolism of the Bird's Nest Stadium and the Water Cube Aquatics Centre was more important than delivering sustainability. London's Olympic Stadium used one quarter of the amount of steel in the Bird's Nest, which is now used only occasionally, and only half of the Water Cube has been converted for leisure use. London 2012 learned the lessons of previous Games, particularly Munich 1972 and Barcelona 1992, both of which used the power of the Games to invest in permanent infrastructure that laid the foundations for new quarters for their cities. London 2012 also addressed the need to focus seriously on sustainability.

As a new organisation, the ODA had to write all its corporate policies and strategies. It took the opportunity to 'rewrite the book'. Working with stakeholders across the board, including key environmental organisations, businesses, universities and community groups, the 'rewrite' was encompassed most comprehensively in its *Sustainable Development Strategy*.[12]

(continued on page 84)

DELIVERING THE PARK WITH CONSISTENCY AND FLEXIBILITY

Ian Galloway OBE
Programme Director, CLM, 2007–11

Matt Heal
Head of Parklands and Public Realm, CLM, 2006–9

Our pitch for the project was on the basis that we offered something different. CLM's unique bid was a blend of three separate companies – CH2M Hill International, Laing O'Rourke and Mace – that had complementary skills, but little overlap. We had individual cultures and used different processes that gave us a lot to choose from to meet the peculiarities of the programme and the delivery standards that the ODA demanded. The computer-based Programme Delivery Management System, for example, was built from scratch using the best tried and tested procedures from each organisation and those tailored for delivery of the ODA's programme.

On signing the contract in September 2006, the immediate need was to get the power lines underground as swiftly as possible. Of course there was always the desire to get the Olympic Stadium underway quickly, but the power lines sterilised both the Olympic Stadium and Olympic and Paralympic Village sites, posing a significant risk to the programme. The location and design of the tunnels for the power lines had to be fast tracked, and the complex mix of legal issues for access and planning was particularly challenging.

We knew the site was contaminated but had no idea to what extent. We needed a comprehensive

Diggers processing contaminated soil on the Aquatics Centre site in September 2007. An extensive programme of groundwater monitoring was undertaken across the Park as part of the decontamination and remediation works.

Demolition of the Capital Print buildings in October 2007. These buildings, located within the footprint of the Stadium, were some of the first to be removed on the Park.

The south of the Park looking west towards the City of London in March 2010. The construction of the 2012 Gardens on the western bank of the Waterworks river has just started on site.

picture as rapidly as possible and pushed hard to start the site investigations wherever we could get access. Close behind was the start of the earthworks programme. This had to be built up incrementally and by the time we completed the landform we were on version 13 of the topography plan. The masterplan also remained live for a long period. Positions for some of the key venues had to be revised from the original bid. The International Broadcast Centre/Main Press Centre (IBC/MPC), for example, was moved from the south of the Olympic Stadium, to the far east of the Park, before finally settling in the north-west corner. The

refinement process was to ensure that the masterplan would maximise legacy opportunities and provide the greatest value in the long term. Most ideas were run offline initially, tested, and then only included once agreement had been achieved across the programme. During this time the ODA's Communications team was great at presenting key messages to stakeholders and the wider public, for example the 'big build', the 'big four' (Olympic Stadium, Aquatics Centre, Velodrome and IBC/MPC), the 2-4-1 programme and key milestones.

A key stage in the delivery of the masterplan was when we moved into the design and delivery of

infrastructure and venues. The Park was divided into separate projects. This was when things began to really take off. There were more than 30 capital-build projects that brought a new level of detail, and the need to coordinate multiple design and contractor teams. Once the entire delivery programme was mapped out we went through each stage in detail to reduce it by three months. This was to ensure that we would complete a year ahead of the Games to allow for testing.

The utilities – gas, water, electricity, heating, cooling, telecommunications, foul and potable water – were probably the hardest to programme, design and deliver. They not only had to be coordinated with each other, but also with the bridges, venues, landscape and public realm and especially the topography, along with other structures, while ensuring that stringent accessibility requirements were met. Should they be put in early or late, in a common trench or separated? Ultimately they were separated but installed in broad corridors. Having agreed that installing them later would be too disruptive, they started early in the construction programme. This proved to be the right decision.

Almost as complex was the Parklands and Public Realm project. It had an interface with virtually every project on the Park. While most of the venues were relatively isolated, the parklands and public realm connected everything. A lot of the venue architects wanted to design the setting for their own buildings and had their own view on how the parklands should look, but the ODA wanted consistency and so adopted an integrated approach across the entire site. The packaging of this project across the Park made an important contribution to achieving this goal.

Project management is a process that continually tries to limit change. So the introduction of a significant variation in the detailed design of the Park was a big issue. At the same time that those changes were being proposed, there was increasing concern about the likelihood of a growing surplus of soil. This would have been incredibly expensive, difficult and highly unsustainable to take off site. The Parklands and Public Realm design team managed to establish a revised landform that used much of the surplus material on site. This was one of the single biggest and certainly the latest major design change across the entire Park. It was achieved in the nick of time and could only just be accommodated given that so many other projects were already procured and underway.

It is an immense achievement to have collectively delivered something as large and complex as the Park on time, and particularly without significant injuries, logistical issues or industrial disputes. While it was important to establish agreed processes and operate consistently from the outset, over time the reporting systems have been refined to meet the evolving needs of the ODA as client and, ultimately, the Government and other funders. Mitigating risk requires flexibility to deal with challenges as they emerge, but it was essential to take the time needed do things properly. The ODA invested heavily in design and procurement to give teams time to do what they are good at, and provided the structure for individuals to deliver at the highest level.

The Olympic Stadium 'island' site looking south towards Canary Wharf in June 2008. The formation of the 'bowl' of the Stadium can be clearly seen.

It was inspired by the ten cross-cutting themes in *Towards a One Planet 2012* and the over-arching *London 2012 Sustainability Policy and Plan*.[13] One Planet Living assessments are based on ecological and carbon footprints as indicators of sustainability. An ecological footprint is a measure of the area of land needed to support a person, an organisation, a city or a country; or to support the production of a product such as a bicycle. It measures both the natural capital resources consumed and wastes produced that the environment has to absorb. A carbon footprint is a simplified proxy for an ecological footprint measuring just the quantity of greenhouse gases that contribute to global warming.

True to its commitment to be the first sustainable Olympic and Paralympic Games, London 2012 was the first to commission a carbon footprint study assessing their impact.[14] The study assessed both the embodied and the operational carbon impacts of the Games. It was intended more to guide decision-making than set standards and led to some surprising conclusions, one of which was that two thirds of emissions are embodied in the venues and infrastructure and therefore expended before the Games commenced. Laying to rest the assumption that air travel is the greatest emitter of carbon for the Games, it confirmed that the focus on legacy, permanence, efficiency and embracing the temporary was absolutely correct. No less than 55 per cent of emissions were down to the construction works undertaken by the ODA. Carbon footprinting is an emerging methodology. By undertaking the study, LOCOG and the ODA mainstreamed carbon footprinting and at the same time advanced and developed methodologies through delivering the Park. The carbon footprint study came quite late in the day for the ODA; the larger lesson therefore is that ecological and carbon footprint studies should be the precursor to any development project from inception through masterplanning, detailed design, construction and operation to guide decision-making and establish targets.

PRIORITY THEMES

By common consent the ODA's six priority themes cemented the remarkable and successful delivery of the Park. Projects traditionally measure sustainability through primarily environmental objectives using industry standards such as BREEAM, Code for Sustainable Homes, CEEQUAL and LEED.[15] The ODA's Sustainable Development Strategy moved it from the aspirational to the deliverable and measurable. Its 12 sustainability objectives from carbon emissions to equalities and inclusion (see table opposite) were distilled down to the six priority themes addressing health, safety and security; design and accessibility; legacy; sustainability; equality and inclusion; and employment and skills. The themes set out the targets and key performance indicators that were embedded in every brief and contract. They were managed and monitored at every stage of the programme from brief to completion of construction and business close out, forcing designers, contractors and suppliers to challenge conventional practice. Never before had sustainability been so comprehensively and pragmatically addressed.

London 2012 overarching themes	12 Olympic Delivery Authority objectives											
	Carbon	Water	Waste	Materials	Biodiversity and ecology	Land, air, water, noise	Supporting communities	Transport and mobility	Access	Employment and skills	Health and well-being	Inclusion
Climate change	✓	✓		✓	✓		✓	✓				
Waste		✓	✓	✓			✓					
Biodiversity and ecology		✓			✓	✓						
Inclusion						✓	✓		✓	✓	✓	✓
Healthy living				✓	✓		✓	✓		✓	✓	

The ODA cross-referenced its 12 key sustainable development objectives with London 2012's overarching sustainability themes. Project delivery focused on the ODA's six priority themes: health, safety and security; design and accessibility; legacy; sustainability; equality and inclusion; and employment and skills.

Independent scrutiny of the ODA's sustainability targets was achieved in several ways. Rigorous conditions were attached to planning approvals, including Section 106 Agreements that formalised sustainability targets.[16] The independent planning committee required the ODA to provide a formal report on progress against those targets annually. Also, for the first time, health, safety and the environment were put under combined leadership throughout construction. Directors from each of the principal contractors on the Park were required to be members of the Safety, Health and Environment Leadership Team (SHELT), which was charged with delivering 'The safest, healthiest and greenest Olympic and Paralympic Games'.[17] Contractors were also required to prepare Environmental Management Plans setting out standards for monitoring environmental quality and The Code of Construction Practice[18] required them to be 'good neighbours' by liaising with local residents throughout construction.

Designers and contractors were required to use the Building Research Establishment's (BRE) Green Guide to Specification of materials. And in another first, the ODA worked with BRE on a bespoke version of its Environmental Assessment Method (BREEAM) for use on permanent sports venues. All permanent venues on the Park achieved an 'Excellent' rating.[19] The ODA also required that all apartments in the Olympic and Paralympic Village achieve Code for Sustainable Homes Level 4 – the highest rating – and, again remarkably, they did. It also required submission for CEEQUAL awards, which are aimed at improving sustainability in civil engineering and public realm projects – every project achieved a 'very good' rating and eight won 'Excellent' Awards including the Greenway, which achieved the highest ever CEEQUAL score of 97 per cent. Contractors were required to sign up to WRAP's (Waste and Resources Action Programme) Halving Waste to Landfill Initiative and to abide by the Code of Construction Practice. On appointment, contractors were issued with Implementation Guidance for Project Teams (IGPT) setting out detailed requirements that would ensure the ODA achieved targets across the Park. As an example, the number

Priority theme indicators	Target	Status (as of December 2011)
Carbon		
Carbon reduction	50%	58%
Renewable energy	20%[1]	10%
BREEAM		
BREEAM [2] – Olympic Park permanent venues	Excellent in legacy	On track to achieve Excellent[3]
BREEAM – Lee Valley White Water Centre	Very Good in legacy	On track to achieve Very Good
BREEAM – Retail and Academy	Very Good in legacy	On track to achieve Very Good
BREEAM – Polyclinic	Excellent in legacy	On track to achieve Excellent
Water		
Water reduction	40%	60%
Sustainable Urban Drainage Systems compliance	Compliant	Conditions discharged
Waste		
Reused or recycled (demolition)	90%	98.5%
Reused, recycled or recovered (construction)	90%	99%
Materials		
Recycled aggregate	25%	42%
Recycled content (Waste Resource Action Programme net waste tool)	20%	34%
Responsibly sourced materials	80%	86%
Timber from sustainable sources	100%	100%
Unhealthy/barred materials	0% non-compliance	0%

Priority theme indicators	Target	Status (as of December 2011)
Biodiversity		
Habitat creation and area covered (hectares)	45	25ha for Games >45ha for legacy
Habitat creation nest/roost boxes	675	568 for Games >675 in legacy
Land, air, water and noise		
CEEQUAL[4] – 20 projects	Very Good	On track to achieve and exceed Very Good[5]
Considerate constructors scheme	4 or more in each section	4 or more in each section
Transport		
Sustainable transport (deliver 50% by weight by rail/water)	50%	67%

4   CEEQUAL – Civil Engineering Environmental Quality and Assessment Award Scheme.
5   13 projects have achieved Excellent, one off-Park project has achieved Very Good (construction-only award), and the remaining six are on track to achieve Excellent or Very Good.

Summary table of progress in delivering the priority sustainable development themes through to December 2011. Published in *Delivering Change*, London 2012 Pre-Games Sustainability Report, LOCOG, April 2012.

1   During 2011 the renewable energy target was adjusted in planning from 20 per cent down to 9 per cent through a Section 73 amendment, discussed further on opposite page.
2   BREEAM – Building Research Establishment Environmental Assessment Method.
3   The Aquatics Centre, Velodrome, Copper Box (formerly known as the Handball Arena) and Eton Manor have all achieved BREEAM Excellent. The Olympic Stadium and the International Broadcast Centre/Main Press Centre are on track to achieve Excellent in legacy.

of bird and bat boxes that venues, bridges and structures had to install across the programme to achieve biodiversity targets was set down. More generally though, setting sustainability targets, but not how they should be delivered, engaged and energised the whole supply chain and was instrumental to the ODA's achievements.

The Commission for a Sustainable London 2012 was established specifically to provide independent scrutiny of London 2012's programme. It published annual reports on the ODA's performance and occasional thematic reviews. After five years' work, Shaun McCarthy, the Chair of the independent Commission, lauded the ODA's achievement: 'Construction is nearing completion and I commend the Olympic Delivery Authority for their professional approach throughout. Not only have they delivered wonderful facilities ahead of schedule and under budget; they have also delivered unprecedented sustainability standards through a rigorous approach involving the on-site teams and management. The ODA's performance in this area should be game-changing for the construction industry. I look to the Government, the Mayor of London and construction firms to follow the ODA's example, which shows that quality, value, deadlines and sustainability are not incompatible but mutually supportive.'[20]

ENERGY, WATER, WASTE

By ensuring excellent insulation, airtight construction and optimising natural heating, cooling and lighting, energy demand was reduced by 15 per cent over and above the standards required at the time. This was a real challenge to designers and contractors unused to such stretching targets. The new state-of-the-art combined district heating, cooling and power plant – the largest in the UK at the time – achieved a 20 per cent reduction in CO_2 emissions across the Park. To assure that the 'Lean, Mean and Green' targets were not just a 'paper exercise', the ODA required the operational testing to verify airtightness, insulation and the efficiency of heating, ventilation and air-conditioning equipment. The target of 20 per cent energy produced by renewable sources was the only sustainability target the ODA did not achieve. The original proposal to install a wind turbine at Eton Manor failed due to changing regulations during the project and there was not enough time to envision, design and deliver any alternative. In lieu, the ODA invested in two community retrofit programmes, prompting the Commission for a Sustainable London 2012 to note, 'These programmes have the potential to be a model for future initiatives including meeting the national zero-carbon targets after 2016.'[21] Renewable energy sources were, however, incorporated throughout the Park: the power plant has a biomass boiler; the Main Press Centre has photovoltaic panels on its roof; 170 panels are integrated into lighting columns in the Park; and there are seven small vertical helical wind turbines integrated with the 25m-high lighting masts on the concourse above the 2012 Gardens.

The ODA's Integrated Water Management approach considered all aspects of water from river water quality, flood risk and water habitats, to potable and non-potable water supply and demand. Potable water use was reduced by 57 per cent through the installation of water-efficient fittings, rainwater harvesting, filter backwash recycling and the construction of the UK's largest non-potable network supplied with reclaimed wastewater or 'blackwater', treated to a water quality that exceeds bathing-water standards. The 'black water treatment plant', another first for the ODA and its partner Thames Water, takes wastewater from the Northern Outfall Sewer, which runs beneath the Greenway, and treats it using the latest technology before pumping it through a dedicated water mains network into the Park for reuse. It provides enough non-potable water to flush more than 80,000 toilets each day. As well as being used for toilet flushing in the main buildings and venues, it is used to irrigate the parklands and fields of play within venues and for heating and cooling operations in the Energy Centre.

The ODA adopted the 'reduce, reuse, repair, recycle' mantra to drive its approach to waste. A central on-site waste consolidation centre was set up to process segregated construction waste from all the 17 primary contractors across the Park. Segregated materials included timber, bricks and solid concrete, construction plastic, metal and office waste. Site-won material was recycled as engineering fill and used in temporary road and pavement construction and in the gabions across the Park, on the Greenway and in the parklands. More than 80 per cent of spoil on site was cleaned and reused on the Park. A total of 98.5 per cent of demolition waste was recycled or reused. In addition, eight buildings were dismantled and re-erected elsewhere. Approximately 2,000 tonnes of waste was removed from the site by barge. Even the foundations for the Aquatics Centre, the Copper Box and the Olympic Stadium used concrete made with more than 30 per cent of recycled materials.

SUSTAINABLE MATERIALS AND BIODIVERSITY

To assure the ODA's sustainability targets for materials were achieved, there was a dedicated 'materials manager' within the Delivery Partner's sustainability team who worked with designers, contractors and suppliers, constantly pushing at the limits of best practice. This level of ownership and technical support was critical to raising awareness of the contribution materials make to the emissions. For example, rationalisation and efficiencies through design alone reduced concrete demand by 65,000 cubic metres – an 11 per cent overall reduction in volume – saving 20,000 tonnes of embodied carbon. The ODA appointed a single concrete supplier who set up a batching plant on site, which reduced the number and frequency of deliveries, secured supply and facilitated the development of sustainable concrete mixes. Of the 400,000 tonnes of concrete used on the Park, the mix contained approximately 170,000 tonnes of recycled and secondary aggregate, a saving of approximately 30,000 tonnes of embodied carbon in addition to the elimination of over 70,000 road vehicle movements. Emissions were also cut by delivering 67 per cent by weight of materials to site by rail and barge against a target of 50 per cent – again reducing the number and frequency of delivery trucks.

Another innovative example of reducing emissions was the upper compression ring of the Olympic Stadium, which is made from surplus steel gas supply pipes – this saved 9 tonnes of carbon dioxide emissions. The Copper Box, initially named the Handball Arena, is an innovative example of material efficiency. The distinctive, box-shaped top of the

arena is wrapped in 3,000 square metres of copper cladding. The ODA worked with the manufacturer of the copper cladding to ensure it had a high recycled content. Sixty-five per cent is from production scraps. Additionally, to demonstrate that the copper was responsibly sourced, the ODA helped the manufacturer audit its full chain of custody from mine, to manufacture, to delivery to site. Only environmentally and socially responsible materials were used on the Park. The Timber Supplier Panel established by the ODA assured that 100 per cent of timber came from certified and sustainable sources. Some 20 per cent of materials by value came from recycled or secondary sources; 25 per

Investing in a new lock at Three Mills allowed larger barges to use the waterways to transport construction materials and equipment into the Park and remove waste. A temporary wharf was built opposite the Aquatics Centre site on the Waterworks river.

An on-site recycling plant in November 2007. Significant cost savings were achieved through the processing and recycling of materials generated by the demolition of existing buildings and the remediation of the site.

cent of aggregates by weight came from recycled or secondary sources; 90 per cent of demolition materials by weight were reused or recycled and 90 per cent of construction waste was diverted from landfill.

More than 45ha of new wildlife habitat was delivered, about half for the Games and the remainder through the transformation of the Park following the Games. The river corridors are of particular value, containing important habitats including wetlands, wet woodlands, ponds and swales. However, it was not only the parklands that contributed to biodiversity targets. The Olympic and Paralympic Village, Aquatics Centre, Eton Manor and Main Press Centre have more than 15,000 square metres of living roof. As a result of an integrated approach to the project, the ODA restored the waterways and provided an extraordinary range of habitats for wildlife and people. The parklands landscape accepts, absorbs, stores and utilises rainwater, minimises flood risk, maximises opportunities for a rich ecology and provides shading and cooling to reduce the effects of the urban heat island. The ways in which the parklands provide a working landscape are described further in Chapter Three. The parklands at the heart of the Park were a key element of the masterplan contributing to both the sustainable Games and legacy.

DIVERSITY, EQUALITY AND INCLUSION

As described in Chapter One, one of the reasons the Park was located in this part of London was due to the significant levels of deprivation. The ODA set new standards not only for the environmental aspects of sustainability, but also for the social and economic aspects. It carried out and published Equalities Impact Assessments on every project to improve its work by assessing potential impacts on equality target groups, ensuring, as far as possible, that steps were taken to eliminate or minimise any negative consequences and to maximise opportunities that promoted equality. Legislation required that these assessments address race, disability and gender. However, the ODA went much further, assessing all the equality strands of race, disability, sexual orientation, age, faith/religion and gender.

EMPLOYMENT AND SKILLS

In an area of high unemployment and poor educational and skills levels, the ODA used its construction programme to engage with the local community and get them into work. The statistics are telling. More than 46,000 people worked on the Olympic Park and Olympic and Paralympic Village in total and more than 12,000 at peak. 10 per cent of the workforce were previously unemployed and local people from the five Host Boroughs (Greenwich, Hackney, Newham, Tower Hamlets and Waltham Forest – Barking and

Cement pour for the main foundations of the Aquatics Centre in September 2008. The specification and supply of sustainable concrete achieved significant reductions in embodied carbon across all construction projects.

Dagenham was awarded Host Borough status later in the construction project) made up 15.6 per cent of the construction workforce on the Olympic Park, and 24.2 per cent of the construction workforce on the Olympic and Paralympic Village — beating the ODA's target of 15 per cent. On the Olympic Park, 15 per cent were from Black, Asian and Minority Ethnic backgrounds. A total of 457 apprentices worked for the ODA on the construction programme. Overall, 3,559 training places were provided through the National Skills Academy for Construction, which the ODA set up.

In an effort to enhance equality and inclusion, the ODA introduced the Women into Construction Project, which included a work-placement initiative, offering newly qualified women an opportunity to gain experience of working on site. The project brokered 270 women into employment, with 83 women experiencing work placements. A total of 674 women received employment support as part of this programme. In 2010, Opportunity Now, part of Business in the Community, recognised the ODA's gender equality programme with its Innovation Award. Opportunity Now praised the fact that women working on the Park were empowered and supported to use their skills to further develop their careers. Semra Kamil Yusuf, a participant in the Women into Construction project, said 'gaining employment has changed my life tremendously as I was very depressed and had a lack of confidence. This has helped me financially, emotionally and socially.'

Photograph of female workers employed on the Park, taken with London Assembly member Jennette Arnold on the Greenway in December 2009. The Women in Construction project provided a significant number of newly qualified women with on-site construction experience.

In a wider effort to engage with communities, events were held with stakeholders and local community groups to consult them on the plans for the venues and infrastructure for the Games. There were quarterly community meetings providing construction updates in four areas around the Park. The Olympic Park Engagement Network (OPEN) held twice-yearly events, hosted by the ODA's Chief Executive, for individuals, communities and businesses surrounding the Park. There was a 24-hour Construction Hotline for members of the public and an education programme providing schools with tours of the Park and health and safety workshops. More than 300 local schools visited the Park and nearly 7,000 children and young people attended workshops. The ODA hosted daily bus tours of the Park, and more than 280,000 stakeholders and members of the public saw progress first hand.

DESIGN, ACCESSIBILITY, HEALTH AND SAFETY

The ODA knew that good design was essential to achieving venues, infrastructure, parklands and public realm that were not only sustainable and functioned well, but were also beautiful. Its Design Strategy set out clearly what the ODA would do to ensure it delivered a beautiful and accessible Park, and this is covered in more detail in the next chapter. The Park is both beautiful and one of the most accessible developments ever delivered. The ODA achieved this by employing in-house accessibility specialists to advise on all aspects of design and construction and by engaging with key stakeholders and disabled people on accessibility issues from design through to completion. The ODA's Inclusive Design Standards provided project teams with guidance on how to deliver the principles as set out in its *Inclusive Design Strategy*. The standards aimed to create environments where people have the same quality of experience, irrespective of how they engaged with the physical environment.

The Built Environment Access Panel provided expert technical and strategic advice to the ODA and its project teams. It comprised a group of disability and inclusive design experts in the design and planning fields drawn from a range of government, private and voluntary sector organisations. The Access and Inclusion Forum was established to give ODA project sponsors, managers and design teams, advice and feedback on proposals from the point of view of users and experts in disability, age, gender, faith and specific impairment requirements. The Forum included representation from a lead organisation of disabled people within each of the original five Host Boroughs, as well as the Borough Access Officers, a representative from a number of other impairment-specific organisations and other key external stakeholders. All projects were presented to these panels for review and comment during each design stage and prior to submission of planning applications.

The ODA's health and safety record was exemplary. More than 76 million hours were worked on the Park over five years. During this time the accident frequency rate was

Workers on the Velodrome constructing the cable-net roof in April 2010. The ODA invested heavily in the health and safety of the construction workers on the Park to minimise personal injury, with the added benefit of reducing delays to the construction programme.

comparable to the average for all British employment rather than just for construction and with no major environmental incidents. At 0.16 it is lower than all UK employment that recorded 0.21 in 2010/11 and 0.5 for the UK construction industry for the same period. Significantly there were no accidental fatalities which meant that construction workers on the Park were only as likely to suffer accidents as workers in offices and shops. It showed that through careful planning, the implementation of strategies that have a proven track record and with clear leadership and focus, even the most complex of construction programmes, with immoveable deadlines and fixed budgets, can be safe. Health and safety was addressed systematically – the ODA was the first Delivery Authority for a Games to have its health and safety management system certified against the internationally recognised Standard OHSAS 18001. Also, and uniquely, the ODA brought together design, construction, health, safety and environmental standards. It recognised that excellence across these sectors would be achieved not only by the implementation of effective systems and processes, but also by the leadership of the directors and senior staff of every contractor and the active engagement of all personnel.

A complex steel cross beam is carefully lifted into place to form one of the main structural elements of the Aquatics Centre roof in March 2009.

Additionally, through Park Health, the ODA provided occupational hygiene and medical facilities on site. It provided a degree of care and campaigning not previously experienced in the industry. Activities supporting healthy living included cycle route maps, cycle to work days with cycle mechanics available to service bikes, the provision of 400 cycle parking bays and healthy-eating events. The presence of a physiotherapist on site was also instrumental in reducing the number of lost days due to musculoskeletal disorders. Apart from the human concern that everyone should arrive home safely every evening, the ODA's performance on health and safety arguably contributed to it delivering on time and under budget. Human and environmental accidents cost time and money. Time spent on health, safety and the environment represented a sound investment rather than an additional cost.

LEGACY

It was the focus on legacy that drove long-term sustainability benefits. Regenerating a largely derelict, contaminated, poorly connected part of London and building a sustainable infrastructure will have multiple, long-term social, economic and environmental benefits. Some 75 pence in every £1 was invested in permanent infrastructure ready for legacy development. The carbon footprint study confirmed that the ODA was responsible for 55 per cent of all carbon emissions from the London 2102 programme, the biggest contributors being the permanent venues and infrastructure. Designing the Park from a legacy standpoint assured the biggest sustainable achievement, which was using the power of the Games to 'invest once and invest wisely'. The ODA broke the mould in delivering sustainable venues and infrastructure that will provide the locus for more than 20,000 people in the years to come. The International Olympic Committee (IOC) President Jacques Rogge recognised this, saying: 'London has raised the bar on how to deliver a lasting legacy. We can already see tangible results in the remarkable regeneration of east London. This great historical city has created a legacy blueprint for future Games hosts.'[22]

The ODA quickly established itself as a credible authority. It defined its scope of work, budget and programme, wrote policies and strategies and agreed priority themes setting out challenging sustainability targets that could be managed, monitored and reported on in an open, independent and transparent manner. While it was doing all this, it was also on site demolishing buildings and dismantling overhead pylons, tunnelling for the underground power lines, translocating species and habitats and decontaminating land. In addition, it was refining the masterplan and designing and detailing the utilities, structures, bridges, highways, venues, parklands, waterways, wetlands and a new topography that were all emerging concurrently on drawing boards and computers. This could only be done through exceptional planning, management and design.

Panoramic views of the entire site looking north taken in November 2007.

November 2008 as the structure of the Olympic Stadium emerges.

July 2009 with the roof structure of the Aquatics Centre, just right of centre, almost complete.

November 2010 with the form of the Olympic and Paralympic Village clearly visible.

December 2011 with Orbit nearly complete.

April 2012 as all the venues go through a series of test events.

The perennial meadows, riverside spectator lawn, wetlands and river Lea in the north east of the Park during the Games in July 2012.

CHAPTER THREE

CHAPTER THREE

Planning and Designing the Park

Once the bid was won in the summer of 2005, the masterplan for what became the Queen Elizabeth Olympic Park inevitably underwent a new level of development driven by the reality of implementation. It was reassessed according to the distribution and location of venues, Games-time operation, its overall sustainability, general efficiency, fitness for legacy and cost. Yet despite all this pragmatism, the Olympic Delivery Authority's (ODA's) deep commitment to design led to some award-winning jewels of architecture that were individual and poetic. This commitment extended beyond architecture to infrastructure, utilities and some stunning works of art. But the parklands and public realm astonished most – they were the crown within which the 'jewels' were set.

How many masterplans did it take to complete the Park? This question is more complicated than it might at first seem. One official answer is three: one for the Games in 2012, one for transformation immediately following the Games, and one for long-term legacy development beyond 2013. So far so unusual – this was the first time an Olympic Park had been designed for legacy, and then for the Games. A second official answer, in terms of formal planning applications, is two: one for the bid approved in November 2004, and a second following the bid's success in 2005 that was approved in September 2007. A third, and unofficial answer, is a 'known unknown'. Details within the Games masterplan were tweaked virtually up to the completion of the Park.

The Games masterplan was essentially very simple: the parklands at the heart based along and around the waterways; the 'front of house' concourse and bridges accommodating spectators entering the Park and moving to and from venues; the loop road providing access to the 'back of house' service areas for each venue; and the security fence with entrance plazas. The Transformation masterplan reversed this plan, creating a fully connected Park that was a part of the existing urban fabric.

EVOLUTION OF THE MASTERPLANS

The Games masterplan was always a 'work in progress', constantly being updated throughout the project in response to conditions discovered on site, the inevitable changes in the locations and sizes of structures and venues and the vicissitudes of political and cost pressures. It was also updated to capture improvements in value, efficiency, sustainability and in response to the London Organising Committee of the Olympic Games and Paralympic Games' (LOCOG's) emerging temporary overlay design requirements for the Games – it was responsible for the design and delivery of all temporary facilities required to stage the Games. But remarkably, despite the detail of the Games-time masterplan changing constantly, the legacy masterplan approved in 2007 did not change throughout the ODA's work up to the approval of its detailed transformation planning applications in April 2010. The consistent focus was on delivering the infrastructure for the Games, but driven by the requirements of the legacy masterplan.

The first intimations that changes to the bid masterplan might be necessary came from Chair of LOCOG, Sebastian Coe on 12 October 2005: 'It's a big jigsaw. It's a multi-faceted project ... it's very important to get all these things nailed down at the very beginning. The things that have caused grief over a seven-year implementation phase is [sic] when actually the strategy has consistently and continually changed. This is something that we want to deal with now.' Those changes soon came with the appointment of the EDAW Consortium led by landscape architect Jason Prior in January 2006, comprising EDAW plc, Buro Happold, Foreign Office Architects, HOK Sport and Allies & Morrison. It was charged with refining the masterplan it had prepared for the bid, and submitting a new application to enable construction of the Park to commence. Newly appointed Chief Executive Sir David Higgins knew that 'getting the site infrastructure and landscape right is a key task for the Olympic Delivery Authority over the next two years. It is not only critical for the Games but also to frame one of the most significant regeneration legacies for a generation.'[2]

It took six months to prepare the 2007 application comprising 15 volumes, including an Environmental Impact Assessment, Design and Access Statement, Statement of Community Involvement, and so on, with some 1,000 drawings. At around 10,000 pages, it was the largest planning application ever submitted in Europe. Resubmission was an impossibility given the immoveable deadline. Consequently, in order to manage the dynamic and fast-moving process of refinement, realignment and change, an innovative town planning process was agreed between the ODA's Town Planning Promoter Team

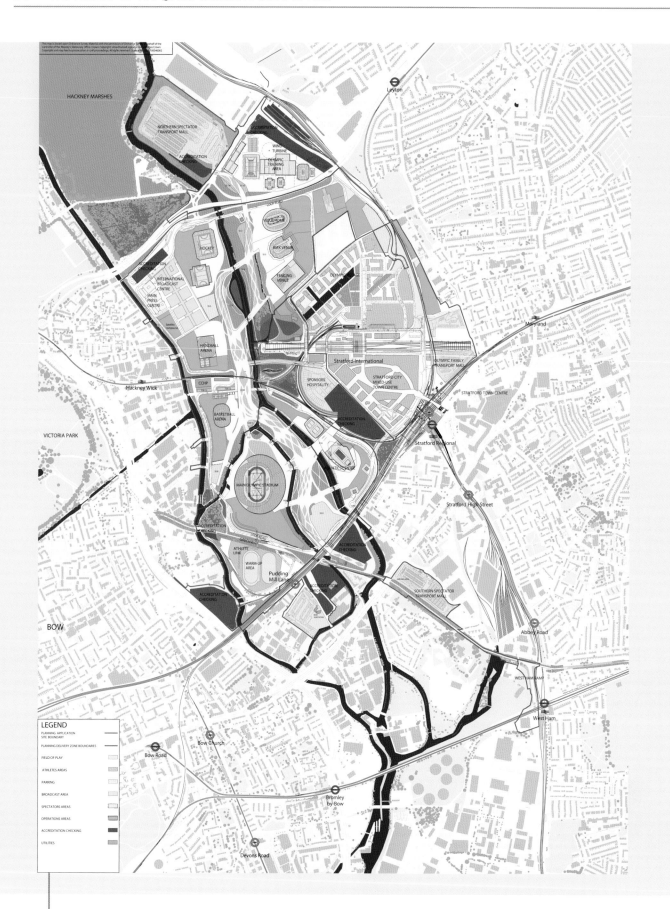

Illustrative Olympic Masterplan (left) and Illustrative Legacy Masterplan (right) submitted as part of the Olympic, Paralympic and Legacy Transformation Planning Application in 2007. It was the largest planning application in Europe, submitted on 7 February 2007 and approved on 28 September 2007.

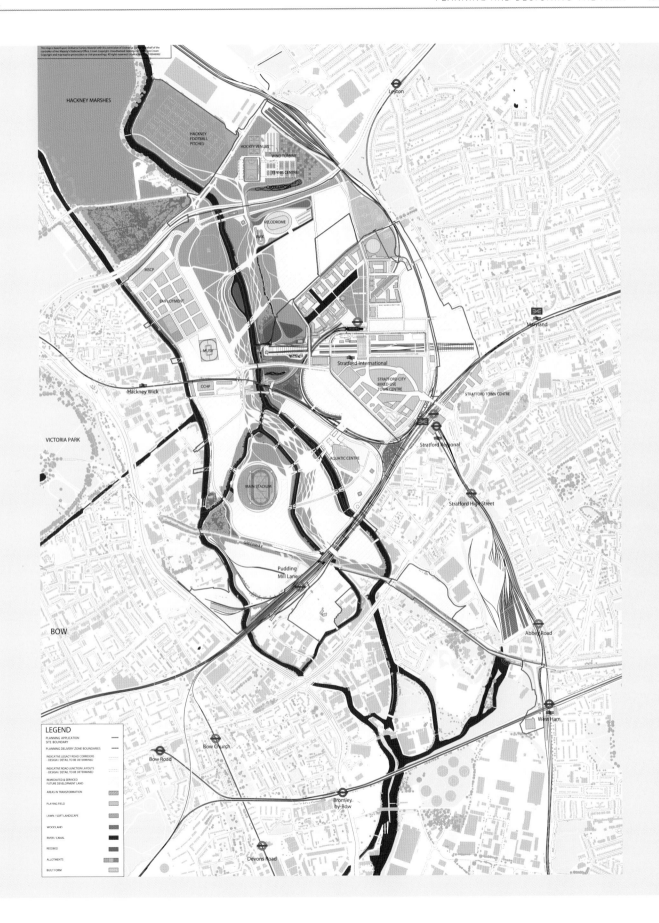

HACKNEY MARSHES

HACKNEY
FOOTBALL
PITCHES

HOCKEY VENUES

WIND TURBINE

TENNIS CENTRE

WATERPORT

VELODROME

MSCP

EMPLOYMENT

MUSE

Stratford International

STRATFORD CITY
MIXED-USE
TOWN CENTRE

Maryland

Hackney Wick

CCHP

CCHP

Stratford Town Centre

STRATFORD TOWN CENTRE

VICTORIA PARK

AQUATIC CENTRE

Stratford Regional

MAIN STADIUM

Stratford High Street

GREENWAY

Pudding
Mill Lane

Abbey Road

BOW

West Ham

LEGEND

PLANNING APPLICATION
SITE BOUNDARY

PLANNING DELIVERY ZONE BOUNDARIES

INDICATIVE LEGACY ROAD CORRIDORS
- DESIGN / DETAIL TO BE DETERMINED

INDICATIVE ROAD JUNCTION LAYOUTS
- DESIGN / DETAIL TO BE DETERMINED

REMEDIATED & SERVICED
FUTURE DEVELOPMENT LAND

AREAS IN TRANSFORMATION

PLAYING FIELD

LAWN / SOFT LANDSCAPE

WOODLAND

RIVER / CANAL

REEDBED

ALLOTMENTS

BUILT FORM

Bow Church

Bow Road

Bromley
by-Bow

Devons Road

(TPPT) and its 'arm's-length' Planning Decisions Team (PDT), which was, effectively, the local planning authority.[3] The 'slot in/slot out' process was a legally robust mechanism that meant that changes could be made to the masterplan without recourse to a completely new application. It was a 'jigsaw' approach that allowed for elements of the 2007 masterplan to be removed ('slotted out') and new replacement pieces to be put in their place ('slotted in'). Applications were supported by a Statement of Superseded Development that precluded the ODA from implementing that part of the development being superseded.[4] On notification of a 'slot in' application the PDT assessed the likely impact and confirmed whether it could be made. The TPPT then submitted an Environmental Impact Assessment 'screening opinion' to ensure that the PDT could assess the likely environmental impacts that might result from the application. Once the 'slot in' applications were approved, the masterplan was updated to provide a new baseline for both planners and designers. The new baselines ensured that both the original planning permission received in 2007 and the Environmental Impact Assessments were not compromised, and that everyone was working to the latest plan.

It was clear that a lot of work had been going on in the background. On 30 January 2006 Higgins announced the first revisions: 'The revised plans improve quality and security of the Olympic Park site as well as construction times.'[5] The Olympic and Paralympic Village was now more integrated with the Stratford City Development, allowing construction on the Village to start earlier than anticipated. The Stratford City masterplan had been a separate planning application submitted by Westfield, and approved at the same time as the Park masterplan. This was to assure it could go ahead even if the bid failed. With the bid won, this revised Park masterplan consolidated the two, allowing much better integration with the Stratford City development, and a more compact Park. Additionally, and partly in response to the clamour of complaints prompted by the Compulsory Purchase Orders, the amount of land now required for the Games meant that 80 businesses supporting around 1,000 jobs no longer needed to relocate.

The detailed planning and design of the Park was now steaming ahead. At the same time the London Development Agency (LDA) was progressing the Olympic Park 'fringe area' masterplans alongside the regeneration strategy for the whole of the Lea Valley from the Park down to the Thames. The Lower Lea Valley Opportunity Area Planning Framework, prepared by EDAW, was launched by the LDA and Thames Gateway Development Corporation on 16 May 2006. Yvette Cooper, then Minister for the Department for Communities and Local Government, said: 'We have always been clear that the Olympic legacy should be to strengthen the regeneration of the Lower Lea Valley. These plans show how it is possible to improve the quality of life in the city – with beautiful parks and green spaces as well as more affordable homes.'[6] One of the priorities for the Development Corporation coming out of the planning framework was the implementation of the Lea River Park which would see the completion, via the Olympic Park, of the Lee Valley Regional Park's 42-kilometre (26-

Illustrative Transformation Masterplan prepared in 2008. This shows the permanent venues that remain after the Games, the removal of the concourse, extended parklands and future development plots in beige.

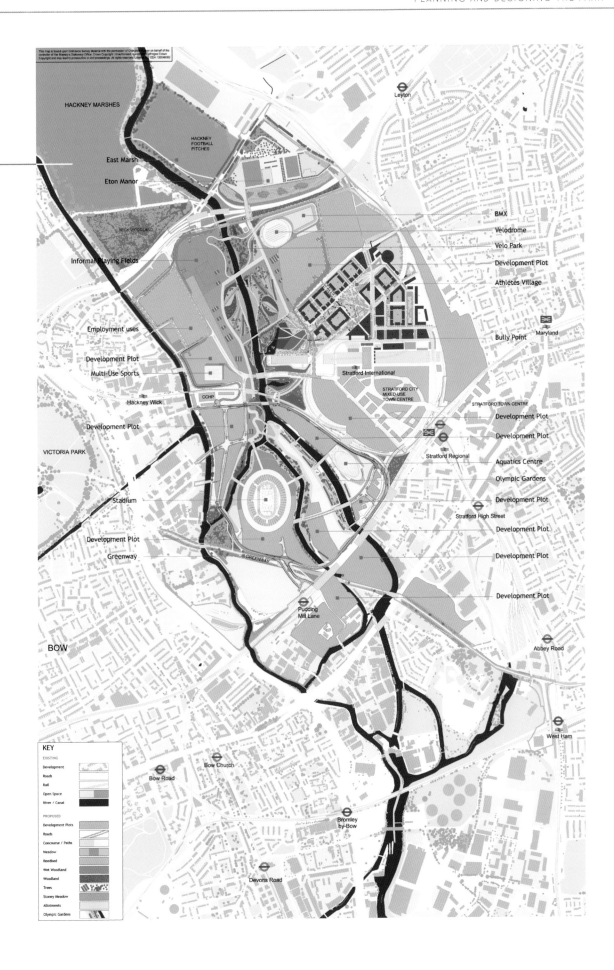

This map is based upon Ordnance Survey Material with the permission of Ordnance Survey on behalf of the controller of Her Majesty's Stationery Office. Crown Copyright. Unauthorised reproduction infringes Crown Copyright and may lead to prosecution or civil proceedings. All rights reserved. Licence No. OSA 100048092

HACKNEY MARSHES

HACKNEY FOOTBALL PITCHES

East Marsh

Eton Manor

WICK WOODLAND

Informal Playing Fields

Employment uses

Development Plot

Multi-Use Sports

Hackney Wick

CCHP

Development Plot

VICTORIA PARK

Stadium

Development Plot

Greenway

GREENWAY

Pudding Mill Lane

BOW

Leyton

BMX

Velodrome

Velo Park

Development Plot

Athletes Village

Bully Point

Maryland

Stratford International

STRATFORD CITY MIXED-USE TOWN CENTRE

STRATFORD TOWN CENTRE

Development Plot

Development Plot

Stratford Regional

Aquatics Centre

Olympic Gardens

Development Plot

Stratford High Street

Development Plot

Development Plot

Development Plot

Abbey Road

West Ham

Bow Church

Bow Road

Bromley by-Bow

Devons Road

KEY

EXISTING

Development

Roads

Rail

Open Space

River / Canal

PROPOSED

Development Plots

Roads

Concourse / Paths

Meadow

Reedbed

Wet Woodland

Woodland

Trees

Stoney Meadow

Allotments

Olympic Gardens

mile) footpath and cycle path all the way from Ware in Hertfordshire to the Thames.[7] The extraordinary vision for the East London Green Grid and the Thames Gateway Parklands, with the Olympic Park as a major catalyst, was becoming a reality.

In June 2006 the ODA published its latest masterplan. Although the changes were not as radical as those announced in January, they were similarly driven by the need to improve the Park both for the Games and for legacy use. It was recognised that the strategy of only building permanent venues with viable business plans in legacy would lead to higher-quality facilities – investing once and wisely – and emphasise the long-term commitment to create a new piece of the city. Significantly, the International Broadcast Centre (IBC) and Main Press Centre (MPC) were now to be permanent. There would be indoor sports facilities left in legacy in Hackney with a number of options still being tested, including retaining the Copper Box as a major sports venue, and modifying two of the southernmost buildings of the IBC into a multi-purpose arena and a six-court sports hall. The facilities for Paralympic Tennis now north of the A12 road would be combined with the two hockey pitches to be relocated there from the temporary hockey venue at the Riverbank Arena after the Games. This would form a new and permanent tennis and hockey complex on the Eton Manor site in Waltham Forest, and offer the opportunity for a mix of other sporting facilities that could be used by local communities. Combined with the VeloPark and the improvements to Hackney Marshes this amounted to a significant sporting legacy in the north of the Park. And finally, the temporary Sponsors' Village was relocated to give great views over the Park.

The Park in Games mode was anchored in the north by the Velodrome and in the south by the Olympic Stadium, enhancing the concept of a strong cluster of sports to the north. There was now also space at the Stratford site for additional security and spectator facilities close to the Olympic Stadium. These changes also made the Park more sustainable because the plan now more closely matched the existing topography of the site. Although the topography of the site was changed considerably, by clever design the cutting and filling of earth was balanced across the Park. This meant that no non-contaminated material left the site, saving money on land-fill tax charges, and also reducing vehicle movements. In sum, the new masterplan would enhance the Games experience for athletes, spectators, media and sponsors alike, be more sustainable, and improve legacy infrastructure. With these changes approved by the International Olympic Committee (IOC) – a not insignificant hurdle – the ODA could move on to the next stage of the project, which was to secure the necessary planning permissions and set out the scope, cost and programme for the Park in the Programme Baseline Report.

Between June 2006 and February 2007, a number of further refinements were made to the masterplan that included adding photovoltaic arrays on the Main Press Centre, incorporating combined cooling, heating and power and biomass boilers in the Energy

Illustration of the fringe-area masterplans for development and regeneration projects surrounding the Olympic Park prepared by Design for London and the Olympic Park Legacy Company (now London Legacy Development Corporation) in 2011.

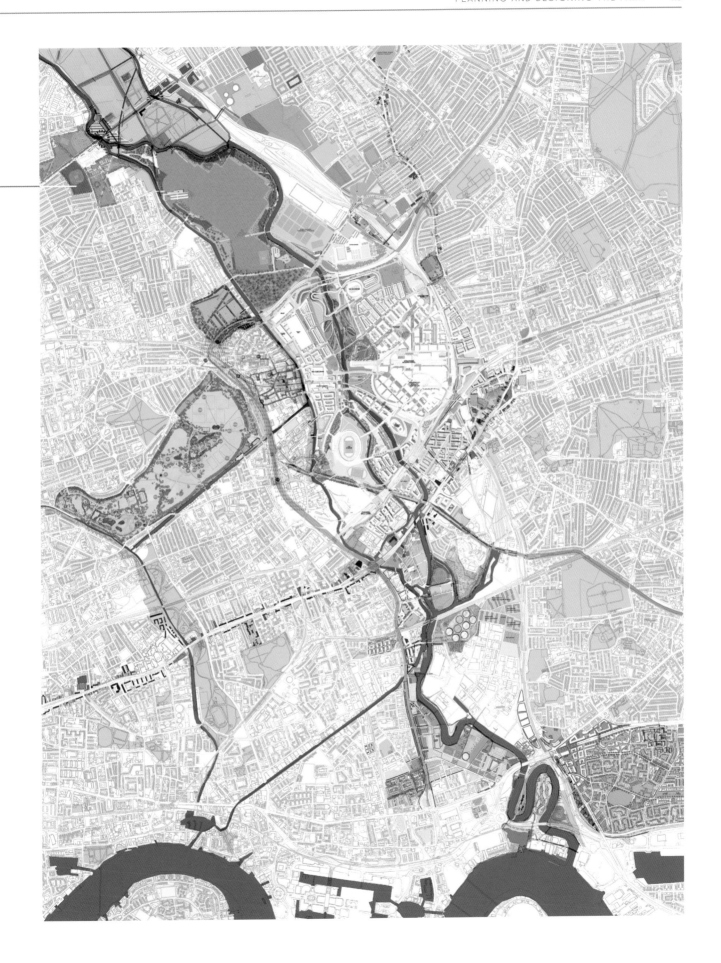

Centre, and revising the Games infrastructure of bridges and land bridges to minimise transformation, and further benefit legacy. The two land bridges originally proposed at the northern and southern ends of the Park were deemed too big, too challenging technically and too expensive. The land bridges carried people and the landscape over roads, railways and other infrastructure. The alternative solution in the north was a series of more traditional bridges for both Games and legacy. In the south, temporary decking over the canals was designed, sections of which remain in legacy to create towpath connections where none existed before. Two planning applications were submitted in February 2007. The first, 'Site Preparation', enabled groundworks on site to commence. It covered earthworks, remediation of land, demolition, works to river walls, highways and utilities. The second, Olympic Facilities and Legacy Transformation, covered venues, bridges, other infrastructure and parklands, and their subsequent transformation for post-Games legacy. To the sounds of the celebrating teams, they were granted planning permission in September 2007, providing the baseline for all subsequent detailed planning, design and implementation. It really was now time to design.

EVOLUTION OF DESIGNS

The ODA's commitment to design was reinforced by the appointment of ODA Board member Sir Nicholas Serota, Director of the Tate, as design champion. The ODA's design strategy *Designing for Legacy* developed the Design Principles set out in the 2007 planning application that, alongside the myriad of other ODA policy documents, established a framework for detailed briefs to be written for each project with targets for sustainability. A huge amount of effort went into researching, writing and consulting on the briefs for each and every project. Exemplar projects were identified, visited, assessed and lessons logged, these included previous Olympic Stadia, venues and Parks. In the case of the parklands, the Commission for Architecture and the Built Environment (CABE) collated and assessed previous Olympic Parks, and arranged study tours of the central Royal Parks, Victoria Park, West Ham Park, Thames Barrier Park, Gunpowder Park, Northala Fields in Ealing, the Ecology Park at Greenwich Peninsula and others. It was recognised that getting the brief right at the beginning of the project would save time and money and reduce risks. Rigorous formal and informal internal design reviews took place over several years. Independent external reviews were undertaken by a dedicated London 2012 Design Panel established by CABE with Design for London. CABE endorsed the masterplan, being 'impressed by the scale of ambition in delivering an Olympic Games in London' and believing that 'the unique combination of parklands in the context of a major industrial city has the potential to make this site the most memorable Olympic venue yet.'[8]

A huge public consultation programme was run, which included early engagement with the local community, and throughout the Host Boroughs, London and the UK all in a very

A Technical Fora consultation event held by the ODA for Eton Manor in June 2009. One of many consultation events held with stakeholders and communities in the Host Boroughs surrounding the Park.

short space of time. More than 220 consultation events were undertaken, including 44 public drop-in sessions in the original five Host Boroughs, 38 community sessions, 95 technical and political stakeholder meetings and 44 public information stands. Art events engaged with, and captured the imagination of, local communities and ensured their contributions. These included a workshop with Royal College of Art students on gabions (recycled concrete-filled wire baskets used to retain bridge abutments and blend into the landscape), and for artworks that were eventually incorporated into the 2012 Gardens – the *Garden Decode* mobile phone app and Turner Prize-winning artist Grenville Davey's *Inter Alia*. Formal, internal ODA design review sessions were challenging, enlightening and invigorating. Designers presented their work and were scrutinised by project sponsors, project managers and the priority theme team leaders. No aspect was left untouched, no questions left unanswered, no possibilities left unaddressed. All proposals were assessed against the ODA's objectives and priority theme targets including design and accessibility, legacy, sustainability, equality and inclusion, employment and skills, buildability, cost, programme, environment, health and safety, and security. External Technical Fora were held where designs for venues, infrastructure, structures, bridges, highways, parklands and public realm were presented, absorbed and interrogated by up to 200 key stakeholders, specialists and experts in their fields from London and across the UK. They represented every aspect of the design and delivery of regeneration projects from health and safety to accessibility. The ODA wanted to ensure that it was getting everything right at the beginning, that everything had been considered, that everyone had been given an opportunity to contribute, and felt engaged and a part of it. The Technical Fora were innovative and inclusive events that helped to smooth significantly the passage of projects through the planning system. No designs went

(continued on page 120)

A POST-INDUSTRIAL PICTURESQUE

George Hargreaves
Design Director, Hargreaves Associates

The character of the Park is palpable and beautiful. It references the heritage of the picturesque while developing a strongly muscular approach that takes us beyond earth-art by weaving in ecology and sustainability. Certainly there is the whiff of the large parks of the 18th century with the mix of prospect and refuge, circulation and topography, but unlike the great parks of history, which had geomorphological bones, here we must put bones in place to carry the Park forward. This is critical since many surfaces will be transformed immediately after the Games and on into the future. The challenge of contemporary, post-industrial park-making is that we are given dead sites and blank sites where everything has to be reformed and made new.

I've never had a greenfield site to work with and never been afraid to change the interface between water and land. By shifting the tectonic plates of the landscape we have created much-needed verticality for the Park, but everybody wants to get to the water so we peeled back the landform to reveal the river, ensuring that it is visible and accessible. By removing Henniker's Ditch we have been able to widen the river corridor fourfold and create substantial wetlands, and so the Park has a much better and richer ecology. The particular emphasis on biodiversity in the brief included some ambitious targets, but rather than fighting these, the challenge was to keep working the design and keep going back to it to finally make it work. This was particularly true for the rain gardens and perennial meadows.

When we started, the concourse was too large. My experience from the Sydney 2000 Games allowed us to challenge the crowd modelling and in doing so free up more space for the Park. A key lesson is that you have to challenge everything and question the given. For the south of the Park, which is much more urban in character, reducing the size of the concourse brought us the opportunity to create the 2012 Gardens that run for over half a mile. We wanted to create something horticulturally and conceptually unique and that referenced the particularly British passion for collecting plants throughout the world. It was

A clay model of the northern Park prepared by LDA Design.Hargreaves Associates during the detailed design stage, which ran from March to November 2008.

An early stage in the construction of landforms in the north of the Park in March 2010. Contractors are part way through building the sculptural landform and are placing topsoil on the largest of the elliptical mounds adjacent to the Olympic and Paralympic Village at top left in the picture.

created by a strong collaboration across the design team and this element of the masterplan was one of the great 'ah-ha' moments of the project. This we couldn't have done some 10 or 15 years ago. In the States we are trying to advance our horticulture and the 2012 Gardens takes us across this frontier by developing a more diverse structure and more complex form of art.

The initial design brief set such collaboration at the heart of the design process, asking for a large multidisciplinary design team with a mix of landscape, engineering, horticultural and ecological skills. From the outset we faced some positive tensions for the design and to make this work we had to get the diagram set and agreed first. Then, building a big model of the Park

The near-complete 'muscular' landform in the north of the Park in March 2011. In the foreground is the largest of the incised, elliptical mounds with a grove of birch trees and topsoil ready for planting of a perennial feature meadow opposite the semi-circular spectator lawn.

got the design process going and having the model and spending time with it was key. With more than 30 people working on the project during some of the most intense stages, we chose to pair up the staff from different practices – a lesson we developed at Sydney. Teams have learnt from each other and friendships have continued, which is somewhat unique.

I have never done so much mixed planting in my life; so much biodiversity in my life. The Park is my most muscular so far and in layering in the ecology, the rain gardens and meadow planting makes it different to other parks. Such complex planting works, but you first have to have a strong ground plane to work with. It marks a new stage in making post-industrial landscapes, yet still builds on the tradition of the English park.

Looking south across a perennial feature meadow towards the Olympic Stadium in September 2011. This meadow was planted on the south-facing slope of the largest of the incised elliptical mounds.

forward for planning approval without the signatures of ODA and LOCOG directors, heads, project sponsors and managers, priority theme team leaders, planning and design managers and more. It was a huge and impressive design management exercise. Compliance or otherwise of designs was all recorded in the Project Status Reports, which were reviewed at monthly project board meetings – red or amber was no good, only a green light got all the signatures and was built. Once designs were approved, any changes that affected the budget, timescale for delivery or risks had to be approved by the project board, then the ODA's Change Board.

The masterplan design concept at the bid stage was of an architecturally homogeneous Park similar to that of the Munich 1972 Games. But unlike, say, Rome or Paris, London itself has never had a masterplan. Sir Christopher Wren had a go at a 'grand plan' after the Great Fire of London in 1666, but it was never implemented. London's character derives from an eclectic mix of building sizes, types, styles, ages and urban typologies slowly accreting over time. Diversity was key to its character. Turner Prize-winning artist Grayson Perry observed during a visit to the Park that it is extremely difficult to create a sense of place and character in big developments such as the Park that are largely built in one go. That sense of a 'real place' usually emerges over time and gets better with the

View of the construction of one of the access shafts to the two deep-bore tunnels that were dug underneath the Olympic Park. A hugely complex engineering project, it was the first contract let, the day after the bid was won, commencing construction of the Olympic Park. Once the tunnels were complete the pylons could be dismantled allowing the placement of over 13km of overhead power lines underground.

View across the Olympic Stadium site looking south towards Canary Wharf in February 2008. The Stadium site was one of the earliest to be cleared. Contaminated soil was excavated to accommodate the construction of the sunken Stadium bowl, then remediated and reused elsewhere on the Park.

patina of age.[9] To assure diversity and eclectism, it was agreed that the Park should have venues designed by different architects, each having its individual character, seeking to create a sense of place, becoming landmarks and loci for future communities to revolve around. The Park should also be ecological: of its place, of its time, of its community – a place for people and wildlife. It should also embed art as 'a part of it', not as an 'add on'. As Serota noted, 'Art can reference the accumulation of memory and experience which gives a place a sense of identity. These elements are not "nice to have" – they are the foundation of any vibrant and successful community.'[10]

Design work commenced on the venues, structures, bridges, highways and the parklands and public realm. But the first priority for the ODA was to complete the design and the construction of the two 6km tunnels so that the power lines could be put underground, and the 52 pylons dominating the site dismantled. What would normally have taken four years was done in just two. This huge undertaking, initiated by the LDA, was delivered on time and on budget – the first big construction win for the project. It laid down the challenge for two equally huge and complex follow-on civil engineering projects: the 'enabling works' – that included the demolition, decontamination and preparation of the 'platform' ready for the construction of the venues and other infrastructure; and the 'utilities' – providing a whole new infrastructure for energy supply and distribution of electricity, gas, potable and grey water, sewage, heating and cooling networks and telecommunication systems. The legacy masterplan determined the layout of this 'unseen' infrastructure: the vision had been set and approved. Through demolition and remediation this chaotic landscape was being transformed, a coherent Park was beginning to emerge for both Games and legacy alongside the designs for the venues.

THE AQUATICS CENTRE

In January 2005 it was announced that architect Zaha Hadid, working with S & P specialist swimming-pool architects and engineers Arup, had won the competition to design the Aquatics Centre. It was commissioned as an iconic piece of architecture in support of the bid. It had a spectacular 11,000-square-metre sinuous roof inspired by the flow of water in the adjacent Waterworks river. Keith Mills, the Chief Executive of London 2012 at the time, said: 'This is an outstanding design that will create a spectacular building, delivering the essential "wow" factor for the 2012 Olympic Games and Paralympic Games … It gives the community a lasting sporting legacy.'[1] The completed Aquatics Centre comprises a 50m competition pool, a 50m training pool and a competition diving pool. The roof is supported on just two concrete cores to the north and a 22m wall to the south.

November 2009 view of the nearly complete roof structure of the Aquatics Centre designed by Zaha Hadid Architects. The 3,000-tonne steel roof has a longer single span than Heathrow's Terminal Five and rests on just two concrete supports at its northern end and one wall at the southern end.

The temporary wings increase the seating capacity to 17,500 for the Games that, once removed, will leave a permanent capacity of 2,500. The wave-like roof won the British Constructional Steelwork Association Award in 2010. However, because it was designed prior to the research and publication of the ODA's policies and strategies, particularly the Sustainable Design Strategy, it did not benefit from the rigorous informed brief writing, sustainability targets and early design review process that so positively influenced all other venues, infrastructure, parklands and public realm from inception to completion. This made it a much more difficult project to deliver. The lesson is that getting the brief right at the beginning, with all the requirements, targets and performance criteria clearly established, is crucial to a smoother design and delivery process.

The completed wave-form roof of the Aquatics Centre with the 15,000-capacity temporary wings under construction in February 2011.

February 2011 view of the Olympic Stadium, designed by Populous, looking north across the Park. The shard paving pattern was laid with the graphic design extending to the Stadium seating.

THE OLYMPIC STADIUM

The Olympic Stadium is the centrepiece of every Games, hosting the Opening and Closing Ceremonies and the Athletics events. At the time the design brief was being drawn up, there was no interest from any Premiership football club in taking over the Stadium after the Games – the only possible user that could fill an 80,000-capacity stadium. London had recently seen the completion of Wembley Stadium (a project that had well-publicised problems of cost, construction and late delivery that bred much scepticism about the ODA's ability to deliver) so there was no need, no business case for another large stadium in London. Consequently, and extraordinarily, the Olympic Stadium was designed to be largely demountable, leaving a permanent 25,000-capacity home for athletics, combined with other sporting, community and educational uses. Embracing the temporary was a thoroughly pragmatic response to legacy needs. In October 2006, Sir Robert McAlpine was named as the preferred bidder to design and build the Olympic Stadium. The omens were good. Team Stadium, as it became known, had already designed and built the universally praised Emirates Stadium for Arsenal Football Club on time and on budget. It was made up of Sir Robert McAlpine, architects Populous (specialists in sports architecture having designed Sydney's Olympic Stadium), structural and building services engineer Buro Happold, and landscape architect Hyland Edgar Driver. The eagerly anticipated design was revealed in November 2007. It was utterly unique and innovative.

An Olympic Stadium with such a large demountable structure had never been attempted before. To save space and drive efficiencies, the majority of spectator facilities were moved outside the main structure. The result was the lightest stadium of its size in the world – four times less steel was used than in Beijing's 'Bird's Nest'. Architect Rod Sheard said: 'The design is a response to the challenge of creating the temporary and the permanent at the same time – that is the essence of the design for the stadium.'[12]

THE VELODROME

Triple Beijing 2008 gold medal-winning cyclist Chris Hoy unveiled designs for the Velodrome on 8 September 2007. Beside the 6,000-capacity Velodrome is a BMX Track that will be converted for both competitive and general public use after the Games. A one-mile road cycle circuit and mountain-bike tracks will also be added. Combining cycling facilities for all disciplines in one 'hub', they will form what will arguably be the world's best VeloPark, to be owned and run by the Lee Valley Regional Park Authority. It will also have a café and terrace offering fantastic views over the Park and the London skyline.

The design team for the Velodrome comprised Hopkins Architects, Expedition Engineering and BDSP, along with Grant Associates as landscape architects who were appointed following a design competition. It was the first venue on which construction was completed on the Park and handed over to LOCOG in February 2011. In October

The footprint of the Velodrome can be seen emerging in the north-east of the Park in November 2008. Across the site the soil remediation programme was well underway. The river Lea prior to remediation can be seen at the top of the image.

December 2011 aerial view of the Velodrome, designed by Hopkins Architects, looking across the river Lea. The Park's landform was carefully designed to both frame and provide a setting for each individual venue in addition to providing access, habitats and a multiplicity of other functions.

2011 it won the British Construction Industry's Better Public Building Award – a prestigious accolade that recognises the best of British design and service. Mike Taylor the lead architect was ecstatic: 'When we originally won this commission we not only wanted to create a world-class Velodrome for London 2012, but also set ourselves the challenge to try and design a building as elegant and efficient as a bicycle. It was only possible because architect, engineer, client and contractor all worked together as one and we are all extremely proud of the finished building.'[13] The venue also won a commendation for sustainability, the Award for Sports Structures, and the Supreme Award from the Institute of Structural Engineers in 2011. It is, in the opinion of many people, the most beautiful building on the Park. It is also arguably the most sustainable.

COPPER BOX

The exterior of the Copper Box is clad with more than 3,000 square metres of mostly recycled copper. It was designed by Make Architects with PTW and Arup.[14] During the Games the arena hosted Handball, Goalball and the fencing element of the Modern Pentathlon. In legacy it will cater for a wide range of indoor sports, including basketball,

December 2011 view of the completed Copper Box. Designed by Make Architects, it will be transformed into a 3,000-seat multi-use sports and events venue after the Games.

handball, badminton, boxing, martial arts, netball, table tennis, wheelchair rugby and volleyball. It will also include a health and fitness club with changing facilities and a café, all for use by the local community. In contrast to its mono-colour exterior, it has a vibrant and multi-coloured interior, inspired through workshops with students from the Royal College of Art, and light pipes in the roof to let in natural daylight and reduce energy consumption. The square in front of the venue has a bosque of London plane trees and, overlooking the parklands, 9m-high individual letters in glass and steel spelling the word 'RUN', a sculpture by artist Monica Bonvicini – famous for her see-through toilet *Don't Miss a Sec*.[15]

INTERNATIONAL BROADCAST CENTRE / MAIN PRESS CENTRE COMPLEX

The modern Games are huge televisual events. The IBC/MPC complex was the 24-hour media hub for around 20,000 broadcasters, photographers and journalists who brought the Games to an estimated four billion people worldwide. The ODA selected a consortium of Carillion and Igloo to deliver the IBC/MPC for both the Games and its transformation for

December 2011 aerial view looking south-west across the IBC and MBC. The buildings provided a media hub for 20,000 journalists, photographers and broadcasters during the Games. The London Legacy Development Corporation is responsible for their use following the Games.

legacy. Its flexible design can accommodate a range of potential uses after the Games for either a single tenant in the whole building or on each floor, or multiple tenants on each floor. During the Games, a 200m-long temporary 'high street' between the MPC and IBC offered outlets such as banks, newsagents, travel agents and a post office. Five jumbo jets could be parked inside the IBC wing-tip to wing-tip. The MPC has 29,000 square metres of 'green' office space with four storeys of workspace for journalists and photographers, and state-of-the-art utilities, power and digital connectivity for both Games and legacy. The London Legacy Development Corporation is responsible for the future use of the 80,000 square metres of buildings with the potential to generate thousands of new jobs.[16]

ETON MANOR

Eton Manor was one of the most difficult parts of the Park to plan in detail. Eton College had been running a mission and a club for disadvantaged boys in Hackney Wick, which was expanded to include the Eton Manor Boys' Club and the allotments in the north of the Park. The sports centre for the Eton Manor Boys' Club was established in 1924, its

December 2011 view looking south across the Olympic Park with Eton Manor, masterplanned by Stanton Williams with LDA Design. Hargreaves, in the foreground. Following the Games, Eton Manor is transformed into a community sports facility with tennis courts, hockey pitches, allotments, mountain-bike tracks and space for 5-a-side football pitches.

final incarnation as a community sports centre was closed 2001. Since then, it had been vandalised and become badly dilapidated. Architects Stanton Williams along with LDA Design.Hargreaves Associates were charged with designing three distinct modes for Olympic Games, Paralympic Games and legacy. After the Games, the site becomes the Lee Valley Hockey and Tennis Centre, owned and managed by the Lee Valley Regional Park Authority. The sporting complex will have a clubhouse retained from the Games, two competition hockey pitches, a tennis centre with four indoor and six outdoor courts, provision for 5-a-side football pitches, allotment gardens and mountain-bike tracks. The main hockey pitch includes 3,000 permanent seats with flexibility to expand the total capacity to 15,000 for elite hockey events. Adjacent to the main entrance to the clubhouse is a garden with two relocated war memorials to Eton Manor Boys' Club members who fought and died in the First and Second World Wars. They were removed from the site for protection during construction. The 'Old Boys' were very supportive of the Games and pleased beyond measure that the site would return to its roots as a sports hub for the community. The ODA worked extremely closely with them and the War Memorials Trust on the removal, conservation and new setting for the memorials. Through a series of site visits, discussions, presentations and workshops that were at times very emotional, everyone's wishes were accommodated.

The 2007 masterplan located the replacement allotments on Eton Manor. Initially, a 120m-tall wind turbine was to be accommodated there as well. Following months of anguished feasibility studies, heated debates and masterplanning options, the wind turbine was cancelled when the preferred bidder pulled out at a very late stage. New wider safety legislation that applied to design elements of the particular wind turbine proposed, including a new requirement for an internal operator lift, came into effect. Consequently, the preferred bidder's turbine supplier for the project felt unable to comply with these new regulations before the Games and withdrew from the project.[7] By this time, internal ODA studies had tested the location of the allotments in every feasible place on the Park. Relations with the Manor Gardening Society were becoming fraught as the Society felt time was passing and they were being ignored. Discussions with the Society were restarted, and the proposed solution was to locate half of the allotments on Eton Manor, and half in the south of the Park adjacent to legacy housing development and a railway – a fairly traditional location for allotments. Despite objections by the Chair of the Manor Gardening Society, who argued that splitting the allotments was inappropriate, and that the Society had not been consulted fully, the planning committee approved the plans in 2010. The ODA immediately embarked on another series of site visits, meetings, discussions and workshops, working very closely and positively with the Manor Gardening Society on the detailed design of the allotments, which were concluded to everyone's satisfaction in mid-2011.

One of the perceived reasons for the failure of the previous Eton Manor sports centre was its isolation – essentially it was an 'island' site bound by main roads. In legacy it will be reconnected to the surrounding areas by two pedestrian and cycle bridges. David Higgins summed it all up: 'The Eton Manor site is steeped in sporting history. We want to recapture this and regenerate the area with well-designed, world-class facilities fit for the Olympic and Paralympic stage. The new facilities along with the new bridges and new walking and cycling routes better linking them into the local community will mean that London 2012 will leave a significant sporting legacy in the north of the Olympic Park for generations to come.'[18]

BASKETBALL ARENA

The 2006 masterplan proposed three temporary venues on the Park: Basketball, Water Polo and Fencing. On announcing the search for designers of the Basketball and Fencing Arenas, Alison Nimmo, the ODA's Director of Design and Regeneration, said: 'We are looking for solutions that combine design flair and innovation with practicality and cost efficiency. At the same time we are investigating how these facilities could be best utilised after the Games.' Soon after this announcement, a decision was made to locate Fencing in the nearby existing ExCeL centre, a much more cost-effective solution. In November 2007, the ODA announced the appointment of a multi-disciplinary team for the Basketball Arena, comprising Sinclair Knight Merz, architects Wilkinson Eyre, and KSS Design Group. The ODA's Chief Adviser on Architecture and Urbanism, Ricky Burdett, said: 'Temporary structures of the scale and impact of the Basketball Arena need to be designed with elegance, simplicity and intelligence. The design team were selected for their ability to integrate structural integrity with architectural expression, backed up with experience, capacity, creativity and a deep understanding of the complex brief.'[19]

The Basketball Arena's portal frame steelwork under construction in May 2010. Designed by Wilkinson Eyre Architects, it was the largest temporary building erected for any Olympic and Paralympic Games. It will be demounted and reused following the Games.

The 12,000-capacity arena is the largest temporary venue built for any Games and hosted not only Basketball, but also Wheelchair Basketball, Wheelchair Rugby and Handball. It was also used as a holding area for athletes awaiting the Opening and Closing Ceremonies. The venue's 'back of house' area was shared with the Velodrome and BMX Track to make the most efficient use of space and resources. This included two further practice courts in temporary accommodation and areas for catering, security, waste management and the media. The brilliant white, dramatically sculpted external membrane provided a canvas for spectacular lighting shows – the Park's equivalent of Beijing 2008's Cube. The Arena was designed to be demounted after the Games and re-erected elsewhere.

February 2011 aerial view of the Basketball Arena and north Park landscape under construction. The Arena will be removed after the Games, and a new Park pavilion and playground designed by Erect Architecture and LUC landscape architects built within the extended Parklands.

WATER POLO ARENA

The last venue to be completed by the ODA on the Park was the distinctive, wedge-shaped temporary Water Polo Arena. Designed by David Morley Architects with Max Fordham and Buro Happold, the main structure was built by the ES Group based in Silvertown close to the Park – it specialised in building stages and support structures for major

events, including the 2010 Ryder Cup. It was a wonderfully appropriate appointment. The company was previously based on the Park site, and had had to be relocated as part of the compulsory purchase programme. The sloping roof of the Water Polo Arena was made from air-inflated recyclable phthalate-free PVC cushions that provide extra insulation and reduce condensation. The venue was wrapped in a distinctive silver membrane with translucent shard-shaped panels. To give visitors entering the Park a clear view of the Olympic Stadium, the architects proposed a unique design that sloped upwards from 6m to 25m. It also meant the referee's raised table used in Water Polo did not obscure the view of spectators, who sat on the opposite side of the pool. Its asymmetric shape gave the best sightlines for viewing Water Polo. It provided step-free access without the need for lifts and reduced water use by 40 per cent through low-flow taps and showers and waterless urinals. Designed to be taken down after the Games, it incorporated a plethora of reusable elements available through the rental market to promote reuse and reduce construction waste.

The first permanent bridge being lifted into place in the north of the Park in October 2009. Over 30 new bridges and connections were built for use both during and after the Games.

UTILITIES, STRUCTURES, BRIDGES AND HIGHWAYS

Most clients would view utility buildings as, well, utilitarian. But not the ODA. At the launch of designs for the Park's main pumping station by John Lyall Architects, Simon Wright, the ODA's Director of Infrastructure and Utilities, said he believed that: 'Design excellence runs through the heart of the project, and the early designs in place for the pumping station show that we can use innovative architecture in functional buildings in the Olympic Park, not just the world-class sporting venues we are building.'[20] CABE agreed. Following the launch of the designs for another piece of the Park's utilities infrastructure, the Primary Substation designed by NORD Architecture, they congratulated 'the client and architects for producing a real piece of architecture out of an everyday brief. We think this is an object lesson in how even relatively minor parts of the Olympic programme can benefit from committed design thinking.'[21] It won a Royal Institute of British Architects Award for architectural excellence in May 2010.

The Energy Centre designed by John McAslan & Partners followed and is both striking and sustainable. It includes biomass boilers using woodchip and gas to generate heat, and a Combined Cooling Heat and Power (CCHP) plant to capture the heat generated by electricity production. It provides domestic hot water and heat to all venues and buildings within the Park for both Games and legacy. Part of this infrastructure is housed within an existing Victorian building at Kings Yard, which was retained and renovated as an important part of the cultural heritage of the Park. Even temporary electrical substations were timber clad to fit in with the Park's design ethos.

The majority of bridges throughout the Park were designed with two spans, a permanent section for legacy, and an adjacent temporary section to accommodate the huge crowds during the Games. The original concept for massive 'land bridges' connecting the Park at its northern and southern ends was dropped early on due to practical considerations and cost constraints. Arguments raged, however, about the 12 new permanent bridges across the waterways. Should they be individually designed bringing character and sense of place – Venice was cited! – or of a consistent design, low-key and blending seamlessly with the landscape of the Park? The low-key approach won the day. The bridges are of a consistent and simple design except for one, the central and most prominent bridge connecting the northern and southern halves of the Park. A design competition was held and was won by Heneghan Peng Architects with Adams Kara Taylor Engineers. The purpose of the bridge during the Games was to accommodate hundreds of thousands of spectators moving between the northern and southern halves of the Park. It is 40m wide and completely covers Carpenters Road Lock below it. Extraordinarily, this fine bridge was not seen in its full glory until after the Games. In legacy, the temporary infills were be removed and the landscape sculpted to reveal the stunningly elegant, mirror steel, 4m-wide permanent 'zigzag' bridge framing the restored, historic lock below. Yet another example of legacy driving Games-time design.

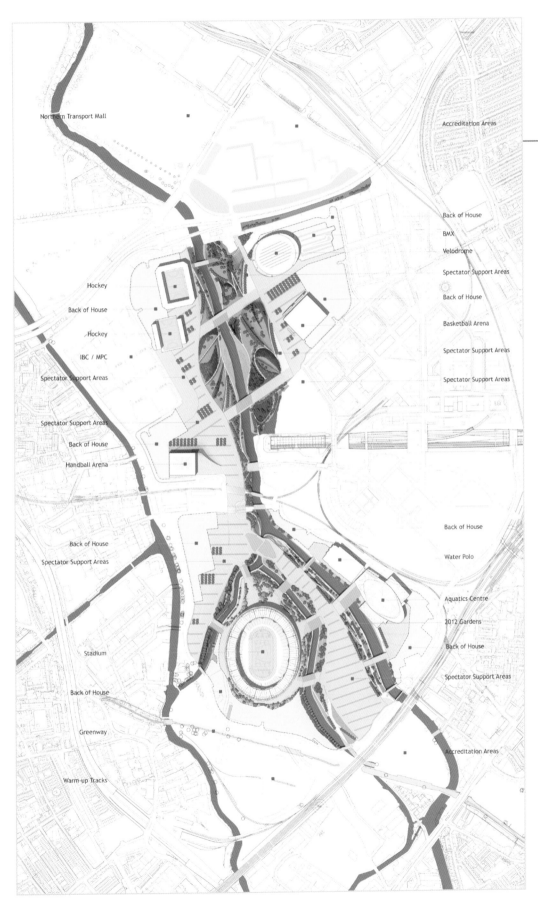

Northern Transport Mall

Hockey

Back of House

Hockey

IBC / MPC

Spectator Support Areas

Spectator Support Areas

Back of House

Handball Arena

Back of House

Spectator Support Areas

Stadium

Back of House

Greenway

Warm-up Tracks

Accreditation Areas

Back of House

BMX

Velodrome

Spectator Support Areas

Back of House

Basketball Arena

Spectator Support Areas

Spectator Support Areas

Back of House

Water Polo

Aquatics Centre

2012 Gardens

Back of House

Spectator Support Areas

Accreditation Areas

The Games Parklands and Public Realm Masterplan by LDA Design. Hargreaves Associates and approved in February 2009. The team had just six months to prepare detailed designs, gain all client and stakeholder approvals and submit them for planning in September 2008.

PARKLANDS AND PUBLIC REALM

Everything revolved around the parklands at the heart of the Park. Along with the iconic venues, they had to characterise the Games. In legacy, they would reach out into east London connecting adjacent neighbourhoods. They had to become east London's equivalent of a Royal Park combining, as examples, the glory of the Avenue Gardens at Regent's Park, the wilder landscapes of Richmond Park, and with the capability of hosting big events like Hyde Park. They had to be a 'working landscape': managing and ameliorating flooding, the urban heat island effect and pollution; sequestering carbon; enhancing wildlife; and collecting, cleansing and utilising water. They had to restore the landscapes that were largely contaminated, degraded, inaccessible and weed infested, and the waterways that had become largely unnavigable, weed infested and dumped with old cars, tyres and other post-industrial detritus. They had to be spectacular for the Games and in legacy be an international, metropolitan, regional and, most importantly, a local destination. They had to be a place for communities to come together and celebrate their differences and commonalities. They had to promote development and enhance land values. They had to encourage walking and cycling, tackle obesity, and promote physical and mental health and well-being. They had to be educational, re-establishing connections between people and the ecological services on which we depend for all our needs.

The 2007 EDAW masterplan established a bold Park structure for both Games and legacy. They set out inviolable principles for a city-scale infrastructure with the Park at the heart. They proposed one Park with two halves. The northern half was more open, ecological and community focused. The southern half more constrained, urban, vibrant and the big destination. Everything was being done to ensure that the vision was delivered – great venues and infrastructure, sustainability, a focus on legacy and an exceptional Games. The Park now needed a stunning landscape design.

The ODA sought a world-class landscape architect and design team. In March 2008, a consortium of LDA Design.Hargreaves Associates was appointed to take up the challenge. Landscape architect George Hargreaves was the design director. Large parks and post-industrial sites form a substantial part of his portfolio of completed works. Also, having been the masterplanner for Sydney 2000, he understood the weird and wonderful world of requirements for a Games.[22] The brief for the parklands and public realm was explicit: 'It will be a new kind of Park for the city. Built around and between the existing infrastructure and developments within the valley. It will become a part of the surrounding city, rather than being set aside and protected from surrounding urban structures and activities.' In other words: a 'total landscape'. An exact opposite of the Olympic Park for the Beijing 2008 Games.

The technical requirements of the brief were onerous. The project had to satisfy LOCOG's specifications for operating the Games – essentially accommodating up to

250,000 spectators per day and the entire temporary overlay required to support them. It had to achieve minimum 'levels of service' for crowd flow, comfort and safety – a highly sophisticated computer crowd-flow model was run to assess and assure this. It had to comply with the ODA's accessibility standards. For example, no gradients should be greater than 1:21, preferably 1:60, benches had to have backrests, there had to be resting places every 50m and handrails next to any steps with alternative ramp access immediately adjacent. This was on a site where there was an average 10m level difference between the concourse and the waterways! It had to be capable of a safe and cost-effective transformation for legacy development, essentially leaving 102ha capable of designation as Metropolitan Open Land (London's planning equivalent of a Green Belt designation). No less than half of the 102ha had to be habitat as set out in the Biodiversity Action Plan (BAP) — 45ha was the area of designated habitat existing on the site prior to any development. As the Park was set within a river valley, it received storm water flows from the wider urban area. The parklands, therefore, had to meet the requirements for online storage of flood waters. The team also had to consult with dozens of stakeholders. The challenge was immense. They had six months in which to prepare designs, get them approved by the ODA and its stakeholders, and submit a detailed planning application.

The ODA consistently challenged its design teams, but the LDA Design.Hargreaves team countered: no one was expecting such radical proposals. They triggered a lot of debate and assessments of feasibility. Firstly, in a heartening triumph of human intuition over computer modelling, they spotted that in comparison to Sydney there was too much concourse for the crowd numbers and flows. The concourse is the vast hard landscape carrying spectators to and from all main entrances and exits to the Park, and then to and from the venues within the Park. They thought it could be substantially reduced. This meant that the edges of the concourse could be pulled back, thus reducing the angle of the landscape down to the river. This would result in a more accessible and useable soft landscape sloping down to the waterways, which would also be easier to design as habitat. It meant cost savings in reduced earthworks, remediation and extent of hard landscape. It also meant that the waterways were much more visible from the concourse.

The team's next big move in the north of the Park was – unbelievably – to fill in the Channelsea river, a designated 'main water course'. This 'river' was in fact a remnant at the bottom of a steep-sided valley, and water only flowed through it following heavy storms. Essentially, it was a huge drainage ditch, appropriately named locally as Hennicker's Ditch. But to 'ditch the ditch' was a 'no-no'. Firstly, to the ODA's engineering teams who had completed their groundwork plans, remediation strategies, utility and drainage designs based on retaining it, and secondly to the Government's Environment Agency whose national policy and duty it was to protect designated 'main water courses'.

(continued on page 145)

A NEW BENCHMARK FOR URBAN LANDSCAPES

Andrew Harland and Neil Mattinson

Senior Partners, LDA Design

The design brief for the Park was comprehensive and called for both world-class and young emerging design talent. As lead landscape consultant, we built a large and comprehensive team with two separate design practices and over 20 specialists including ecology, meadow planting, horticulture, arts, lighting, irrigation, soils, planning, consultation and management. George Hargreaves was the lead designer and Sarah

Early design diagrams illustrating the landscape framework for the Park prepared by LDA Design. Hargreaves Associates. The primary design objective was to establish the parklands as the unifying element integrating all the venues within a single Park, and then extending it to the surrounding neighbourhoods through the transformation of the Park immediately following the Games.

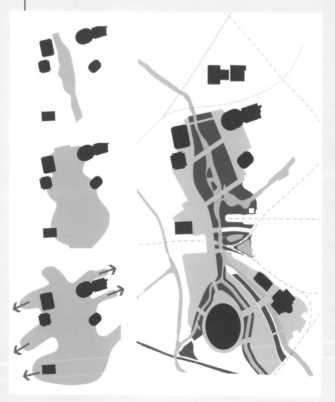

Price, whom we met as she was starting to build her reputation, led on garden planting design supported by professors Dunnet and Hitchmough. After appointment and having reviewed the needs of the client we focused our core team down to around 12 and had to quickly establish a clear, committed and collaborative working relationship between us all. We all knew there would be no second chance. This was the London 2012 Games, the world and the world's media would be watching – failure was way too great to contemplate.

Straight away we ran a number of design workshops to agree what elements of the scheme were fixed or could change. We wanted to create more landscape within the same cost and had to achieve this within six weeks. Our greatest technical challenge was to get the crowd modelling right and build a strong case to fill Henniker's Ditch. George Hargreaves's design signature is about large parks and bold landforms that create vistas and surprise and integrate landscape with architecture. So he started by building a clay model, which was entirely the right thing to do. It tested the landform, helped to define its scale and was a simple practical way to balance material, cut and fill.

In making big shifts to the existing masterplan we had to minimise risk and ensure that there was no impact on the headline budget or programme. The ODA's John Hopkins as client and Matt Heal as the CLM Delivery Partner attended many of our workshops. They understood the design intent and were very supportive, but also very challenging. We had to demonstrate that many of the design elements – including the lighting,

Wet woodland planting and spectator seating in the north of the Park. The landform was designed to create settings and frame views of the venues. The landscape setting for the Velodrome seen here is particularly striking.

timber and soils – were sustainable, appropriately specified and buildable, and had to prepare detailed reports to defend our proposals. We were challenged hard by other design teams and particularly from the Velodrome on the landform. They considered it way too excessive and CLM saw it as being very complex, difficult to construct and vulnerable to bad weather. But once construction had begun and people were getting out onto site the penny dropped and they started to really understand the vision and see how the landscape would draw the venues together into a single and unified composition.

There was a danger that the sustainability targets, and particularly those agreed in the outline planning permission, could have been overplayed to force a certain design response. Early on there was a lot of emphasis on numbers and percentages, such as the 45ha requirement for biodiversity. These were worked through in detail during the design development, which included a lot of consultation with environmental stakeholders and community groups. A particular focus was British Waterways, the Environment Agency and Thames Water as statutory consultees, alongside the Eton Manor Old Boys' Club and the Manor Gardening

Society. It all took time, but we slowly gained trust by maintaining continuity and adopting a collective attitude to delivering the design intent. It was also unusual to have the Town Planning Promoter Team as a separate but related organisation to the client and the planning authority. They were fundamental to gaining the necessary approvals and contributed as much to the successful delivery of the project as the consultant planning agent whom they managed.

The layering and sophistication of the ecology, including the vast reed beds, fish refuges, otter holts and kingfisher walls, make the Park a very important new benchmark for the design of urban landscapes. But in many ways it can also be considered as continuing the development of ecologically structured landscapes across the city. London has an established track record with ecology parks, and more recently with contemporary urban parks including Gunpowder Park further north in the Lea Valley, Northala Fields in Ealing and Southwark's Burgess Park. They have all taken a minimalist approach to the use of resources, overlaid sustainability systems on physical systems and worked with nature as a landscape system. But for the Queen Elizabeth Olympic Park this is all taken to a far more significant level.

After the Games a key issue will be how local communities will embrace the Park and start to use it and love it. What will be particularly interesting to see is how the Park is able to project an image of a new sustainable community; perhaps adding to our country's much admired and envied collection of great garden cities.

Curved timber seats in the 2012 Gardens in the south of the Park. All timber for the construction of the Park was supplied from certified sustainable sources that had to be monitored by the design and contractor teams though the entire supply chain.

The eastern half of the wetland bowl in the north of the Park in March 2011. The sophisticated ecological design for the Park included refuges for fish in reed beds and wet woodlands. The channel and refuges can be seen clearly on the picture.

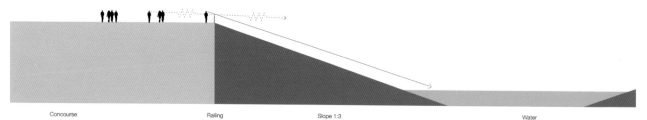

Concourse   Railing   Slope 1:3   Water

River visibility: Stage C proposals

■ The river is only visible from the edge of the
   concourse. The river valley sides are steep
   and difficult to access.

Concourse   Slope less than 1:3   Water

River visibility: Stage D proposals

■ By laying back the valley sides the river can be
   seen from further back within the concourse
   area. Earthworks help to frame and shape
   views so create a 'Picturesque' landscape.

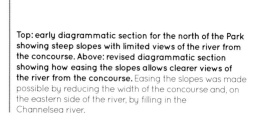

KEY

⟶ open views

⇢⋀⋀⋀⟶ obstructed views

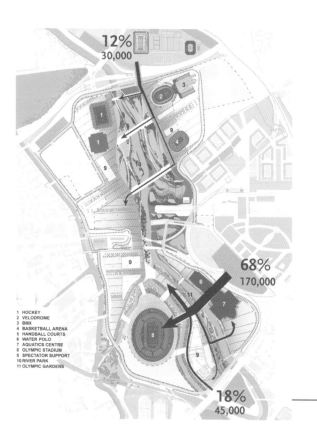

12%
30,000

68%
170,000

18%
45,000

1 HOCKEY
2 VELODROME
3 BMX
4 BASKETBALL ARENA
5 HANDBALL COURTS
6 WATER POLO
7 AQUATICS CENTRE
8 OLYMPIC STADIUM
9 SPECTATOR SUPPORT
10 RIVER PARK
11 OLYMPIC GARDENS

**Top: early diagrammatic section for the north of the Park
showing steep slopes with limited views of the river from
the concourse. Above: revised diagrammatic section
showing how easing the slopes allows clearer views of
the river from the concourse.** Easing the slopes was made
possible by reducing the width of the concourse and, on
the eastern side of the river, by filling in the
Channelsea river.

Crowd flow projections for the Park during the Games.
The vast majority of the 250,000 visitors per day
approached the Park from the Stratford transport hub to the
east of the Park, arriving between the Aquatics Centre and
the Water Polo Arena via a bridge crossing roads, railways
and a river.

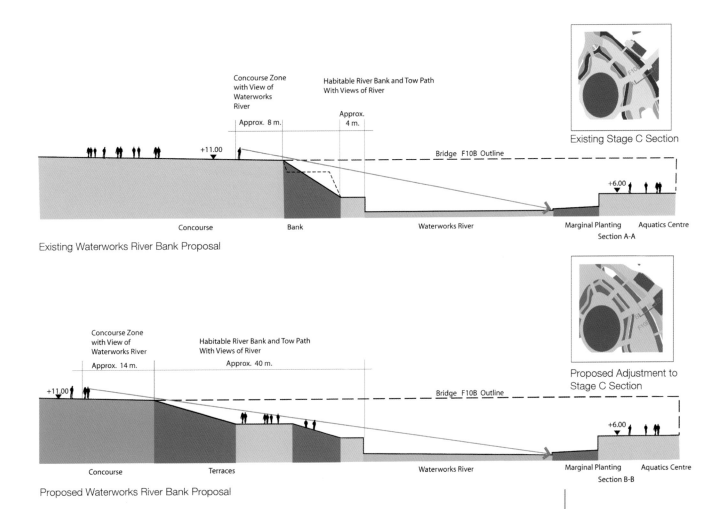

Concourse Zone
with View of
Waterworks
River

Habitable River Bank and Tow Path
With Views of River

Approx. 8 m.

Approx.
4 m.

+11.00

Bridge F10B Outline

+6.00

Concourse   Bank   Waterworks River   Marginal Planting   Aquatics Centre
Section A-A

Existing Waterworks River Bank Proposal

Existing Stage C Section

Concourse Zone
with View of
Waterworks River

Habitable River Bank and Tow Path
With Views of River

Approx. 14 m.

Approx. 40 m.

+11.00

Bridge F10B Outline

+6.00

Concourse   Terraces   Waterworks River   Marginal Planting   Aquatics Centre
Section B-B

Proposed Waterworks River Bank Proposal

Proposed Adjustment to
Stage C Section

The team had been working with a big clay model of the Park. They knew that a heroic, honed landform was necessary to characterise the Park as a distinctly human-made artefact. It should be iconic and of a scale to match the Games venues and infrastructure and, eventually, long-term legacy. They also knew that there was an emerging and substantial excess of spoil, and that it would be much cheaper to retain this on site to create these huge landforms. Money could also be saved by designing open swales to carry water from the concourse down to the river from porous paving rather than putting it in pipes underground. With check dams constructed from granite curbs recycled from the site, these rich wet and dry 'bio-swale' habitats would help to meet BAP targets and, with extraordinary planting design, look fabulous. Truly a sustainable urban drainage system for the 21st century, nothing like this had been done before. The swales recharged 'frog ponds' with loggeries piled and laid in straight lines again to celebrate the human intervention, but no less ecologically sound. Wet woodlands were proposed that utilised the daily rise and fall in the river levels to keep them wet – a very rich habitat that again contributed to achieving the BAP targets for the Park, and looked great.

Top: early diagrammatic section for the Waterworks river in the south of the Park showing steep slopes with limited access. Above: revised diagrammatic section showing how easing the slopes allowed the terraces for the 2012 Gardens to be formed. Easing the slopes was made possible by reducing the width of the concourse.

Two wetland bowls had always been proposed in the EDAW masterplan. The team now designed them between geometrically sculpted land bridges dissecting the north of the Park. The wetlands would be planted with aquatic species predominantly collected from the site prior to remediation, and grown in coir mats for ease of planting. Marginal aquatic plants fringed the majority of the waterway edges throughout the Park, enhancing ecological connectivity and aesthetic appeal. The wetlands were also part of the flood-risk management system. Again as part of the EDAW masterplan, the Waterworks river that flows beneath the Aquatics Centre was widened by 8m to increase flow capacity during floods – this strip was also planted with marginal aquatic plants. The widening of the river – and the storage capacity of the drainage swales, soft landscape, frog ponds and wetland bowls proposed by the landscape team in the north Park – helped to protect the venues and infrastructure within the Park, and 5,000 properties outside the Park, from flooding. In legacy, the north of the Park will be more community oriented, with a pavilion and playground designed by Erect Architecture and landscape architects Land Use Consultants. It is on the main footpath and cycle route connecting new and existing neighbourhoods either side of the valley.[23]

The Channelsea river, also known as Hennicker's Ditch, photographed in 2008. It was culverted following detailed negotiations with stakeholders, particularly the Environment Agency, Natural England and the London Wildlife Trust. This allowed a more continuous landscape in the north of the Park on the east side of the river Lea, providing greater accessibility, usability and the creation of diverse habitats.

An early design development model for the parklands prepared by LDA Design.Hargreaves Associates illustrating the emerging sculptural landform and gently sloping paths to the river edges.

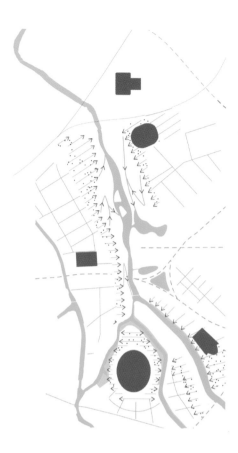

Diagrams of the surface
water drainage system
for the Park for the Games
(left) and in legacy (right).
They illustrate the strategy
for taking water from the
upper levels through swales,
ponds and wetlands before
releasing it into the river.

surface water drainage (games)

surface water drainage (legacy)

A check dam constructed
from granite kerbs recycled
from the site. Planted
with native species, the
drainage swales hold back
water regulating flow after
heavy rainfall while creating
valuable and diverse wet/
dry habitats.

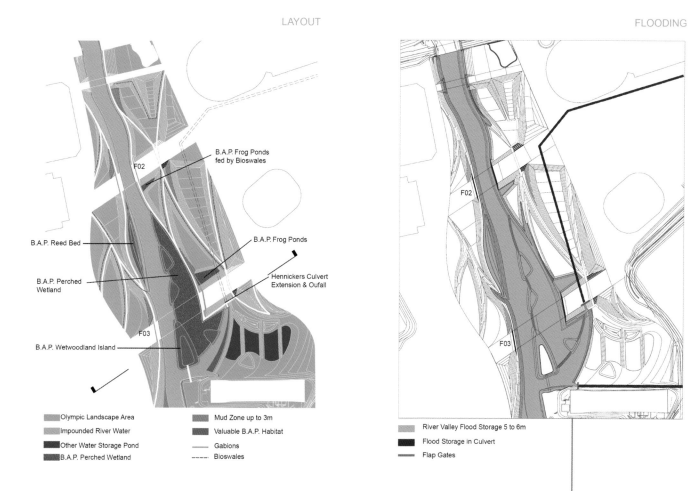

F02

B.A.P. Frog Ponds
fed by Bioswales

B.A.P. Reed Bed

B.A.P. Frog Ponds

B.A.P. Perched
Wetland

Hennickers Culvert
Extension & Oufall

F03

B.A.P. Wetwoodland Island

Olympic Landscape Area		Mud Zone up to 3m	
Impounded River Water		Valuable B.A.P. Habitat	
Other Water Storage Pond		Gabions	
B.A.P. Perched Wetland		Bioswales	

F02

F03

River Valley Flood Storage 5 to 6m	
Flood Storage in Culvert	
Flap Gates	

In contrast to the more open, ecologically based landscape in the north of the Park, the south is much more constrained and 'urban' because of the three waterways that split off from the river Lea running through the middle of the north of the Park. Pulling back the slopes, as in the north of the Park, improved visibility and accessibility to the waterways. The City Mill river and Old River Lea create the Stadium 'island' in the south of the Park. They were designed by the Olympic Stadium's landscape architect HED as naturalised river valley slopes, ensuring the ecological continuity from the north to the south of the Park, and eventually all the way to the Thames. In direct contrast to the character of the north of the Park, the LDA Design. Hargreaves Associates team proposed the remaining part of the south of the Park as an urban festival site, a pleasure ground of the 21st century continuing the tradition of British models such as the 19th-century Vauxhall Gardens, and the 20th-century Festival of Britain Gardens. This is where 70 per cent of spectators arrived for the Games, and the majority of non-local visitors will arrive in legacy. They proposed the 0.8km (half-mile) long 2012 Gardens designed in collaboration with team's garden designer Sarah Price, and urban horticulturalists from Sheffield University, Professors James Hitchmough and Nigel Dunnett. The Gardens comprise four sections, each representing a global climate zone: Europe, North America, Southern Hemisphere and Asia.

An early flood capacity diagram for the wetland bowl and Bulley Point in the north of the Park. At times of peak rainfall the landscape is designed to flood and then release water slowly back into the river network to minimise flood risk. The diagram on the left illustrates normal flows, the one on the right during a 1:100-year flood plus an allowance for climate change.

(continued on page 158)

View of the north of the Park showing the completed sculpted landform of the central section in February 2011.

The detailed landscape masterplan for the north of the Park prepared by **LDA Design.Hargreaves Associates.** This illustrates the sculpted 'muscular' landform and wetland bowl created by re-profiling the original steep river embankments and culverting the Channelsea river/Hennicker's Ditch.

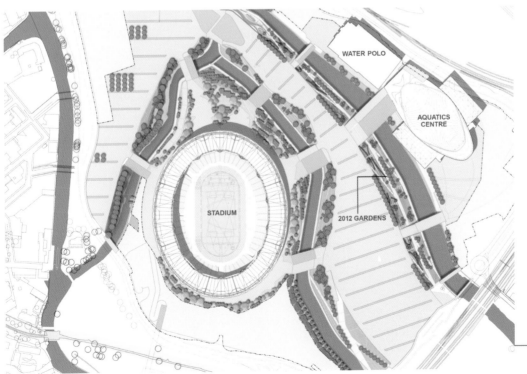

View of the south of the Park taken in December 2011. From left to right the Aquatics Centre and Water Polo Arena either side of the main entrance to the Park, the Waterworks river and 2012 Gardens, the central concourse with Orbit, mast lights and the bridge connecting the north and south of the Park, and finally the City Mill river, Olympic Stadium, Old River Lea and Great British Garden.

The detailed landscape masterplan for the south of the Park prepared by LDA Design. Hargreaves Associates comprising the terraced 2012 Gardens, the horticultural centrepiece of the Park, set between the Olympic Stadium and the Aquatics Centre, the naturalised river valley slopes surrounding the Stadium. The Great British Garden to the north west of the Stadium was a later addition.

Planting strategy for the north of the Park proposing predominantly native tree and shrub species, with a significant proportion of wetland and wet woodland plant communities.

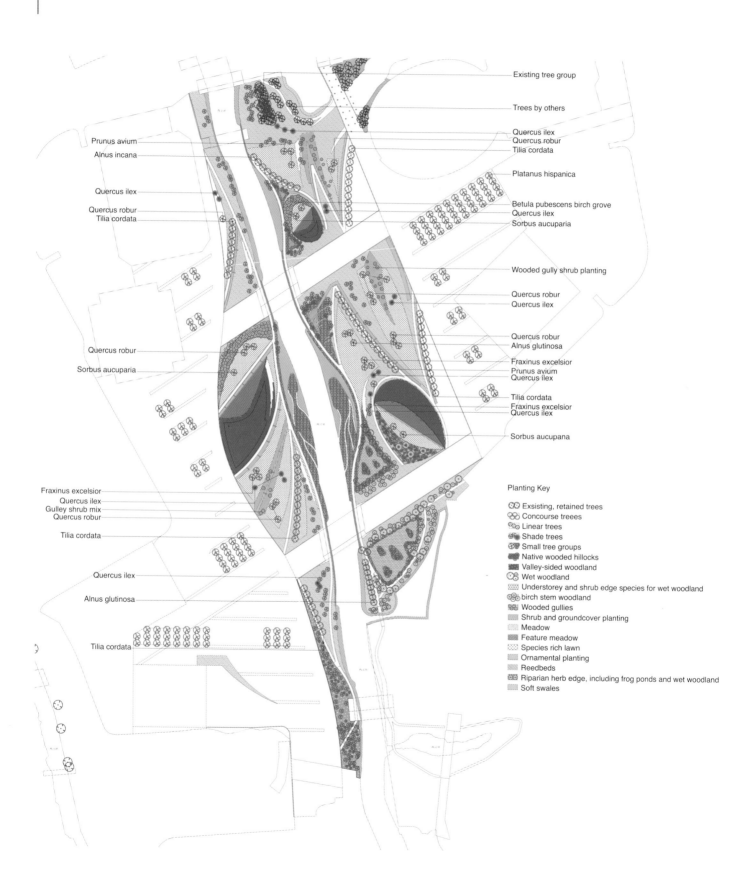

Existing tree group

Trees by others

Quercus ilex
Quercus robur
Tilia cordata

Platanus hispanica

Betula pubescens birch grove
Quercus ilex
Sorbus aucuparia

Wooded gully shrub planting

Quercus robur
Quercus ilex

Quercus robur
Alnus glutinosa

Fraxinus excelsior
Prunus avium
Quercus ilex

Tilia cordata
Fraxinus excelsior
Quercus ilex

Sorbus aucupana

Prunus avium
Alnus incana

Quercus ilex

Quercus robur
Tilia cordata

Quercus robur

Sorbus aucuparia

Fraxinus excelsior
Quercus ilex
Gulley shrub mix
Quercus robur

Tilia cordata

Quercus ilex

Alnus glutinosa

Tilia cordata

Planting Key

- Exsisting, retained trees
- Concourse treees
- Linear trees
- Shade trees
- Small tree groups
- Native wooded hillocks
- Valley-sided woodland
- Wet woodland
- Understorey and shrub edge species for wet woodland
- birch stem woodland
- Wooded gullies
- Shrub and groundcover planting
- Meadow
- Feature meadow
- Species rich lawn
- Ornamental planting
- Reedbeds
- Riparian herb edge, including frog ponds and wet woodland
- Soft swales

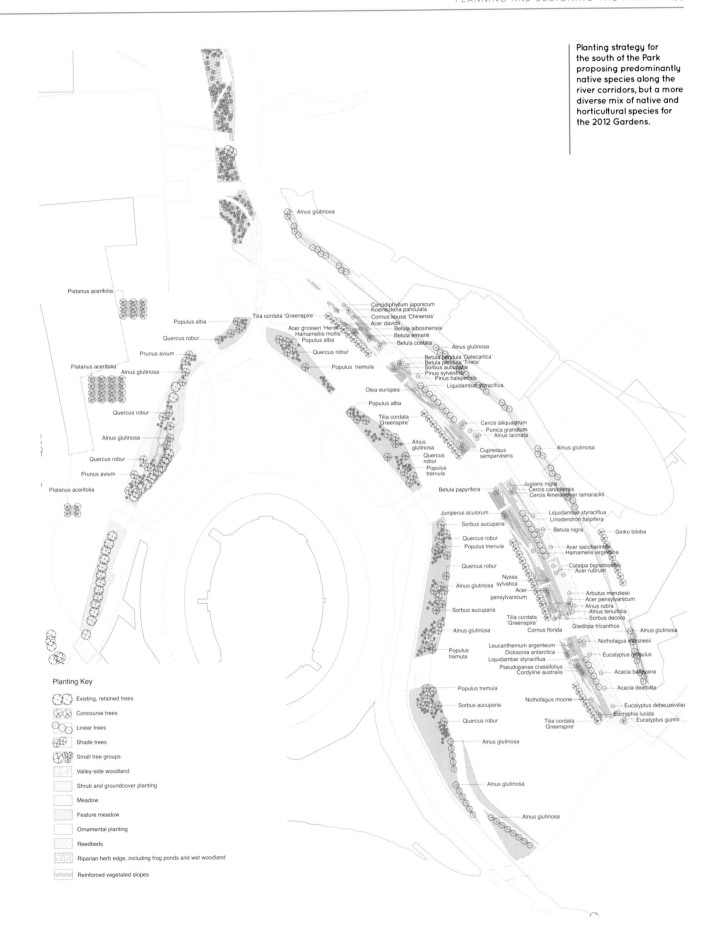

Planting strategy for the south of the Park proposing predominantly native species along the river corridors, but a more diverse mix of native and horticultural species for the 2012 Gardens.

Planting Key

- Existing, retained trees
- Concourse trees
- Linear trees
- Shade trees
- Small tree groups
- Valley-side woodland
- Shrub and groundcover planting
- Meadow
- Feature meadow
- Ornamental planting
- Reedbeds
- Riparian herb edge, including frog ponds and wet woodland
- Reinforced vegetated slopes

LAYERING HORTICULTURE AND ECOLOGY ACROSS THE LONDON 2012 GARDENS

Sarah Price
Garden Designer

For me, work on the 2012 Gardens blew everything up to a monumental scale. It was the first time I had worked in such a large, fast-track commercial context. It took time to establish roles and develop a creative working relationship and it was unusual to have three planting designers working so closely together on one scheme. The fit with the University of Sheffield's Nigel Dunnett and James Hitchmough was natural and, in fact, Tim Richardson, writing on my past work at Chelsea, had drawn parallels with the Sheffield School and their ecologically structured aesthetic to perennial planting.

Initially George Hargreaves was keen that the Gardens built a linear and chronological sequence of planting that embraced the concept of botanical families. He was very definite about the timeline for the Gardens and the need for a strong visual image, especially as they were a central part of the arrival sequence to the Park. The majority of visitors would start at Stratford and make their way to the Olympic

The mix and composition of perennial flowers and grasses in the North American Garden evokes the character and ecological structure of prairie landscapes.

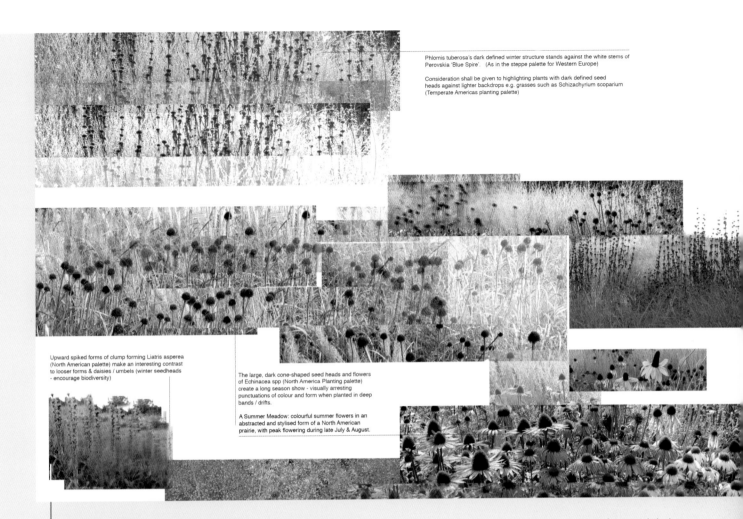

Phlomis tuberosa's dark defined winter structure stands against the white stems of Perovskia 'Blue Spire'. (As in the steppe palette for Western Europe)

Consideration shall be given to highlighting plants with dark defined seed heads against lighter backdrops e.g. grasses such as Schizachyrium scoparium (Temperate Americas planting palette)

Upward spiked forms of clump forming Liatris asperea (North American palette) make an interesting contrast to looser forms & daisies / umbels (winter seedheads - encourage biodiversity)

The large, dark cone-shaped seed heads and flowers of Echinacea spp (North America Planting palette) create a long season show - visually arresting punctuations of colour and form when planted in deep bands / drifts.

A Summer Meadow: colourful summer flowers in an abstracted and stylised form of a North American prairie, with peak flowering during late July & August.

Early planting design collage prepared by Sarah Price in September 2008. This illustrates innovative ecological and aesthetic layering of perennial plants across the 2012 Gardens.

Stadium, walking over the bridge and looking down on the Gardens. The overall form of terraces and ramps provided a good structure to work with, but we wanted to add something different. Nigel, James and I began by emailing each other images of plants and plant communities growing in the wild such as the Drakensberg in South Africa with its striking field groupings of red-hot pokers.

James suggested focusing on Britain's long history of introducing plants from around the world – a tradition that dates back to the 14th century and the collecting of grassland species from central Europe. We also wanted to highlight that by using these plants from around the world, and by placing them in a naturalistic planting context, you can establish a richer resource for biodiversity through complex and varied spatial arrangements. We started to develop an approach to the layering of plants and plant communities, including species with leafless stems and open forms. This allows sunlight to filter through to the lower levels to establish a mosaic of intermingled plant communities. This approach to planting is a very British contribution to the Park and in many ways takes us back to the work of William Robinson in the 1870s. His 'Wild Garden' introduced naturalised planting principles that are also beautifully expressed in the Dutch Heem parks in Amstelveen. These provided a strong point of reference for the planting of the Gardens as well as for the wider Park and in particular the meadow plantings.

The design development was on a very fast track and much of my time was spent communicating our planting ideas to the design team and wider audience.

I developed the spatial layout for the Gardens while Nigel and James split their responsibility for specific continents relating to their particular research interests. They took a very strong scientific and ecological approach. Together we developed our planting ideas through the mathematical distribution of plant types, which I then composed into a series of collages for all four continental zones.

I developed the layout of the hedges from George's rough sketch of hedge forms that took its inspiration from the Olympic Rings. From these hedge forms, I elaborated structural bands of planting, using plant palettes that complemented the selections from James and Nigel. These areas of structured planting provide backdrops that fade into or overlay their more loosely planted fields. There was a continual battle within the team between creating more structural planting strips and more field. As the scheme developed, a balance was struck and the naturalistic and formal horticultural elements of the planting became more focused. What was clear in the design process, as is often the case, was that the most interesting ideas are created when people work in the periphery of established approaches.

The planting plans had to be prepared in a few weeks and were first drawn by hand then by computer, before being finally checked and issued for construction. The plans were complex and I thought they would require a lot of my time on site working with the contractor. If it wasn't for Des Smith, the Head Gardener, who went home and made a watercolour of the scheme to help him visualise what the design was

Initial detailed design sketch for the North American Garden in the 2012 Gardens prepared by Sarah Price. It illustrates the structured blending of perennial plant forms and groups vertically and horizontally.

Maturing planting in the North American Garden in September 2011. The planting includes multi-stem *Malus* 'Evereste', the cream *Heuchera villosa* and golden *Rudbekia fulgida deamii*.

trying to achieve, it would have been much harder to set out and complete the planting in the two months that we had.

Although the Gardens have a big visual impact it is interesting how difficult they have been to photograph. For me their power is in their experiential quality. After we had completed the planting I clearly remember the first time I walked through the upper terrace in the North American Garden and on under the bridge to the Southern Hemisphere. Even though I knew the designs back to front, actually being there and experiencing

the immense contrast between the plant communities was thrilling. Some of the Southern Hemisphere plants are weird in form and when growing on mass have an incredible day-glo intensity.

The Gardens are extremely ambitious and will be very influential in the way native and non-native plants can be used in public spaces and urban parks. In breaking new ground in planting design, I hope we will have shown that there is a far richer palette of plants that can be enjoyed by both wildlife and people.

They are a new kind of garden, not only in terms of their design and the unusual plant species and combinations, but also in terms of their biodiversity value. All the flowering plants were proposed because they also produce lots of nectar and diverse habitat for invertebrates.

The Games are about gathering people from all over the world to celebrate sports, arts and culture. Spectators visiting the gardens saw plants from their home regions, as will the diverse communities who live in this part of London in legacy. They will all have that magical sense of being a world away. The Gardens celebrate the age-old, great British passion for collecting plants from around the world and cultivating them in their gardens, like the Chelsea Physic Garden founded in 1673 by the Worshipful Society of Apothecaries of London for its apprentices to study the medicinal qualities of plants, and the Royal Botanic Gardens, Kew, founded in 1759 and now holding the world's largest collection of living plants. The vision was that the south of the Park will establish itself as a cultural hub for east London on a par with central London's South Bank. Along with the ArcelorMittal Orbit, Britain's largest public sculpture, by Anish Kapoor and Cecil Balmond (an extraordinary 115m-high visitor attraction with a look-out platform at the equivalent of a 23rd floor), James Corner Field Operations' playground, event spaces and visitor centre, and the 2012 Gardens, it is hoped that the south of the Park will be on everyone's 'must see' list.

Planting in the Southern Hemisphere Garden featuring layered strips and drifts of plants. The planting design was inspired by the character and form of native ecological communities found within each continent.

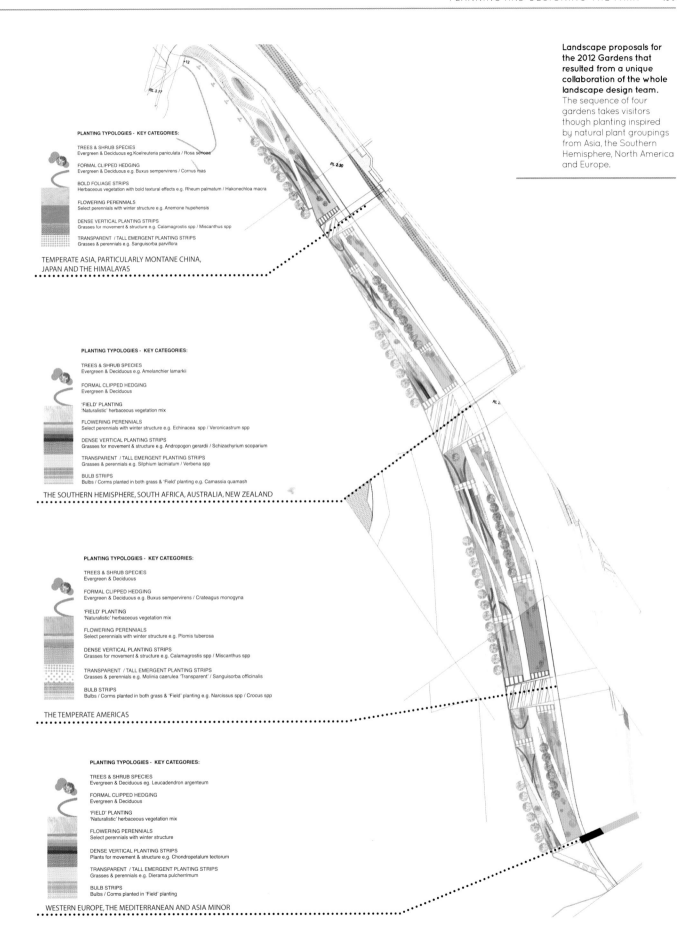

Landscape proposals for the 2012 Gardens that resulted from a unique collaboration of the whole landscape design team. The sequence of four gardens takes visitors though planting inspired by natural plant groupings from Asia, the Southern Hemisphere, North America and Europe.

PLANTING TYPOLOGIES - KEY CATEGORIES:

TREES & SHRUB SPECIES
Evergreen & Deciduous eg.Koelreuteria paniculata / Rosa sericea

FORMAL CLIPPED HEDGING
Evergreen & Deciduous e.g. Buxus sempervirens / Cornus mas

BOLD FOLIAGE STRIPS
Herbaceous vegetation with bold textural effects e.g. Rheum palmatum / Hakonechloa macra

FLOWERING PERENNIALS
Select perennials with winter structure e.g. Anemone hupehensis

DENSE VERTICAL PLANTING STRIPS
Grasses for movement & structure e.g. Calamagrostis spp / Miscanthus spp

TRANSPARENT / TALL EMERGENT PLANTING STRIPS
Grasses & perennials e.g. Sanguisorba parviflora

TEMPERATE ASIA, PARTICULARLY MONTANE CHINA, JAPAN AND THE HIMALAYAS

PLANTING TYPOLOGIES - KEY CATEGORIES:

TREES & SHRUB SPECIES
Evergreen & Deciduous e.g. Amelanchier lamarkii

FORMAL CLIPPED HEDGING
Evergreen & Deciduous

'FIELD' PLANTING
'Naturalistic' herbaceous vegetation mix

FLOWERING PERENNIALS
Select perennials with winter structure e.g. Echinacea spp / Veronicastrum spp

DENSE VERTICAL PLANTING STRIPS
Grasses for movement & structure e.g. Andropogon gerardii / Schizachyrium scoparium

TRANSPARENT / TALL EMERGENT PLANTING STRIPS
Grasses & perennials e.g. Silphium laciniatum / Verbena spp

BULB STRIPS
Bulbs / Corms planted in both grass & 'Field' planting e.g. Camassia quamash

THE SOUTHERN HEMISPHERE, SOUTH AFRICA, AUSTRALIA, NEW ZEALAND

PLANTING TYPOLOGIES - KEY CATEGORIES:

TREES & SHRUB SPECIES
Evergreen & Deciduous

FORMAL CLIPPED HEDGING
Evergreen & Deciduous e.g. Buxus sempervirens / Crateagus monogyna

'FIELD' PLANTING
'Naturalistic' herbaceous vegetation mix

FLOWERING PERENNIALS
Select perennials with winter structure e.g. Plomis tuberosa

DENSE VERTICAL PLANTING STRIPS
Grasses for movement & structure e.g. Calamagrostis spp / Miscanthus spp

TRANSPARENT / TALL EMERGENT PLANTING STRIPS
Grasses & perennials e.g. Molinia caerulea 'Transparent' / Sanguisorba officinalis

BULB STRIPS
Bulbs / Corms planted in both grass & 'Field' planting e.g. Narcissus spp / Crocus spp

THE TEMPERATE AMERICAS

PLANTING TYPOLOGIES - KEY CATEGORIES:

TREES & SHRUB SPECIES
Evergreen & Deciduous eg. Leucadendron argenteum

FORMAL CLIPPED HEDGING
Evergreen & Deciduous

'FIELD' PLANTING
'Naturalistic' herbaceous vegetation mix

FLOWERING PERENNIALS
Select perennials with winter structure

DENSE VERTICAL PLANTING STRIPS
Plants for movement & structure e.g. Chondropetalum tectorum

TRANSPARENT / TALL EMERGENT PLANTING STRIPS
Grasses & perennials e.g. Dierama pulcherrimum

BULB STRIPS
Bulbs / Corms planted in 'Field' planting

WESTERN EUROPE, THE MEDITERRANEAN AND ASIA MINOR

Sowing annual display meadows on this scale had never been done before. This is the 'Olympic Gold' annual meadow being trialled for the second season in September 2011.

The ODA wanted the planting in the Park to be as colourful and festive as possible during the Games. The Opening Ceremony on 27 July 2012 was too late for a large majority of flowering plants that tend to bloom in spring and early summer. The two Sheffield University professors are world-renowned for their work on urban meadows. Their innovative approach to 'dynamic landscapes' that appeal to both people and wildlife was a requirement of the brief. The final overlay on this extraordinary design for the Park included two kinds of meadows. In the north, there are primarily perennial meadows that take two seasons to establish, are terrific for wildlife and, when in flower, look spectacular. To assure that they were in flower for the Games, they were suppressed by cutting, and then encouraged to flower with irrigation and fertiliser. In the south of the Park, golden annual meadows were sown just three months before the Games, and then transformed into perennial meadows for legacy. The annual meadows were trialled to prove to sceptics both within the ODA and externally that it could be done. The result is something that has never been done or seen on this scale anywhere before – a huge, spectacular, colourful and floriferous landscape that is great for people and for wildlife.

The proposals for the parklands were approved and implemented, but as they affected every project on the Park, it was a fraught process – late on in the programme the ship was turned 90 degrees. The crucial meeting took place at 8am, 21 May 2008 over coffee

May 2010 annual and perennial meadow trial beds that were sown and maintained on site for two years. Soil types, species mixes, irrigation and levels of fertiliser for different mixes were trialled, as well as sowing times and cutting regimes, to ensure flowering during the Games.

and croissants in the design team's office. The ODA's Chief Executive and Directors of Design and Infrastructure pored over the clay model. The concept made immense sense, but could it be achieved? It was decided to try. The rest, as they say, is history: the detailed planning application was submitted in November 2008 and approved on 24 February 2009[24] and construction commenced. Detailed transformation proposals also prepared by the team were approved by the planning committee on 27 April 2010. The ODA's planning and design work was now substantially complete. Meanwhile, construction moved relentlessly towards its completion one year ahead of the Games.

A perennial feature meadow in the north of the Park, in June 2011. These feature meadows used a repeating grid of nine non-native plant species to provide maximum visual impact during the Games.

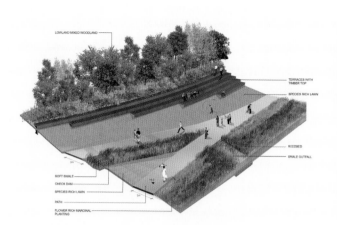

The terraced seating adjacent to the riverside path in the north of the Park. A sequence of gently sloping footpaths connect the riverside path, seating terraces and spectator lawns to the higher-level concourse. Left: visualisation submitted with the planning application in September 2008. Right: pictured in 2012.

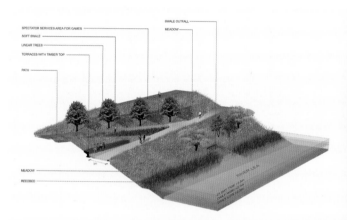

The river edge and terraced seating in the north-west of the Park. The sustainable surface water drainage route from the Concourse flows along the swale and outfalls into the river within the reed margin, completing the drainage cycle. Left: visualisation submitted with the planning application in September 2008. Right: pictured in 2012.

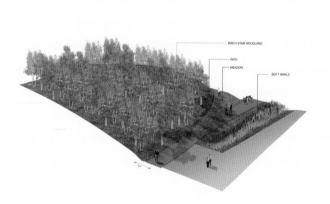

Birch stem woodland with understorey in the north of the Park. The white stems of the birch trees provide a stunning visual display and enhance the sculptural landform. In legacy oak and wild cherry trees will grow and take over from the birch providing long-lived, rich woodland habitat. Left: visualisation submitted with the planning application in September 2008. Right: pictured in 2012.

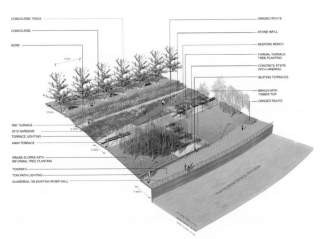

The 2012 Gardens in the south of the Park comprise semi-mature trees along the edge of the concourse, footpaths with gentle slopes providing easy access down to the river promenade, themed planting, spectator lawns, steps, seating, lighting and artworks. Left: visualisation submitted with the planning application in September 2008. Right: pictured in 2012.

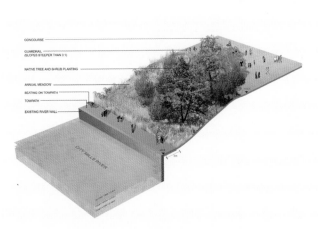

During the Games in the south of the Park, colourful annual meadows complemented a mosaic of native tree and shrub plantings along the City Mill River. Following the Games, the annual meadows are replaced with perennial meadows to assure the long-term ecological value of the riparian corridor. Left: visualisation submitted with the planning application in September 2008. Right: pictured in 2012.

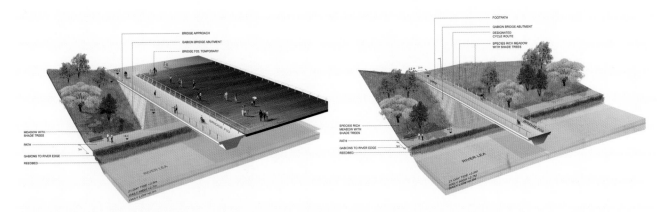

Illustration of the width of a typical bridge is reduced through the removal of the temporary section after the Games.

The Southern Hemisphere 2012 Garden during the Games in July 2012.

CHAPTER FOUR

CHAPTER FOUR

Constructing the Park

With the bid won, the planning application approved, the land in the ownership of the Olympic Delivery Authority (ODA), and designs well underway, demolition commenced in July 2007 and the first contract for construction was let in July 2008. It was one of the largest, most complex construction projects in Europe. The ODA's Demolish, Dig, Design milestones progressed to the three phases of the Big Build – Foundations, Structures and Completion. Archaeological excavations and the translocation of 2,000 newts, other animals and habitats were followed by the eradication of invasive plants, demolition, decontamination, the restoration of the waterways and the building of a completely new infrastructure of utilities, roads, bridges, temporary and permanent venues and the extraordinary parklands.

Mayor Ken Livingstone was known to have a soft spot for newts. So the translocation of around 2,000 of them at the very beginning of construction in July 2007 brought the ODA political capital as well as public goodwill. It was needed. There was broad scepticism that the ODA could deliver what became the Queen Elizabeth Olympic Park on time and within budget. It had published its programme baseline report setting out the scope of its works, the budget and overarching programme milestones beginning with Demolish, Dig, Design 2007–8, then moving to the Big Build – Foundations 2008–9, Structures 2009–10, and finally Completion 2010–11 a year ahead of the Games. Yet, despite nearly 80 per cent of the British public supporting the Games, there was no shortage of sceptical politicians and members of the press predicting ever-rising costs, recriminations, bail-outs and ignominy.[1] In November 2006 the *Observer* wrote that, 'In July 2005 luminaries of London's bid team, such as David Beckham and Steve Redgrave, hugged each other in delight in Singapore when London won. Back home, thousands watching on big screens in Trafalgar Square joined in the celebrations. The mood is different now. Scepticism has replaced exhilaration.'[2]

The precedents did not bode well. Pickett's Lock, also in the Lea Valley to the north of the Park, was Britain's abandoned attempt to build a 45,000-seat National Athletics Stadium for the 2005 World Athletic Championships. Wembley was the world's most expensive stadium, delivered a year late amid much acrimony. Additionally, the UK economy was booming. Contractors were busy, so there was a real fear that they would not risk bidding for such high-profile, time-constrained projects, and that there were just not enough skilled workers to deliver £150 million worth of work per month at peak spend. As it turned out, the global financial crash in 2008 eased the construction market substantially, and the reality was that London 2012 hit the ground running – just the day after London won the bid, the contract to remove all 52 of the 65-metre-high electricity pylons that dominated the landscape of the Park was signed.

Fish being translocated from Pudding Mill river in the Park in 2007. New habitats were created to accommodate species at the Old Ford Wood within the Park, and the Waterworks Nature Reserve just to the north of the Park. Additionally, one hectare of habitat in mitigation for that lost within the Park was created on East Marsh immediately north of the Park.

PREPARE

With an immoveable deadline and a predicted peak workforce of 10,000, the General Secretary of the Union of Construction, Allied Trades and Technicians (UCATT) warned of 'an industrial relations disaster'.[3] The ODA had to head this off. In September 2007, following detailed discussions, the ODA signed a Memorandum of Agreement with the leading trade unions Unite, GMB and UCATT that set out a framework for good industrial relations. The Trades Union Congress General Secretary welcomed the Agreement: 'Our ambition is to see that this world class event generates high quality well rewarded jobs, with the highest standards of health and safety, equal opportunities, skills and training and sustainability.'[4] As a mark of this achievement, there were no major industrial relations disputes during construction. The importance of the agreement was crystallised when as late as February 2012 Len McCluskey of the Unite union sparked a huge political controversy by saying that strikes during the Games were being considered. Deputy Prime Minister Nick Clegg said, 'People will just be gobsmacked, appalled, at Mr McCluskey's remarks.' Ed Miliband, Leader of the Opposition said, 'Any threat to the Olympics is totally unacceptable and wrong.'[5]

With an anticipated 2,000 main contracts to be let, the ODA moved swiftly to get the procurement of contractors and suppliers right.[6] As a public body, it was subject to a complex set of procurement regulations, with specific guidelines on transparency, fairness and non-discrimination to ensure competition. Any whiff of unfair or corrupt practices would be disastrous. In 2007, following consultation with over 60 contracting groups across the UK, it published its Procurement Policy. It complied with EU and Public Contracting Regulations and set out how procurement would support the ODA's approach to managing risk and opportunity, and obtaining value for money. Defining the procurement approach at an early stage in the programme established confidence within the industry.

The ODA committed to use the New Engineering Contract 3 (NEC3) for the majority of its procurements. It also committed not to simply award contracts according to lowest price, but to take into consideration a 'balanced scorecard' of selection and award criteria. These addressed the ODA's priority themes of design and accessibility, employment and skills, equality and inclusion, health, safety and security, legacy and sustainability. In addition, the ODA required its primary contractors to advertise subcontracting opportunities on the CompeteFor website, which generated over 8,000 opportunities. The ODA monitored the financial stability of its contractors and suppliers, working to prevent insolvencies. In 2006, the Chief Executive David Higgins summed up the ODA's bold intention to change the way the construction industry worked: 'The ODA has a finite lifetime. Our work programme can be the catalyst for change across industry and it is my hope that the standards we set will encourage continuing improvements and innovation to 2012 and beyond.'[7]

In addition to its sophisticated and rigorous planning system, the UK has an equally sophisticated and rigorous regulatory system for building and construction overseen by local authorities. The Park covered four boroughs, each with its own regulatory department, so to streamline the approvals process and assure consistency, three joint organisations were established to grant approvals for construction. The Joint Local Authorities Building Control oversaw Building Regulations approvals ensuring that they were safe, healthy, accessible and sustainable. The Joint Local Authority Regulatory Services regulated food safety, health and safety, highways, licensing, parking, pest control, pollution control, public health, safety at sports grounds, street naming, street scene enforcement, trading standards and waste management. And the Olympic Infrastructure Technical Approval Authority brought together the often conflicting design requirements of the Host Boroughs and Transport for London into two Comprehensive Design Guides (Games Mode and Transformation) for use by the respective design teams. Every project had to achieve the approval of these authorities.

To deliver on all its promises, the ODA had to embed sustainability and environmental management right through procurement, contract, design, planning, construction and communication. It had to ensure a safe, healthy, secure site for its workforce, and be a good neighbour to the residents at the edge of this huge construction programme. Soon after receipt of the planning permissions in September 2007, it published its first *Health, Safety and Environmental Standard* – it was the first time the three agendas had been brought together. The standard reflected current best practice such as Constructing Excellence, but also included the ODA's *Construction Commitments*, and its *Sustainable Development Strategy*. A *Code of Construction Practice* complementing the Standard was also published. It set out the measures that were to be followed by the ODA and its contractors with regard to the management of the Park during construction, and included sections that dealt with management of noise, dust and air quality, waste, ecology and lighting.[8]

To get 10,000 workers, freight trains, barges and a truck every 20 seconds into and out of the Park every day through airport-standard security was a potential logistical nightmare. The 'behind the scenes' logistics team was critical – it was like running a small town. It ensured the provision of power, roads, buses, food, healthcare, religious centres and the policing of a safe working environment for everyone on the Park. As there was no car parking provision on the Park, public transport timetables were changed to increase early morning peak services to the Park. Every person entering had special ID cards, regulars also had a biometric hand scan, and bags were scanned on entry. Every truck had a full screening at one of two off-site logistics staging and searching areas, followed by an ancillary check on entering the Park. Up to eight freight trains a week, along with barges, brought in heavier materials and removed waste, dramatically reducing construction traffic on local roads. All deliveries were phased and coordinated. Once inside the Park, site workers took on-site buses to their destinations. In addition to a central canteen, health centre and police station, every project had its own canteen and welfare facilities. Workers soon got to know where the best canteens were located.

FROM THE GROUND UP

It was important not to erase the history, ecology and memory of the site through demolition and construction. The ground, contaminated by years of industrial processes, had hindered any development that was too small, too piecemeal. The scale of the Park allowed a comprehensive approach to bringing the land back into use for all future generations. Despite being neglected and weed strewn, it had a remarkable history waiting to be uncovered, and some unique and valuable habitats and species to be saved. There may indeed have been 4,000 holes in Blackburn, Lancashire, but before demolition and decontamination could be fully commenced, 3,500 holes had to be dug or drilled at 25m intervals across the site to find out what soils, ground conditions, and levels and types of contamination were there. In tandem, the ODA was creating an archaeological record preserving the past history of the Park, its origins and the story of the varied communities who had contributed to its distinctive character – another part of the ODA's legacy.[9] Between 2005 and 2009, a programme of archaeological and historical investigations was undertaken to record, map, excavate and analyse the importance of the Park's location through history as an abundant and safe river crossing.

The Museum of London dug many archaeological trenches and found evidence of prehistoric, Roman, Viking and medieval settlements. More than 140 trenches were dug and investigated. They found evidence of Iron Age settlers who lived in thatched circular mud huts on what would have been a small area of dry land in a valley of lakes, rivers and marshes. Four Iron Age skeletons were discovered buried in graves thought to be 3,000 years old. Roman pottery and a coin dated AD 330–335 were found buried behind a wooden river wall. They were the first evidence of Roman activity associated with the rivers of the valley itself, and again highlighted its significance through history. A year-long 'Discover' project gave local people an insight into the past of the Park through school visits, a community dig, and roadshows across the boroughs. Current East Enders were learning about the very first East Enders.

The valuable species and habitats that had emerged largely undisturbed on the site were surveyed and then protected or translocated. Japanese knotweed, Himalayan balsam, giant hogweed and floating pennywort were mapped and sprayed with a water-soluble weed killer. The eradication programme ran from the start to the finish of the construction and due to their persistence will continue in legacy.[10] In addition to the translocation of the 2,000 newts that so pleased the Mayor, toads, lizards and fish were also moved to the Waterworks Nature Reserve three kilometres (two miles) north of the Park. Seed was

collected and cuttings taken of over 160 species ready to be grown-on off-site and then brought back into the Park."

There was healthy competition within the ODA project teams to be first off the blocks with any activity. The first earthworks commenced in May 2007 on the site of the International Broadcast Centre (IBC) and Main Press Centre (MPC) Complex in the north of the Park. In January 2008, the ODA announced that two-thirds of site demolition was complete and that it was accelerating the clean-up. Five state-of-the-art soil-washing machines were soaking, sieving and shaking contaminants out of 2 million cubic metres of soil, 24 hours a day, seven days a week. Contaminants included petrol, oil, tar and heavy metals such as arsenic and lead. An innovative bioremediation technique was used to clean up nearly 50,000 tonnes of soil contaminated with petrol and oil. Warm air, nutrients and water vapour were pumped through the soil in specially constructed bioremediation beds to increase the number of microorganisms and speed up the natural 'composting' process. After a few weeks the soil was clean enough for reuse.

From 2008 to 2009 five soil-washing machines worked around the clock. The use of site-won materials, including washed sands and gravel, resulted in significant savings and allowed more than 80 per cent of the contaminated soil to be reused.

A full-scale soil analysis laboratory was set up on the Park with a team of 60 scientists, technicians, engineers and data management staff using state-of-the-art analytical equipment to test up to 80 samples of soil a day. Project managers waited anxiously for results, as serious contamination meant delay. In the end, only three per cent of concentrated waste from the whole decontamination process was taken to a licensed landfill. Some 80 per cent of the 2 million cubic metres of spoil excavated, along with more than 200,000 cubic metres of spoil from the power-line tunnels, was reused on the Park to create platforms for venues, future development plots, and the earthworks for the extraordinary landscape. It was an epic decontamination and clean-up process that set a new benchmark for the industry worldwide.

Most people live their lives without giving a second thought to the extraordinary web of underground tunnels, pipes, ducts, cables and pits on which our civilised lives depend. Utilities are the predominantly unseen 'backbone' of any neighbourhood, town or city. In April 2008 the ODA awarded a key contract to deliver a 6-kilometre water network, 6.5km of gas pipes, 22km of telecommunication ducts, and 18km of high-voltage electrical cables access. Cables and substation installation was a separate contract. They were delivered by one contractor in a common utilities trench for efficiency and to save money. A further contract was awarded for the design and construction of the primary sewer and pumping station and associated 1.2m-diameter, 1.8km-long tunnel to collect, convey and discharge foul sewage flows. Another contractor was appointed to design, build, finance,

Construction of the foul water pumping station in August 2008. A new network of primary sewers was constructed across the Park with the capacity to serve both the Games and all future developments.

own and operate two energy centres and community energy networks providing super-efficient power, heating and cooling systems across the Park and the adjacent Stratford City development for a 40-year period. This 'backbone' of utilities was designed to provide all the service needs of not only the Games, but also the neighbourhoods that will arise on the Park in legacy.

With the site and archaeological investigations, demolition, decontamination and other preparatory works complete or well underway, the three phases of the Big Build – Foundations, Structures, Completion – followed on relentlessly. The venues were rising out of the ground, with the Olympic Stadium first off the blocks three months earlier than planned.[12] The answer to the urgent and ever-present question 'How many days to the Opening Ceremony?' became 'How many days … and nights!'

TYING IT ALL TOGETHER – THE PARKLANDS

As the venues rose out of the ground, the waterways and the parklands also began to take shape … and to surprise. More than 280,000 visitors were taken on bus tours around the Park during construction, and there were audible gasps when they crossed the bridge in the north of the Park and saw the new riverine landscape for the first time. The parklands at the heart, as intended, came to characterise the Park as much as the venues.

The landscape design strategy for the parklands had four major themes. Firstly, a strong green framework of highly refined, structured landforms, planting of semi-mature trees and spectator lawns. Secondly, high-impact planting with strong visual interest and colour across the Park – this comprised large sweeps of perennial, annual and feature meadows, the wetlands, and the Gardens. Thirdly, a mosaic of connected ecological habitats throughout the Park. Fourthly, the majority of the landscape was to remain in legacy. Post-Games changes and modifications were anticipated wherever possible and were integral to the design from the start – for example, the conversion of the spectator lawns to species-rich lawns – to ensure the delivery of the Biodiversity Action Plan (BAP) targets.

To some, constructing a landscape entails 'throwing down some soil and a bit of seed'. In the case of the parklands this is more than a slight simplification. The landscape is a constructed complex of soils, drainage, irrigation, structures, paving, lighting, street furniture, trees, woodlands, wetlands, meadows, lawns and gardens. It touched every other project on the Park. It required the most sophisticated project management and coordination skills. It is a meticulously engineered artefact designed as a self-sustaining, dynamic, multifunctional, 'working' landscape of connected habitats from open water through marginal aquatic edges to woodland.[13] It was literally constructed from the underground up. In addition to the landscape architect's team led by LDA Design. Hargreaves Associates, the ODA appointed Arup and Atkins as landscape engineers and

Preliminary grading of subsoil in the north of the Park in early 2010. The subsoil was a key element of the soils and drainage strategy. The subsoils and nine different types of topsoils sequestered carbon, and absorbed water and nutrients that promoted plant growth.

required that those teams be led by director-level landscape architects. This was to ensure coordination with all other engineering works across the Park, also led by Arup and Atkins, and that the focus on the 'look and feel' of the final landscape was not lost in the frenetic, day-to-day business and technicalities of just getting things built. It was also to ensure coordination with the structures, bridges, highways, utilities and architectural elements that were designed by Allies and Morrison.

The protection and translocation of habitats and species, the collection of seeds and cuttings, the eradication of noxious weeds and the decontamination of existing soils and groundwater, were followed by the layering of subsoils, drainage and topsoils. Different sub-grades were prepared for planting and paving and tested for compaction levels. Soils were ameliorated ready for planting, seeding and turfing. Trenches were dug for high- and low-voltage electricity, gas, lighting, telecommunications, CCTV, irrigation, potable and non-potable water lines. An innovative sustainable urban surface water drainage system (SUDS) was put in. Utilities already laid had to be avoided and protected.

(continued on page 184)

AN INTEGRATED AND SEAMLESS INFRASTRUCTURE

Simon Wright OBE

Director of Infrastructure and Utilities 2006–11
Director of Venues and Infrastructure 2011 onwards
Olympic Delivery Authority

When I started in summer 2006 we were halfway through the site investigations. The masterplan team was up and running and the engineering activities were playing catch-up. It was important that during the scheme design the Park would be buildable and workable and that all practical issues had to be sorted out within an unprecedented timescale. Critical decisions had to be made quickly, an essential feature of successful projects, which created a much-needed momentum in the design chain.

We appointed Atkins and Arup as the engineering teams in the north and south of the Park to lead on all

Construction of the central pedestrian bridge designed by Heneghan Peng Architects – the only bespoke bridge on the Park – which carried spectators to the north of the Park during the Games. The temporary decks of the bridge completely cover the canal and Carpenters Road Lock below.

The completed central pedestrian bridge in June 2011. After the Games the slender central Z-section remained, while the large multi-coloured areas were removed to reveal the canal and lock below in transformation, and the adjacent land excavated and sculpted to create bowls focusing on the bridge and lock.

the tasks relating to the topography, engineering, roads, bridges and utilities, with the responsibility to work very closely with the masterplan team. We also appointed Allies and Morrison, part of the EDAW Consortium, to ensure that the entire design of the infrastructure was coordinated, efficient and sustainable and would seamlessly integrate with the landscape. While the ODA had the formal responsibility to drive the masterplan, much of the coordination was achieved through setting up DIG, the design integration group, managed by our Delivery Partner, that drew all design and engineering leads together. It met fortnightly over two years to unify the look and feel of the project, ensuring a coherent whole. Trust was built up early with a 'no blame' culture and a strong collaborative ethos that created a very

powerful, accurate and reliable team – an approach that went right down through the supply chain.

For the enabling works we faced a complex three-dimensional puzzle across the site while the topography and cut and fill requirements were still evolving. This had a direct effect on the projected costs for remediation. While the site was not as contaminated as the Greenwich Peninsula, where I had worked before joining the ODA, we needed to minimise disturbance and excavation. Defining the landform for the enabling works was an iterative process, driven by both budget and design. We had to ensure the Park was accessible with gentle gradients, while creating a landform that would provide the visual interest, drama and variety demanded by the design team.

One of the largest permanent bridge sections being lifted into position in November 2009. It is part of the primary pedestrian route into the Park from the Stratford transport hubs for both the Games and legacy.

Just as we had it all pinned down, the detailed landscape design team proposed a significant change to reform the valley profile and fill Henniker's Ditch. To be honest, I was against this at the time as we had already refined a scheme that worked technically and financially and this change would be disruptive. But the landscape architects were clear on the benefits, Alison Nimmo was convinced, David Higgins was convinced and he carried the day. With hindsight it was one of the best decisions made on the project.

We also achieved a lot though the infrastructure projects in pushing the boundaries on sustainable design. The trigeneration Energy Centre, combining cooling, heating and power, has been fundamental in helping meet the 50 per cent carbon reduction target. The water recycling plant is a first for Britain of this scale, housed in a good-looking building and developed in collaboration with Thames Water. It draws raw sewage directly from the Northern Outfall Sewer, treats it and distributes it around the entire site, thus helping to deliver a 40 per cent reduction in the use of drinking water. The recycled water is used for cooling by the Energy Centre, irrigation and toilet flushing.

There have also been some interesting engineering

View of the underside of a bridge in the north of the Park. The temporary section with vertical sheet piling can be seen on the left, with the permanent section on the right sitting on top of the sloping, gabion walls filled with crushed concrete aggregate recycled from the demolition in the Park. The bridge is one of the Park-wide '12 for 2012' colour-coded artworks.

feats in the project. Designing split bridges that include temporary sections to boost capacity for the Games but that will be removed in legacy will have a massive effect on minimising the impact of the infrastructure in the Park over the long term. Also, jacking a box culvert for a two-lane highway under the A12 on the northern boundary of the Park while keeping the A12 road open was very difficult, but saved an immense amount of money by not having to close the road and divert traffic.

A real shift in approach has been taken in the design of the utility buildings. We wrote into the tender documents the need for them to be well designed and integrated within the masterplan as they are large prominent buildings. The concession agreements included design briefs with the requirement to employ architects to complete the designs and you can now see the electrical substations and pumping station in neat timber structures that even have poetry inscribed on the facade. They represent a recurring lesson for the infrastructure across the Park. On a practical level the utility buildings look fantastic. They embody good design, performance and functionality and have even won RIBA awards, which I think is a big step forward for the utility industry.

The waterways were dredged and the concrete walls to the canals in the southern Park cleaned and repaired. The Waterworks river was widened and planted with marginal aquatics. In the north of the Park, new bio-engineered river edges resilient to scouring during floods, and new wetlands, ponds, swales and wet woodlands were created.

Some 4,000 8m-high trees were planted in specially dug tree trenches complete with structural soils, drainage and irrigation. Over 20 hectares of concourse were laid out and patterned with a gravel surface dressing using, for the first time in the UK, a sustainable binder for the gravel. Bespoke 25m-high lighting masts with vertical wind turbines were erected in the south of the Park. Hundreds of lighting columns lit the concourse, the permanent ones with photovoltaic panels. Bespoke, sustainably sourced timber benches were built on site by carpenters, along with hundreds of freestanding proprietary benches and seats. This was a constructed landscape in every sense, each square millimetre was designed with purpose and beauty in mind. It was naturalised, not natural. And, of course, once complete it had to be managed and maintained to the standard of London's Royal Parks.

SOILS AND DRAINAGE

Soils and drainage are fundamental to achieving a thriving and viable landscape in the long term. If the soil has the wrong structure and nutrients, is too compacted, too loose, too wet or too dry the planting will never succeed.[14] The ODA's specialist horticultural (not agricultural) soil scientist prepared a strategy that had four strands to support: the landscape design, the creation of ecological habitats, environmental interaction, and water attenuation and filtration.[15] Because soils and vegetation sequester substantial amounts of carbon, they were an important contributor to the carbon targets in the ODA's *Sustainable Development Strategy*. The soil strategy also worked in tandem with the remediation strategy. There were limited reserves of natural topsoil on site, consequently, the remediation strategy was a key factor in soil selection alongside the drainage strategy, the tight programme and sustainability objectives.

No less than nine types of soil were specified for each of the predominant habitat types, ranging from general-purpose subsoil to moisture-retentive and high-permeability topsoils. Overall soil depths were mainly controlled by two factors – the need for cover providing the 'human health' layer, and the anticipated rooting depth of the plants to be established. Low-nutrient topsoil was specified for meadows, shrub and groundcover planting. High-permeability topsoil was specified for the spectator lawns to ensure that they drained quickly after heavy rain and could be used soon after. Multi-purpose topsoil was specified for woodland. Moisture-retentive topsoil was specified for the wooded gullies. Tree sand or structural soil was specified for the semi-mature trees in paved areas. The primary component of the soils was quarry overburden – a recycled waste material.

The moisture-retentive topsoils were material made up entirely from soil washings from a sugar beet factory – another recycled waste product. 'Green compost' was mixed in with the topsoils to provide organic content. 'Green compost' is produced commercially and derived from composting garden wastes, such as grass clippings and tree and shrub prunings. No peat was used on the Park. In addition to reusing the soil already in the Park, nearly 50,000 cubic metres of topsoil, and 36,000 cubic metres of subsoil were brought into the Park, the majority by rail.

The soil scientist was retained to advise through all stages of the project – design, specification, manufacture, delivery and placement – as things can go wrong at every stage. And on a couple of occasions things did go wrong. Topsoils and subsoils were placed to very specific depths. Subsoil, because of its low organic matter content, was used to create rooting depths in excess of 0.4–0.5m. Typically, 0.2–0.3m of topsoil was placed over 0.5–0.6m of subsoil. 'More is better' used to be the industry standard for topsoil depths. This is no longer the case. The nutrients lead to anaerobic and toxic conditions below 0.8m. There were one or two instances where topsoil was placed at greater depths under some large trees. The trees were taken out, the topsoil removed, the subsoil then topsoil

Placement of soils during the construction of the 2012 Gardens in May 2010. The soils were built up from an unremediated sub-base demarcated by an orange geosynthetic 'marker' fabric, then a 'human health' layer, of clean soils, subsoils and finally topsoils for planting.

back-filled to the correct depths, and the trees replanted. If this had not been done, the roots would have eventually grown into the anaerobic soil and died. A potential disaster that would only have become apparent in legacy was averted.

Early in the soil placement programme, horsetail began to emerge – another potential disaster. Horsetail is an ancient plant that, once established, is hard to eradicate. It has roots that can extend for several metres in all directions. Even a small piece will take root and grow vigorously. Work was stopped immediately. Nobody knew how an inert soil, brought straight from a quarry that had been inspected, could be so contaminated. As it turned out, a re-inspection of the quarry revealed that a digger operator had, unbeknown to anyone but himself, extracted soil from an uninspected stockpile that was adjacent to a hedgerow with a healthy crop of horsetail growing within it. The majority of soil that had already been placed was removed completely. That which could not be removed was monitored every day, emergent horsetail was carefully removed by hand, and its position marked with a flag and logged by a Geographic Positioning System (GPS). At the start of the next growing season, all locations were again checked every day – there were very few re-emergences of the horsetail. The meadows specialist advised that any remaining horsetail would soon be shaded and outcompeted by the newly sown perennial meadow species. Another potential disaster was avoided.

Off-site batch blending of the manufactured topsoils for the Park. Nine different soils were designed and specified for the various vegetation types within the Park that required the combination of mineral and organic materials in different ratios.

THE WATERWAYS

British Waterways, the owner of the waterways in the south of the Park, built the new Three Mills Lock about 1.5 kilometres (a mile) to the south of the Park with some funding support from the ODA and others. It allowed large barges into the Park, reduced flood risk by controlling the water levels, and locked out the tide. The Waterworks river, adjacent to the Aquatics Centre, is a flood channel that the ODA widened by 8m to increase flow and support flood management. The 8m widened strip was planted with marginal aquatic plants to ensure ecological connectivity and look good. Ramps and steps provide access from the river walk to river level to support future long-term use of the waterways by boats, anglers and others. Towpaths to all the waterways in the south of the Park were widened and seats added every 50m. The retention and restoration of the characteristic concrete walls lining the canals, Carpenters Road Lock, the adjacent old, pale blue metal pedestrian bridge, mooring bollards and other canal infrastructure evoked a real sense of the previously industrial character of the Park.

The construction of Three Mills Lock also facilitated the design and construction of new wetland and wet woodland habitats as part of the flood management scheme. The landscape is like a huge 'sponge' that accepts, absorbs and utilises rainwater to create rich

Installation of sheet piling in November 2007. This was the first stage in widening the Waterworks river in the south of the Park to improve water flows as part of the Park-wide flood alleviation scheme.

Demolition of the original wall along the Waterworks river adjacent to the Aquatics Centre in April 2008. The 8m-wide strip was planted with marginal aquatic vegetation to assure ecological connectivity of the southern stretches of the river network within the Park.

habitats, storing and cleansing water prior to naturally recharging underlying aquifers or slowly discharging it into the river. In conjunction with the sustainable urban drainage system of porous paving, swales, wet woodlands and ponds, the parklands help to protect not only the Park from flooding, but also another 5,000 properties in the surrounding areas.

A specialist river engineer, in conjunction with the landscape architect team, designed and oversaw the construction of the river edges, wetlands, wet woodlands, swales and ponds. They were all interlinked, hydraulically and ecologically, to fit in with the overall look and feel of the Park.[16] The technical challenge was to design and construct a system to manage water levels and flooding, limit bank side erosion, create a series of connected habitats, and ensure ease of management and maintenance. Two 'wetland bowls' were sculpted and planted with reeds, rushes, sedges and iris during the remediation and restoration of the river.[17] The bowls store water in case of rainfall in the river Lea catchment increasing by up to a 1:100-year event – plus predicted increases due to climate change. Channels, shored up underwater by hazel spiling, provide refuges for fish during flooding and for their spawning.

The permanent bridges throughout the Park are of a simple and consistent box girder construction. The concrete abutments are clad with gabions – wire mesh baskets filled

with recycled crushed concrete from demolition across the Park. The gabions create a simple visual identity and blend easily with the landscape.[18] They proved to be a cost-effective way of achieving a high-quality finish, reusing materials from demolition and creating valuable 'brownfield' habitat.[19] Steeper embankments, particularly under bridges where the risk of erosion was greatest, were also reinforced with steel gabions, but backfilled with heavy soil and sown with a riparian seed mix to blend with the riverine landscape. Large outfall structures were also designed to satisfy technical and ecological requirements and blend with the landscape.[20] The test came with the first flood event. The water overflowed the footpaths and the bowl partially filled. The river raced through the restricted space under the bridges. There was no scouring, the planting, lawns and footpaths all remained in place: bio-engineering at its best.

An abutment of the Park's central pedestrian bridge that spans over the original Carpenters Road Lock. The gabion (wire basket) abutments filled with crushed concrete recycled from demolition waste within the Park are typical of those throughout the Park.

(continued on page 194)

COORDINATING THE FINE DETAIL THROUGH LANDSCAPE ENGINEERING

Tom Armour
Design Director Landscape Engineering, Arup

Bill Grose
Project Director, Arup

Alison Braham
Design Director Landscape Engineering, Atkins

Martyn Lass MBE
Project Director, Olympic Park Site Wide Infrastructure, Atkins

Starting work on the environmental impact assessments in 2006 gave us a really good understanding of the baseline condition for the site. But it took some time to develop a comprehensive picture. We couldn't even complete all the site investigations and get a fix on the extent of contamination until we had full access. At the same time the demolition programme started, which was the first really big challenge. Around 220 buildings had to come down within three weeks to ensure the enabling works could start on time. This could never have been achieved if the London

The Olympic and Paralympic Village during clearance in November 2007. The demolition of most buildings had to be undertaken within three weeks to keep to the construction programme.

Computer-generated still of the south Park from an animation of the whole Park. Clockwise from bottom right to left are the Water Polo Arena, Aquatics Centre, Waterworks River, London 2012 Gardens, main concourse with Orbit and high mast lights with wind turbines, the Olympic Stadium and Great British Garden. These animations and visualisations were an essential element of the design process, ensuring that all design and construction teams had a clear understanding of the final look and feel of the Park.

Development Agency hadn't pre-tendered at least 10 separate specialist contractor panels. Without them in place it just wouldn't have been possible to mobilise that scale of workforce in the time available.

It was unusual to have landscape architects leading the engineering programme for the Park, but this proved to be successful. While specialist engineers took charge of individual technical elements including bridge design, utilities and river engineering, the landscape engineers' role was to lead, steer and coordinate these activities to deliver the look and feel that everyone was expecting. There were no end of issues with integration, aligning utilities and resolving problems with levels for the enabling works, bridges and abutments. We prepared a lot of visualisations to help in this process, which forced us to really work out the detail. They were an essential tool to communicate to the design teams and the planners what we were trying to achieve.

Throughout the project it was always necessary to try and strike the right balance between competing demands of cost, quality and time. Firstly, we have never had a project programme with such an immoveable deadline. So decisions had to be made swiftly. The end point, being one big party, really brought people together! The client had a very visible budget so meeting the immense public and social responsibility goals within that budget was a huge undertaking. Making the Delivery Partner responsible for managing detailed budgets and programme freed up the ODA to focus on quality and in particular design quality. Although we can proudly say we have been able to deliver the Park on time and within budget, we know that in the future this achievement will generally be forgotten – people will see and enjoy the Park without a thought for cost and programme. The quality of the project will be what remains, and what people will really appreciate, and this will be especially true after the Games.

One of the bosques of London plane trees within the concourse in the south of the Park. A key challenge for the landscape engineers was to carefully align and integrate all tree planting with underground utilities.

This has been the most successful project that we have been involved in because most projects, and particularly infrastructure projects, don't generally end up with everything working out as initially planned. This in part is down to good dialogue and a near constant schedule of design and technical coordination meetings. You have to get stakeholders involved early to flag specific conflicts. The benefit of having co-located teams and a designer's representative on site has ensured a quick response to problems as they emerged. All teams had to be open and ready to discuss and debate issues and make changes when needed, though at times we all had to defend certain fixed positions. Knowing when you can and can't compromise requires good judgement focused on the end product. Pragmatism often has negative connotations and there were endless meetings on the fine detail – lining up manholes and moving lights in minimal ways. But this approach had a significant effect on ensuring the quality of the final Park.

Together we have achieved much in terms of delivering a sustainable Park. Increasingly we will see clients and design teams having to make much better judgements than in the past on ecological and environmental issues, and in particular the use of carbon. But in the immediate future the economic problems look to be far greater. There will be much more pressure to build cheaper now and deal with the consequences later. The biggest challenge will be to save money, to understand the cost implications of what you are designing and its affordability over its whole life. But we are increasingly finding the cheapest solution is the most sustainable solution.

The success of the Park will be measured differently at different times, but the litmus test will be how it is managed over the long term. This is no simple challenge. In the UK we have often failed to get this right, as the legacy of the Garden Festivals has shown. Perhaps the greatest test will be how the landscape works as a park and how popular it becomes with the local communities in legacy. Time will tell. But we agree with the Mayor of London, Boris Johnson, who believes that the Park will undoubtedly continue to be the most important regeneration project for London over the next 20 to 30 years.

**View of the Park looking
south in June 2010.**
Working in parallel with the
construction of the utilities
and bridges, the majority
of the landform for the Park,
including the placement of
subsoil and topsoils, was
completed during the drier
summer months.

Planting and establishment of more than 4,000 semi-mature trees across the Park commenced in 2009. The selection of species in the north Park reflected the transition from river edge and wetlands to the upper-valley landscape.

Planting of a semi-mature London plane tree within the concourse in the north of the Park in March 2011. Tree pits were carefully backfilled with a drainage layer then structural tree soil designed to ensure aeration, irrigation and drainage to promote good root growth, and to support paved surfaces preventing settlement.

THE PLANTING STRATEGY

Much of the planting across the Park is utterly unique – nothing like it had been done before.[21] It was an ambitious and diverse response to horticulture, ecology, aesthetics, climate change and plant selection. It embraced new designs and techniques for planting annual and perennial meadows and wetlands, and adopted a sophisticated approach to establishing a rich mosaic of ecological habitats. In the 2012 Gardens a new horticultural, ecological and design aesthetic was pioneered. This could only have been achieved by the integration of soil, ecological and horticultural expertise within the design team. Also, to ensure that the landscape thrived, planting trials to test the most appropriate species and techniques for establishment of the wildflower meadows, the wetlands and river edges were run before specifications were finalised. All the planting was designed and specified to deliver the requirements of the BAP, which promoted local provenance of the vegetation, an important aspect of local, genetic diversity.[22]

Semi-mature trees grown at Hilliers nursery in Hampshire provide immediate impact in the Park particularly for the Games, but also for legacy. They were planted as blocks on the concourse, in lines adjacent to footpaths, and as small groups or single specimens to provide shade on the spectator lawns and elsewhere. Linear trees in the north of the Park were set alongside the footpaths connecting the concourse with the riverside paths. The character of these trees reflects the transition from upper-valley species, including small-leaved lime and wild cherry, to more riverine species, such as white willow and alder. In the south of the Park, linear trees include small-leaved lime located on the concourse above the Gardens, and liquidamber along the mid-terraces of the Gardens. The main concourse tree is London plane, so characteristic of streets and parks throughout London.

Trees providing shade, both clear-stem and multi-stem, were positioned as individuals or groups within lawns or meadows. The positioning of these trees reflects the moisture gradient from drier upper-valley levels to river level. Occasional evergreen species such as holm oak provide winter interest. Other shade trees include common alder, common ash, aspen, wild cherry, mountain ash and a disease-resistant elm. Shade trees located in the Gardens include multi-stemmed birch, crab apple, hawthorn and the golden rain tree, *Koelreuteria paniculata*.

Big trees were planted in small groups on steeper gradients and included field maple, common alder and white willow. Fruiting and flower species such as juneberry and wild cherry were planted near seating areas or, for seasonal display, at woodland edges. The rare and declining native black poplar was a target species in the BAP, consequently 60 single specimens grown from cuttings were planted along the river and in the wet woodlands. As there were only hybrid black poplars within or adjacent to the site, cuttings of native species were taken from one male tree approximately 25km (15 miles) north of the Park, and from two female trees from the Vale of Aylesbury approximately 55km (35

Early establishment of the sculpted wetland bowl and landform 'lenses' in the north of the Park in November 2010. The temporary and permanent bridge sections can be seen clearly in the foreground.

miles) north-west of the Park. While this is not exactly 'local' to the Park, because of the scarcity of genuine native black poplars, it was considered important to re-establish them in their native form. They are naturally solitary trees, so they will be managed down to just six specimens after the Games.[23]

Planting trees in urban environments can be technically challenging as they often conflict with underground utilities and service corridors.[24] The design teams worked closely with utility companies to ensure that where National Joint Utility Group (NJUG) guidelines for tree planting could not be achieved, innovative solutions could be agreed. Technical engineering solutions were developed to accommodate utility corridors and meet the requirements for maintaining a healthy tree stock. This included establishing appropriate volumes of soil, improving aeration, drainage, irrigation, structural stability and mitigating root penetration into utility corridors.

Through workshops with the client, design teams and utility companies, a research-led solution was developed to eliminate the impact of trees on services by providing suitable zones for healthy tree-root growth to minimise their encroachment into utility corridors. This included the need to provide adequate soil type and volume, good aeration and oxygenation, regular water supply, drainage and reinforcement for pavements above tree roots.

THE WETLANDS

The north of the Park, in contrast to the more urban southern Park, is characterised by its wetland, riverine landscape. Marginal aquatic plants line the two wetland bowls carved out of the river at the heart of the northern Park. The adjacent areas of wet woodlands sit to the east of the river feeding off its waters. The wetland plants are dominated by common reed, purple loosestrife, sedges, reed sweet-grass and reed canary-grass, which all require a nutrient-poor soil. The design objective for the wetlands was to create broad swathes of colour and texture, forming strong patterns when viewed from the bridges and concourse above. Purple loosestrife and flag iris were selected for colour within the larger expanses of common reed. Purple loosestrife, pale pink hemp-agrimony and yellow ranunculus in particular were selected to flower during the Games. Hemp-agrimony is also extremely attractive to butterflies when in flower, adding another dynamic layer of colour and display. After the Games, to enhance biodiversity, vigorous species such as the reeds will spread and crowd out the more ornamental species. The Games-time planting patterns will gradually diminish and eventually disappear.

All marginal wetland plants were supplied to site already established as semi-mature plants grown in coir pallets or rolls. Higher up the riverbank, reinforced turf was used to hold marginal species suited to the drier conditions. Many of the 350,000 wetland and marginal aquatic plants were grown from seed and cuttings collected from the Park and its environs prior to work starting. Planting trials were undertaken on site to test different planting techniques, including seeding, plug planting and coir mat planting, and different species were tested for their ability to withstand periodic inundations. The lessons learned led to a reduced species palette, and the plants being grown on specially prepared mats and rolls made from coir – a waste material from the coconut plantations of Sri Lanka –

Rolls of coir mats pre-planted with wetland plants delivered to the Park in September 2010. This planting technique was trialled during 2007 and ensured the rapid establishment of the riverine landscape.

The largest of the frog ponds located in the north of the Park is fed by surface water drainage and the daily rise and fall of the river. The ponds provide valuable habitat for invertebrates, amphibians and reptiles. The emergent plant species were carefully selected to withstand fluctuating water levels.

in constructed lagoons by Salix, a specialist nursery with growing areas in Norfolk and the Gower Peninsula, Wales. This enabled efficient transportation and ease and speed of planting on the site. It was the largest urban wetland planting scheme to date in the UK.

The two areas of wet woodland in the northern Park provide valuable habitat that has become scarce worldwide because so much of it has been drained for agriculture and development. In legacy, the northern of the two wet woodlands will be extended with the removal of the temporary portion of the adjacent land bridge. The wet woodlands comprise fish channels, islands and margins providing a series of connected wet-to-dry

Members of the local schoolchildren's Construction Crew brought together by the ODA to help with the planting of the wetlands in June 2010. Several community planting events were arranged to help build long-term local ownership of the Park.

habitats. Planting is dominated by sedge species to provide strong textural contrast to the trees and shrubs, as well as to outcompete unwanted pernicious weeds brought downstream by the river. Moist conditions in the wet woodlands are maintained by the rise and fall in the river water levels, which also ensures that the herbaceous ground layer has a long season of visual interest. There are two artificial otter holts, two kingfisher banks and a sand-martin bank.

The four ponds across the Park provide a wide variety of habitats for all kinds of plants as well as frogs, toads, slow worms and other reptiles, insects and birds. Two of the ponds are fed by rainwater and two are connected to the river and have distinctive log walls providing ideal habitats for reptiles and invertebrates. As with the wet woodland, their complex wet and dry landform provides rich and diverse habitats. Planting is dominated

Early planting of the wet woodland in the north of the Park, November 2010. The orange netting was used as a temporary deterrent to stop geese and ducks grazing on the emerging wetland plants during their establishment.

by sedges with wildflower turf at the upper, drier edges where low-growing species, with occasional emergent plants, create a relatively transparent, multilayered canopy.

The drainage swales form linear networks that collect surface water run-off from the concourse and paths. Check dams constructed with granite kerbs reclaimed from the site hold the water back, creating rich wet/dry habitats and allowing infiltration and aquifer recharge. They discharge any remaining cleansed rainwater into the frog ponds, wetlands and river. The swales are planted with species that give a clear indication of their function, making them visually distinctive from the adjacent lawns and meadows. When in flower, they form colourful strips of taller vegetation in contrast to the meadows and spectator lawns, comprising purple loosestrife and flag iris.

THE WOODLANDS, MEADOWS AND LAWNS

The sculpted 'wooded hillocks' are planted with typical lowland mixed woodland, with a clear 'ecotone' or habitat transition to woodland edge and tall herb. Particular emphasis was placed on the visual quality of the woodland edge, with flowering and fruiting species providing visual interest and enhancing biodiversity. Initially, the tree canopy will not cast a heavy shade, therefore the ground layer was composed of light-demanding woodland species. Once the tree canopy is established and closed, more shade-tolerant species typical of woodland interiors will establish. The river valley sides connecting the north and south of the Park are planted with native trees. The species reflect the split valley character, with upper-valley species such as silver birch adjacent to the concourse, grading down to riverine species such as common alder, aspen and white willow adjacent to the river.

View of the birch stem woodland following snow in February 2012.

Sculpted landforms of the turfed spectator lawns and incised elliptical mounds with a birch stem woodland in the north of the Park, February 2011. Most of the trees planted in the Park had almost two years to establish before the start of the Games.

The 'birch stem' woodlands provide visually dramatic counterpoints within the overall landscape. The white stems contrast with a dark green groundcover of periwinkle, the colour and texture of the meadows, and the brilliant verdancy of the spectator lawns. A proportion of English oak and wild cherry whips and transplants are included within the framework of the dominant birch stem woodland. These will grow to provide mixed woodland in the long term, the birch trees acting as a 'nurse crop'. Occasional herbaceous groups such as woodland aster, lily of the valley, primula and stitchwort create memorable spring floral displays and diversify the under-storey.

Herbaceous species with dramatic foliage, good stem structures and attractive seed heads are planted in the narrow 'wooded gullies' that slice through the spectator lawns. They provide strong textural contrast and interest lasting through the summer and into the autumn. This also reduces maintenance because seasonal cutting is not required. The dominant species are the tussocky grasses such as tufted hair grass, sheep's fescue and sedges, creating a sheet of vegetation from which other herbaceous and woody plants protrude, such as royal fern, betony, eupatorium and geranium. Hair grasses and some of the other species require more damp or shadier conditions, hence the community is subdivided on the basis of moisture requirements. At the higher outer edges of the gully, conditions are drier and the fescue merges with the hair grasses lower down. Drier forb species such as oregano, which are broad-leaved herb species rather than grasses, play a significant role on these upper slopes, and flowered during the Games. At the base of the gullies, foliage texture with strong ferns and sedges contrasts with the shrubby willows.

Perhaps the most significant contribution of the parklands to horticultural development, landscape design and ecology are the perennial, annual and feature meadows throughout the Park. The ODA wanted to ensure that the Park was as colourful as possible, particularly during the Games, but also in legacy, at the same time, it had to meet stringent biodiversity targets and couldn't 'break the budget'. James Hitchmough and Nigel Dunnett, professors at Sheffield University, have pioneered new approaches to achieve what they term 'Dynamic Landscapes' that are great for people and wildlife.[25] Their research has proven that people love and connect with floriferous landscapes, and they have developed mixes of native and non-native meadow species that provide long flowering periods, look beautiful and are extremely attractive to wildlife, as well as being very cost effective. However, these had never been attempted on the scale of the Park before.

The perennial meadows will eventually provide a beautiful, naturalistic display throughout the Park. They require just one cut per year with arisings removed for composting. During the Games, they dressed the steeper slopes that were designed to discourage public access. Uniquely, they were cut to prevent them flowering in the spring of 2012, and then fertilised to encourage and ensure that they flowered during the Games. Henceforth, they will revert to their natural spring and summer flowering cycle. The golden annual

The annual meadows at peak flowering for the start of the Games in July 2012. Planted on either side of the City Mill river, the meadows provide a stunning setting to the Olympic Stadium.

The Velodrome seen
from the axial path and
adjacent swale in the
north of the Park during
the Games in July 2012.

meadows are different to the perennial meadows. They provided extraordinary, colourful displays either side of the City Mill river in the south of the Park during the Games. Hybrids of corn marigold, prairie tickseed and star of the Veldt provided the dominant golden colour, but the depth of colour was subtly yet dramatically lifted by blue cornflower. After the Games, the annual meadows will be replaced with perennial meadows to achieve the BAP targets. The highly colourful 'feature meadows' are different to the perennial and annual meadows. They sit within the elliptical lens-shaped landforms opposite spectator lawns. They have a long flowering season from summer through autumn. Each feature meadow is dominated by a different colour palette, ranging through red, yellow and blue, reflecting their different aspect and location – spectacular spectacles for spectators!

The 'Fantasticology' meadow was yet another kind of meadow. It was an extraordinary artwork adjacent to the City Mill river, created by Klassnik Corporation, We Made That and Riitta Ikonen. Combining ecological and industrial archaeological themes, the design was a geometric, abstract interpretation of a historic land-use map of the area, comprising red, yellow and blue colour palettes. Throughout the Park, beautiful green spectator lawns stand out in contrast to the colourful and textured meadows – like putting greens in the midst of an angular, wild landscape in the north of the Park, and garden lawns in the 2012 Gardens. The well-drained, sand-based soil profile was constructed and finished with a hard-wearing turf to withstand heavy use during the Games. A night-time irrigation system ensures strong growth and maintains the lushness. They are converted into species-rich lawns after the Games, contributing to the BAP targets.

(continued on page 214)

Local residents and schoolchildren were invited for a picnic and a guided 'walk in the Park' to celebrate the completion of the north of the parklands one year ahead of the Games.

The upper spectator lawns in the north east of the Park adjacent to the Velodrome looking south. These lawns provided an extremely popular place for spectators to rest, relax and watch the huge TV screen showing events from across the Games.

ESTABLISHING ECOLOGICALLY DYNAMIC MEADOWS

Professor Nigel Dunnett and Professor James Hitchmough
Department of Landscape, University of Sheffield

Probably the biggest challenge has been the size of the project. Never before has anybody planted annual and perennial meadows on such a vast urban scale. Just getting round the site in a day during construction was a challenge, but more significant was the difficulty in getting the technical process of sowing and establishment to work. In the early stages irrigation was essential, particularly during the very dry spring of 2011. With the irrigation not fully installed, water extraction from the rivers was a problem, the pumps silted up, at times there was not enough capacity and there was concern that some of the water was saline.

It took a while for the contractors to get their heads around the approach to creating such large meadows. Establishing vegetation by seeding rather than planting, the more traditional way, required a different mindset. Initially there was a lot of hands-on education and training with the contractors who were somewhat sceptical as to whether this would work. But once some of the meadows began to take shape there was a huge change in people's attitudes and the contractors started to take real ownership.

While the techniques for establishing these meadows are now well tested, one of the hardest

Hand sowing the annual meadow trial adjacent to the Olympic Stadium in May 2010. Annual meadows on this scale had never been attempted before. The trials were an important stage in fine-tuning the species mix, the establishment of the meadows, and the time of sowing to ensure peak flowering in late July and August 2012 for the Games.

Trial of annual meadow planting using an 'Olympic Gold' mix of species seen here in July 2011. The main flowering species include corn marigold, prairie tickseed and star of the Veldt and the depth of colour is dramatically lifted by a small element of blue cornflower.

Results of the annual meadow trial in September 2011. Two seasons of trials were undertaken to enable experimentation with the mix and composition of species.

aspects of the project has been to skew the more traditional early summer flowering season to late July and August to ensure peak flowering for the start of the Games. To achieve this we have had to bias species selection, including the likes of the spiny restharrow *Ononis spinosa* and the devil's bit scabious *Succisa pratensis*, to maximise the drama and impact. Meeting these requirements was challenging, calling for an exacting and rigorous management of the systems that dictate plant establishment and growth. Getting it to work with such precision needs a robust methodology allied with some critical points of judgement that are heavily influenced by the weather and the particular characteristics of the site.

Running two years of field trails has been really helpful. The first year helped to determine sowing time and in the second we concentrated on getting the species mix right and attuned to the soil mixes. It was incredibly exciting to turn a corner near the Olympic Stadium and see the first meadow trials in their full glory on 27 July 2010, exactly two years before the start of the Olympic Games. The trials were extremely important to boost the confidence of the client, design team and contractors and were an essential part of

Perennial display planting in the north of the Park, September 2011. Opposite the spectator lawns, within the incised elliptical mounds, the species selected ensured spectacular flowering displays during the Games.

limiting risk across this central element of the Park's planting.

The need to design for the Games and legacy brought real conflict between the short- and long-term objectives for the native wildflower meadows. The soil, for example, needed to be low in nutrient to maintain diversity and limit vigorous grass species, but for the Games we have had to add nitrogen and irrigate at the right time to get the necessary speed and volume of growth in time for the Opening Ceremony. Probably the main issue in legacy will be the interplay between climate and topography. Some of the slopes

in the north of the Park are likely to be very dry in the summer, a bit like the Dordogne. So some species, such as *Succisa pratensis*, may fade out in places, although the mix of species will self-select to either drier or wetter conditions. This is the true nature of meadows: their temporality and dynamic of change is integral with their beauty.

Probably the biggest achievement for the planting has been to shift the biodiversity agenda. We came in midway through 2008 and started by reviewing the planting strategy. The north of the Park was exclusively native with meadow planting throughout.

A multi-species perennial meadow on the slopes adjacent to the Velodrome in the north of the Park in June 2011. In total 12 perennial seed mixes were developed for both dry and moist slopes and specific niche habitats throughout the Park.

Across the design team, and with support from the client, the Park has established a different paradigm centred on making nature pleasing to ordinary people. It was about building the capacity for nature within an essentially urban and public park. In urban areas these debates can be very polarised, but for the Park it was not simply about replicating the river meadow landscapes akin to Constable Country, for Stratford is a very diverse area of London and that richness can be played out across the planting and the individual selection of plant species.

It marks a huge turning point to see a major new urban park being delivered without reference to municipal planting, because this has not been done in this country before. For the first time, the entire landscape and especially the 2012 Gardens expose a mass audience to a different way of doing things. What this does is that it moves the floor. The parklands have substituted a different surface from the traditional mown lawns that are highly carbon dependant, to one that has an intense biodiversity. This will have a huge impact on the future design of parks.

THE GARDENS

The 2012 Gardens line the western bank of the Waterworks river opposite the Aquatics Centre in the south of the Park. They embody one of the fundamental philosophies of the Park – that people and biodiversity can be planned and designed to be both beautiful and functional, and that the sole use of native species is not necessary. The paradox is illustrated by the fact that gardens everywhere are full of non-native plants, and support extremely rich communities of native invertebrates and other fauna. Ecological determinism can sometimes work against the best interests of nature conservation. There are four distinct zones in the 2012 Gardens, each showcasing a major climatic and cultural zone of the world – Europe, North America, the Southern Hemisphere and Temperate Asia. They are arranged in the chronological order they were systematically explored as a source of new plants for gardens in Britain. They celebrate the great British passion for collecting and cultivating plants from around the world and designing them into their gardens. Visitors to the Games, and local residents from all over the world, were able to sense and see plants from their home communities.

As with the parklands, the design of the 2012 Gardens came out of the unique collaboration of the landscape architects, ecologists and academic horticulturalists James Hitchmough and Nigel Dunnett – but with the addition of garden designer Sarah Price. According to

Setting out plants in the North American Garden, one of four world zones in the 2012 Gardens, in May 2011. The unusual and diverse mix of plants were specially grown and sourced by a single supplier from specialist nurseries across the UK. They took four months to plant.

the designers, inspiration for the planting design can be found in three exemplars.[26] Firstly, a style informed by the ecological principles originally inspired by William Robinson's *The Wild Garden* published in the 1870s.[27] Secondly, the 'new' German-style plantings in West Park, Munich, and planting mixes mastered at Hermannshof garden, Weinheim, in the 1980s. And thirdly, the large-scale 'new perennial' public plantings, initially pioneered in the Dutch Heem Parks at Amstelveen, and popularised by horticulturalist Piet Oudolf. Within each garden, plants are structured as naturalistic compositions that represent how they look in the wild. These are then combined with cultural patterns that are more typical of gardens and traditional planting design. As Tim Richardson noted in the *Telegraph*, 'The Olympic Park's planting and design is exciting, innovative and could herald a step-change in attitudes to public plantings in Britain, moving us even farther away from the Victorian tradition of bedding out.'[28]

In the spring of 2009, the Government asked the ODA if it would arrange a national design competition that would capture and celebrate the charm of an ordinary British, domestic garden to be built within the Park. It was very late in the planning and design of the Park, and there was only one location it could possibly fit: on the opposite side of the southern Park to the 2012 Gardens, in the shadow of the Olympic Stadium atop the western bank

Completed planting in the Asian Garden at the northern end of the 2012 Gardens. The structural bands of box hedge and ornamental grasses fade in to the more loosely planted naturalistic fields of layered perennial plants.

Planting in the North American Garden featuring layered drifts of plants including *Heuchera* and *Rudbeckia*. Planting in the four zones of the 2012 Gardens is inspired by the character and form of the native ecological communities found there.

The Great British Garden located to the west of the Olympic Stadium on the opposite bank of the Old River Lea completed in spring 2012. The ODA with the Royal Horticultural Society ran a national ideas competition providing an opportunity for members of the public to directly shape part of the Park. It was won by Rachel Read and Hannah Clegg, who worked with the ODA's world-class team of landscape architects to finalise their design ideas.

of the Old River Lea. The ODA worked with the Royal Horticultural Society on an 'ideas' competition, which attracted over 200 entries. These were then voted on by over 4,000 members of the public. Rachel Read and Hannah Clegg won in the adult and under-11 categories respectively. They developed their ideas with the ODA's landscape architecture team through a series of workshops, approving the final designs before they were drawn up by the team and then created on the bank of the Old River Lea opposite the Olympic Stadium. The Great British Garden weaves together their ideas of an accessible, edible, colourful and playful garden based around gold, silver and bronze 'mini-gardens' and a pond.

In line with the ODA's sustainability objective to reduce potable water demand across the Park, the planting was designed to reduce the need for irrigation. The extensive perennial meadows proposed were a key innovation, requiring irrigation for an establishment period of only two seasons. The 2012 Gardens and the Great British Garden are the only areas that require permanent irrigation. All other areas of vegetation require temporary irrigation for a three- to four-year establishment period only. Various sources of water for irrigation were considered, including river water abstraction, rainwater harvesting, boreholes, potable water and non-potable water. The use of river water was discounted as abstraction from the river network was considered to be at capacity. The use of potable water was rejected as a primary source because of the need to reduce demand, although it was accepted for back-up and top-up events. The use of harvested rainwater from across the Park was not feasible due to the large volumes of water that would have to be stored, and it was mostly being used by the venues anyway. Swales and underground storage across the Park were considered, but dismissed as impractical due to a lack of storage capacity. An assessment of non-potable water demand across the Park for venue toilet flushing, general cleaning purposes and the combined cooling and heating plant and for irrigation supported the decision to invest in a non-potable water recycling plant supplying the whole Park. The Old Ford Water Recycling Plant is a state-of-the-art facility, jointly funded with Thames Water, which takes sewage from the Great Northern Outfall Sewer and treats it to a non-potable standard based on water quality requirements.

SUSTAINABLE MATERIALS AND INSTALLATIONS

With sustainability a key driver of the programme, the selection and use of sustainable materials covered a number of aspects, including responsible sourcing, embodied impacts such as energy and recycled content, health impacts, waste and transportation. As an example, over half of the concourse of 20 ha is converted to soft landscape or development platforms in transformation for legacy. Early in the design process, manufacturers and contractors were invited to demonstrate innovative surfacing solutions to deliver the established design criteria. This allowed the ODA and design teams to assess architectural quality, accessibility and ease of construction, and conduct a full sustainability appraisal

A bosque of plane trees adjacent to the concourse by the Copper Box providing a frame for artist Monica Bonvicini's 'RUN' sculpture.

for each option. Following trials, a pavement build-up was recommended to optimise cost, quality, programme and sustainability. The agreed solution consisted of a recycled Type 1 sub-base, a cold-foamed bitumen base course, a standard hot asphalt wearing course, and surface dressing of UK-sourced gravel chips in a vegetable-based emulsion. Initial analysis indicated this solution could save around 350 tonnes of primary material in comparison to standard construction. Temporary surfaces were constructed with thinner construction depths, which saved on quantities and laying times, and were designed to be recycled in transformation.

With over 2.2km of seating in the Park, combining bespoke and proprietary elements, the selection of materials was given considerable focus. The specification of tropical hardwoods was challenged by the planning authority on the grounds of sustainability and appropriateness. An extensive evaluation, prioritising sustainability criteria, was completed, analysing all seating alternatives including steel, concrete, imported hardwood timber, UK softwood timber and UK-sourced recycled plastic. A simplified life-cycle analysis over a 120-year period, considering carbon footprint, waste generation, emissions/ecotoxicity in disposal and growth rate and renewability, formed part of the full evaluation. The study concluded that hardwood timber certified by the Forest Stewardship Council

A kingfisher nesting bank constructed in the north of the Park on the edge of the wet woodland. This was described in the BAP and was a formal requirement of the planning permission for the Park.

(FSC) was the most appropriate material. An additional outcome of this process, which included extensive discussions with the supply chain, was the identification of a limited quantity of suitable reclaimed timber. As a consequence, 86m of reclaimed Basralocus timber from Dutch flood defences was used to construct benches for the Park. One of the key lessons learned was that sustainable design needs to be driven by the most sustainable material available, rather than searching for the most sustainable material for the element that has been designed – a subtle, but important difference. As awareness and a more comprehensive technical understanding of sustainability develops, so too will the process of sustainable design and construction. However, far from considering this as a failure, one of the major successes of the construction of the Park is that it has provided the impetus in a number of areas for further research to be undertaken by suppliers to enable them to deliver truly sustainable solutions in the future.

The ODA installed 675 bat and bird boxes across the Park. Architects, engineers and ecologists worked together to integrate the boxes early on in the design and construction of the Park's venues, structures and bridges. Innovative and sustainable solutions were developed, such as locating boxes within bridge structures, seldom used in this way, and

Gently curving terraced seating integrated into the sculptural landform in the north of the Park. All timber used for the Park was sourced sustainably, certified by the FSC, and had 'chain of custody' documents from forest to site.

the use of cut-offs from utility pipes from site for birds. Some 66 bat boxes and 178 bird habitats were created within bridges alone on the Park. Other wildlife installations ranged from the otter holts, to compost heaps, loggeries and beehives in the View Tube's garden and Old Ford Wood. Even geometric strips of stone were set in the landscape of the north of the Park and planted with various species of toadflax – the food of the toadflax brocade moth, a 'target species' of the BAP.

COMPLETION FOR GAMES AND LEGACY

Ensuring high-quality construction across the Park was essential.[29] This was particularly the case on the parklands because they were composed of simple materials that were well detailed. The experience on many large landscape projects is that they are squeezed into the time available at the end of the contract, and have their funding cut because of earlier cost overruns. The budget for the parklands and public realm was secured and ring-fenced from the start, and the project managers and programmers worked closely with the ODA and its designers, contractors and suppliers to ensure that there was enough time to deliver good quality during construction. Good quality begins with the selection of the right team and individuals from the start of a project, but ultimately depends on the contractors who build it and the suppliers who provide, manufacture and grow the materials. Leadership, teamwork and an attitude that the quality of materials and workmanship were as important as fitness for purpose and programme was crucial.

Procurement of separate Tier One contractors for the north and south of the Park was a rigorous process that took nine months from start to appointment. BAM Nuttall was appointed as a management contractor in the north of the Park, supported by Frosts Landscape Construction with Land and Water, and White Horse Contractors with Gavin Jones Group. Skanska supported by Willerby Landscapes was appointed in the south of the Park. The aim was to complete excellent-quality work at the first attempt – 'do it once, do it right'. A series of workshops were convened for specific elements of work, for example, semi-mature tree planting, or achieving crystal-cut edges to earthworks, so that each individual knew their role and responsibilities, good communication was established, and better ways of delivery eked out. Lessons were shared between all contractors. 'Benchmarks' were kept on-site. A dedicated 'sample park' was built. This was, effectively a 'mini-Park' intended to provide a point of reference, and show external stakeholders, such as the Planning Decisions Team and the Built Environment Access Panel, what the Park would look and feel like. This proved to be very useful; however, the real lessons were learned in constructing it.

Quality Leadership teams were established to share experiences, raise quality aspirations and discuss how quality could be improved. 'Quality Circles' were also set up so that the workforce could meet on a weekly basis to discuss current issues and challenges. This

Yellow toadflax flowering in April 2012. Strips of brownfield habitat have been created on the south-facing slopes in the north of the Park that include toadflax patches to provide habitat for the toadflax brocade moth.

proved to be a very popular and successful way of involving the workforce and capturing their contributions. Badges and certificates were given to all those who demonstrated their commitment to quality, and although they were only small tokens, they were very much appreciated and helped to ensure that the workforce felt that their commitment to quality was fully recognised.

It was recognised that the parklands would change over time as they matured and would be used (and abused) through the Games and into legacy. It is a unique and innovative landscape the like of which has not been seen before. Consequently, in order to support the future management and planning for the Park, the ODA prepared a 10-year management and maintenance plan that gathered all management, maintenance, operational, governance, funding, finance and biodiversity monitoring requirements into one document.[30] It provided a strategic context, highlighting organisations directly or indirectly involved in the Park's future management, and set out a broad schedule of events and activities that the Park could support. It also set out a full schedule of management and maintenance activities for both the hard and soft elements of the Park. It concluded with a summary of potential staffing, equipment and facility needs that were benchmarked against London's Royal Parks and Central Park, New York.

Planning the Games and their legacy together from the start enabled the ODA to invest 75 pence of every pound it spent on the construction of permanent venues and infrastructure, including the new parklands, which will benefit the area for decades. A remarkable statistic. Following the Games, it will take up to two years to remove the temporary venues, bridges, concourse and other works to transform the Park so it is ready for legacy development over the coming decades. The transformation of the Park will see the parklands double in size. In April 2010, the ODA received detailed planning consent for these transformation works, which led to the procurement of contractors to deliver the transformation construction works, and of semi-mature trees and perennial meadow turf ready for planting. On the substantial completion of the construction of the Park on time and within budget in July 2011, one year ahead of the Olympic Games, the UK's Prime Minister, David Cameron, lauded the ODA's achievement, which he noted was 'all the more remarkable' considering that, 'back in 2005, the Olympic Park site was largely a derelict wasteland. Since then, one of the biggest-ever clean-up operations has given these vast brownfields a complete ecological make-over, with over 100 hectares of new parklands, eight kilometres of waterways and half a million new plants.'[31]

Winter view of the river Lea looking north across the wetland bowl in February 2012. Following the Games the parkland will double in size with substantial sections opened to the general public within a year of the Closing Ceremony of the Paralympic Games.

Left: a computer-generated visualisation of the 2012 Gardens showing the terraced planting, paths and lawns prepared in September 2008. Right: the completed garden in 2012.

Left: a computer-generated visualisation prepared in September 2008 looking across one of the spectator lawns in the northern section of the Park. The gently sloping path is bordered on one side by spring-flowering cherry trees, and on the other, by a swale. Right: the completed Park in 2012.

Left: a computer-generated visualisation of the wetland bowl in the north of the Park looking south across the river Lea. This was prepared in 2008 before the Orbit was proposed. Right: the completed Park in 2012.

Left: a computer-generated visualisation looking south from the bridge to the north of the wetland bowl. Right: the completed wetland bowl in 2012.

The river Lea, wetland edge, spectator lawn and footpaths, perennial meadows and the Velodrome during the Games in August 2012.

CHAPTER FIVE

CHAPTER FIVE

A Walk in the Park

Through the planning, design and delivery of what became the Queen Elizabeth Olympic Park on time, within budget, to multiple stakeholders' satisfaction, and to challenging targets for sustainability, the Olympic Delivery Authority (ODA) established a new benchmark for development everywhere. Powered by the Games, the Park represents a significant step towards achieving One Planet Living. Alongside reflections on the deeper significance of this achievement are lessons for future development and regeneration programmes across the world.

Walk from the renewed and expanded Stratford stations through the Westfield shopping centre, turn a corner and the dramatic curved roof of the Aquatics Centre can be seen overhanging the walkway. Opposite the Aquatics Centre is the inward-sloping roof of the Water Polo Arena forming a 'gateway' to the Park during the Games, and framing a view of the Olympic Stadium beyond. Walk on a little further and the bold scale of the Aquatics Centre roof, defying gravity, becomes apparent. From the bridge over the Waterworks river, Orbit erupts quirkily from the main concourse. The concourse itself is lined by seven tall white masts leading towards the north of the Park, each topped with a 'halo' of lights and a beautifully sculpted wind turbine – one of the few overt symbols of the sustainability credentials on the Park. Lower your eyes and the resplendent 2012 Gardens stretch left and right before you into the distance, an enticing, kaleidoscope of flowers, grasses, herbs, hedges, trees and finely mown lawns. Below is the riverside promenade with shade trees and seats. A margin of native wetland reeds fills the gap where the river has been widened to accommodate increased flood flows and connect

View looking south across the Olympic Stadium and 2012 Gardens towards Canary Wharf in April 2012. The main route into the Park from Stratford is clearly visible on the left leading spectators underneath the dramatically curved roof of the Aquatics Centre.

habitats. The edge of the navigation is marked by the brightly coloured *Steles* – artworks by Keith Wilson that double as mooring posts. Continue walking over the bridge and you arrive on the main concourse – the heart of the south of the Park.

This spectacular sequence of views, experienced by the majority of Games spectators who arrived via the Stratford stations, will have changed little following the transformation of the Park immediately after the Games. The transformation of the Park ready for legacy development following the Games will take up to two years; however, it is intended to open the Park in phases, the first during the summer of 2013 to mark the first anniversary of the Opening Ceremony of the Games. The majority of visitors to the Park in legacy will continue to arrive via the Stratford stations, but the huge Games-time crowds will never again course their way into the Park. Consequently, the walkway is transformed into an extension of the parklands – one of many changes that will turn the Park from a secure compound into an easily accessible Park 'stitched' back into the fabric of the surrounding neighbourhoods. The walkway from Westfield is 40 metres wide. It crosses a railway, the realigned Carpenters Road and the Waterworks river before reaching the main concourse. The Park integrates old and new infrastructure seamlessly. The width of the bridge over the Waterworks river is reduced by half in transformation and, as with all the other bridges over this river, the landscape – in this case the 2012 Gardens – is extended to fill the gaps. The scale of the walkway is reduced dramatically in transformation by the extensive planting of trees, hedges, lawns and flowering meadows edged by seating walls and benches.

THE PLEASURE GARDENS

The south of the Park was planned and designed as a primary destination in legacy for international, national, local and London visitors – a pleasure garden in the 19th-century tradition of Vauxhall, Ranelagh and Victoria. Orbit and the 2012 Gardens will be the big draws, attracting and enthralling visitors. The addition of a café, visitor centre and children's play area creates the hub for the south of the Park. It is where you will be able to buy 2012 memorabilia and discover all the things going on throughout the Park, have a coffee and

View of the 2012 Gardens from the main bridge into the Park next to the Aquatics Centre. Orbit and Olympic Stadium form the backdrop.

cake, hire a bike or Rollerblades, and buy tickets for boat trips in the Park. A programme of large and small festivals and events will celebrate the vibrant multiculturalism of east London's food, music, art, design, culture and fashion. It could be something like a bazaar, a place where you know you can just turn up and something interesting will be happening to suit every age, pocket and desire, every day of the week.

A ride to the viewing platform of Orbit, which is at the equivalent of the 23rd floor of a tower block, ends with exhilarating views across the Park and the capital, an added bonus to the overall experience of Anish Kapoor's extraordinary sculpture, the tallest in the UK. A walk through the half-mile of the 2012 Gardens feels like a journey through the landscapes of the world, the humming and buzzing bees, butterflies and other wildlife adding a dynamic layer to the whole experience. The 2012 Gardens innovative mobile phone app interprets the narrative of the Gardens, the history and provenance of the unusual plants and their combinations, the importance of gardens to wildlife, and the history of plant collecting.

The promenade on the bank opposite the 2012 Gardens – envisioned as Stratford's Waterfront – will be completed with trees, paving and seating during transformation. Ramps to pontoons will provide access to boats and allow the launching of canoes. The site of the temporary Water Polo Arena will eventually be developed with a mix of uses including apartments, and with shops, cafés and restaurants lining the promenade and overlooking the river to the 2012 Gardens. The refurbishment of Carpenters Road Lock will allow boats to navigate the Bow Back Loop for both fun and commerce for the first time in decades. In sum, following the transformation of the Park after the Games, the south of the Park with the 2012 Gardens, Orbit, pavilion, playground, the Aquatics Centre and Olympic Stadium will be a 'must see' major destination for the capital. The eventual development of the waterfront cafés, shops and restaurants on the former site of the Water Polo Arena venue in legacy will be added attractions. The spirit of London 2012, London's 19th-century pleasure gardens, the Royal Parks, Brick Lane, Camden Lock, Borough and Spitalfields Markets and the South Bank all rolled into one.

The reason for such an emphasis on the role of the Park as a destination is because the vast majority of visits following the Games will be to the parklands. All the venues combined can expect up to 2 million visits per annum, whilst Victoria Park just a 15-minute walk from the Park already attracts 4 million visits per year, and that was before its restoration was completed in April 2012. Greenwich Park has 3 million visits per annum, around 50 per cent of which are by locals. The same proportion is likely for the Park, hence the construction of a local community hub in the north of the Park in transformation ready for use in legacy. As a comparison, and to place these figures in a contemporary context, the power of shopping at Westfield next to the Park will attract over 20 million visits per annum.[1] The challenge is to draw some of those into the Park.

Looking down the City Mill river. The gabion walls feathering out from the bridge abutment can be seen in the foreground. Orbit and Olympic Stadium on its platform formed by green walls rise above this restored and refurbished industrial canal.

View looking up the City Mill river. Extensive reed and predominantly native meadow planting greatly improved the ecological connectivity of the old industrial canal network.

POST-INDUSTRIAL MELANCHOLY

Walk across the patterned main concourse towards the Olympic Stadium and you come to the 'rim', a consistent and permanent design feature throughout the Park. The 'rim' defines the edge of the predominantly flat concourse and the slopes down to the rivers and waterways. Several footpaths glide gently down between the bridges to the towpath sitting atop a 2m-high concrete wall forming the canal-like City Mill river. The grittier character of City Mill river is purposely in complete contrast to the formality of the 2012 Gardens. The canal was dredged, and the walls retained, cleaned and repaired along with bollards, some original canal balustrades, an old blue footbridge and Carpenters Road Lock. Built in 1931, the radial rising lock is the only one of its kind on Britain's canal system. City Mill river, navigable again, retains a sense of its industrial past.

Golden flowering meadows dressed the slopes either side of the river in a spectacular Games-inspired show. The Fantasticology meadows drawing on the industrial past of the site provided a quirky geometrical interlude. But keep your eyes focused on the old industrial canal, meadows and woodland, and you could be lost in a post-industrial, melancholic landscape of solitude. Walk south, turn a corner, look up and you can see the towers of Canary Wharf on the horizon. Look up higher, and Orbit and the Olympic Stadium fill your gaze, and place you at the heart of the south of the Park. These extraordinary juxtapositions are woven together from the history and context of the site. Nothing is accidental, be it a view, a habitat or the location of a tree. Every square millimetre of the

Park has been thought about and designed for people, for wildlife, for delight, for the Games, then for transformation ready for legacy development.

The Old River Lea forms the far side of the Stadium 'island'. It has its own special character in contrast to the City Mill and Waterworks rivers. On one side existing mature river-edge woodland has been retained, on the other is the same 2m-high concrete canal wall as City Mill river. An early 20th-century landing has been preserved. Half close your eyes, focus on the water, vegetation and retained canal-side infrastructure, and again it feels like an old industrial backwater. There are newly planted marginal aquatics below the old woodland. There is a new kingfisher bank. The Old River Lea is an unlikely haven for wildlife – herons, kingfishers, swans and coots – right next to the Olympic Stadium.

On top of the far bank, protected and enclosed behind the woodland, is the Great British Garden. The Games-inspired gold, silver and bronze themed gardens are home to a willow wall and tunnel, a small pond, a sundial and swing seat carved with the names of Rachel and Hannah who won the national competition to design the garden. Its character is domestic, colourful and playful. A place where you could expect to chat to your neighbours over the garden fence. But again, lift your gaze and the Olympic Stadium appears above the woodland. A gap in the trees allows glimpses of the high mast lights and wind turbines spinning in the breeze on the main concourse.

The Great British Garden in July 2012. The rich and varied planting, the pond and other features were very popular with children and families during the Games.

(continued on page 238)

TIME WAS OF THE ESSENCE

Dennis Hone
Chief Executive, Olympic Delivery Authority
February 2011 onwards

On my appointment as Chief Executive to replace David Higgins in February 2011 there was a real danger that people would take it for granted that the ODA was well on programme and most of the work was all but complete. Having previously been the Director of Finance and Corporate Services I was fully aware that there was still over £1bn expenditure to manage. It was critical that we didn't lose focus and retained a clear understanding of the scale of the remaining task. The size and complexity of the Aquatics Centre, for example, was always a challenge and we had to undertake intricate final adjustments to ensure the water and ambient air temperatures in the building were balanced for the competing swimmers. This work was finally complete just six days before the scheduled handover, exactly one year before the Games.

Throughout the year of test events, there was a continuing iterative and at times challenging process with LOCOG to ensure its evolving overlay – the facilities needed to host and run the Games – fitted into the Park. We needed to make sure the accommodation for the media, sponsors and spectators had limited impact on the completed Park and venues. Additional paths to increase access were required, some lighting columns had to be moved and fences realigned to ensure everything that was needed on the Park could be accommodated. This all took time and we had to work hard to minimise the knock-on impacts of these changes, particularly on legacy.

As Director of Finance, managing the budget for the entire project was my central responsibility for over five years. As a corporate organisation, all the directors would have been for the high jump if the budget had got out of control, and for me personally it was a career-defining issue. The obvious response would have been to try to limit expenditure across the entire programme. It would have been very easy to nickel and dime all elements to minimise cost. But for the ODA, time was of the essence. If we got behind on programme three things would have happened: firstly, contractors would work double or triple shifts, and the cost implications of 24-hour working would have been exorbitant; secondly, claims from contractors could spiral out of control; and thirdly, there would be an increasing risk of industrial action. The response was in some ways counterintuitive: the best way to save money was to spend it appropriately to maintain programme. To keep on programme was critical for the budget, and I worked closely with Howard Shiplee, the ODA's

The Asian Garden marks the northern end of the 2012 Gardens. The Gardens stretch for almost a kilometre along the western bank of the Waterworks river.

The vibrant annual meadow plantings along the City Mill river looking south at the start of the Games in July 2012. The richly flowering meadows were greatly enjoyed and much photographed by spectators.

Director of Construction, to ensure this was the case. The ODA came in almost £1bn under budget, when one takes into account the unspent contingencies, which proved that our approach was right.

Most of the ODA's remaining work will be complete by the end of March 2013, and it will become a very small organisation as all remaining construction work transforming the Park ready for legacy development immediately after the Games was transferred to the London Legacy Development Corporation. Following the retrofit of the Olympic and Paralympic Village and the preparation of final accounts it will be formally wound up around March 2014. A key responsibility for the ODA was to deliver 102ha of open space. I think what we have produced is a very visual Park, it's almost a throwback to the Victorians with the creation of different views and vistas, a kind of picturesque. All too often landscape is ancillary, but we deliberately gave it equal prominence with the venues, and in many ways the Park has become the principal feature of the entire project. By stitching together all the various elements – the venues, the Village and other buildings, bridges and works of art – we have created the foundation for a thriving community in legacy.

TO THE NORTH OF THE PARK

Follow the line of graceful mast lighting columns with their dynamic turbines northwards, and you cross a sequence of bridges rising and then gently descending into the northern parklands. During the Games, these bridges combined to form a 50m-wide walkway carrying thousands of spectators to the north of the Park, crossing a waterway with a lock, a road and a railway. To assure consistency and emphasise the sense that this is 'one park', the majority of the bridges are of consistent, simple, box girder design with balustrades of stainless steel uprights, toprail and mesh infill. They are supported by gabion baskets filled with crushed concrete recycled from demolitions within the site. The angle of all the sloping gabion abutments and the balustrades is exactly 22 degrees, an attention to detail that ensures harmony throughout the Park. In several instances the gabions feather seamlessly into the landscape, creating habitats for reptiles and other species – a good example of landscape and infrastructure designed as one. There are 12 of these permanent bridges across the four waterways within the Park. The underside of each bridge is colour coded according to which waterway it crosses, and is reflected in the water below. 'Twelve for 2012' is another subtle example of the ODA's mantra: 'art as a part of it, not as an add-on'.

The bridge in the centre of the Park was the only one that was specially commissioned via a design competition. Immediately following the Games, it underwent a dramatic transformation, emerging like a butterfly from its chrysalis. During the Games, it was hardly noticeable that it was a bridge – only the vividly coloured paving giving any clue as to its future reinvention from a 50m-wide monolith to an elegant 4m-wide z-shaped bridge. The top and bottom of the 'z' run between the north and south of the Park, and the connecting piece of the 'z' oversails the restored Carpenters Road Lock below. The concourse and ground underneath it on either side of the lock is scooped out to reveal the bridge that is already in place, to create two grassy bowls planted with trees, focusing on and leading down to the towpath and lock. The underside of the bridge is fabricated from mirrored steel reflecting the lock, the bowl and the canal – an extraordinary experience that blurs visual reality. The bridge is an example of how far the ODA went to ensure that the Park in legacy was not over scaled, and that it had some beautiful insertions. A large nib of the deck of the second bridge, crossing Carpenters Road, is removed in transformation opening up Carpenters Road below. The third bridge over the railway remains in place, but several oval landscape forms with trees, seating edges and meadows are added to the whole sequence of bridges in transformation, creating a distinctive transition between the north and the south of the Park.

From the bridges, there are views of the Energy Centre clad in perforated Corten steel and its substation on the left, followed by the Copper Box. This venue provides a simple and very effective dark backdrop to Monica Bonvicini's exquisitely detailed sculpture spelling out 'RUN' in 9m-high letters, a literary essay in light and reflection. After passing

View looking south across the northern section of the Park towards the Olympic Stadium in December 2011. The fully restored river Lea is surrounded by diverse wetlands and fully accessible, bold geometric landforms.

the Copper Box and turning right onto the first of the two land bridges that cross the river Lea and the landscape of the north of the Park, you catch your first sight of the river and wetland landscape. It is in breathtaking contrast to the south of the Park. Nothing quite like this landscape has been seen before, and very little changes in transformation, other than the landscape expands to fill the gaps once the temporary sections of the bridges are removed. The fully restored river Lea, wetlands and quite extraordinary geometric landforms characterise this diverse, open and ecological landscape connecting seamlessly to the wilder landscapes of the Lea Valley to the north. The heroic landforms create settings for the International Broadcast Centre/Main Press Centre (IBC/MPC), the Copper Box, Olympic and Paralympic Village, temporary Basketball Arena and Riverside Arena (Hockey), and Velodrome. Most striking are the 'land bridges' that extend in straight lines with angular banks from the bridge decks across the landscape connecting east and west concourses during the Games, and the primary footpaths retained for legacy.

An axial path purposely centred on the Velodrome provides one of the most striking and memorable views in the north of the Park.

THE NEW PICTURESQUE

It was William Kent (*c* 1685–1748) who particularly at Rousham delivered the most complete exemplar of the English Picturesque landscape movement, where art and nature are balanced and informed by each other. His 'shaggy' landscapes were a reaction to the ubiquitous, smooth flowing landscapes of Capability Brown (1716–83) whose contrived sequence of views or 'pictures', revealed only by walking through the garden, also took in the broader 'borrowed' landscape. The 'art' that most influenced the English picturesque landscapes were paintings by Claude Lorrain (1604/5–82) and Nicolas Poussin (1594–1665). In a deeply innate, imaginative and fun response to the idea of the picturesque, the ODA's resident artist Neville Gabie created *Freeze Frame* in which he took Georges Seurat's 1884 painting *Bathers at Asnières* and 'produced' an equivalent photographic facsimile on the Park. Paris was rapidly expanding through industrialisation towards the end of the 19th century. Controversially, Seurat's painting depicts workers at leisure, co-opting the banks of the Seine for use as their public park and bathing area. In the background, the new industrial skyline of factories, chimneys and railway bridge can be seen. The painting broke away from the tradition of aristocratic portraiture and the portrayal of classical scenes. Gabie felt there was 'an obvious and surprising physical connection between the two landscapes, but the concept for the work explores the more striking similarities between the social and political contexts of the two. When Seurat painted the *Bathers at Asnières* in 1884 it was seen as a radical image.' He populated his finely choreographed photograph with people (and a dog) who were working on the Park. As Christopher Riopelle, Curator of Post 1800 Paintings at The National Gallery concluded, 'Gabie reinterprets Seurat for a post-industrial age.'[2]

The ODA's artist in residence Neville Gabie's *Freeze Frame,* a choreographed scene populated with workers on the Park photographed in 2011. It is based on Georges Seurat's painting *Bathers at Asnières* (1884).

Georges Seurat's original painting *Bathers at Asnières* (1884).

Descending into this riverine landscape even the quality of the sound changes. The hubbub of the city dissipates, overtaken by the sounds of lapping water, coots hooting and the wind whispering through the wetland reeds. To the right of the footpath is a swale for surface water collected on the concourse and planted with beautiful, taller flowering plants. Arriving at the wetland bowl there is an extraordinary sense of entering entirely another world. It is quiet and strangely intimate. The wetland bowl carved out of the river is rich with reeds, flag iris and purple loosestrife. It looks like it has always been there, and yet it is completely new, completely fabricated. The frog ponds with their geometrically stacked, linear log piles paradoxically have an almost primeval quality: art and nature coming together. The wet woodlands with their fish channels, wet and dry habitats, and kingfisher wall play with texture, light and shade. Everywhere buzzes with wildlife. Within a year of the north of the Park being completed no less than 47 different species of birds had already been spotted within the Park. They include the more common coots, moorhens, mallards, geese and cormorants, but also the more rare cuckoos, owls and kingfishers. Some, like reed warblers and sand martins, also nested there. It is an extraordinarily rich landscape.

In complete contrast, many of the larger spectator lawns appear to rise up to the sky, giving spectacular views over the Park and the city. You feel exposed, elevated, exhilarated. The lawns within the incised mounds conversely make you feel protected and safe, but utterly dazzled by the spectacular flower displays on the opposite facet of the incision. The wooded gulleys cut into the spectator lawns are full of rich and unusual plants and herbs. The sharded slopes are clothed in vibrantly colourful perennial meadows, giving the north of the Park a looser, slightly unkempt feel moderated by the angular landforms. A human invention developing the picturesque, a facsimile of natural ecosystems. A living, working landscape.

In contrast to the south of the Park, the north of the Park is not designed to attract and cater for large numbers of people. It is envisaged as the more local and community-oriented part of the Park. In transformation, a new park hub with a pavilion and a playground is added near the Village next to the main footpath and cycle route that connects it with Hackney Wick. It will have a café, toilets, meeting rooms, rangers' accommodation and classrooms. The Park landscape will be a fantastic 'outdoor classroom'.

A one-mile cycle circuit along with mountain-bike tracks are inserted into the far northern landscape in transformation, which is a smaller version of the main wetland. The Velodrome, BMX track and mountain-bike circuits will combine to create a unique VeloPark in legacy. The eastern riverside path will be extended and pass under the A12 highway. For the first time in decades, you will be able to walk and cycle along the river to Hackney Marshes and Eton Manor. Eton Manor undergoes some major changes transforming into a hockey, tennis and 5-a-side football community sports hub. It will also have the memorial garden to the Eton Manor Old Boys, retaining links with the history of 'The Manor'.

By the time the transformation phase of construction is complete, the area of parklands throughout the Park will have doubled from that for the Games. The majority will have been created in the north of the Park, particularly with the removal of the hockey pitches at the Riverbank Arena and large areas of concourse. The Biodiversity Action Plan (BAP) target for 45ha of diverse habitats, and the planning requirement for 102ha of metropolitan open land will have been delivered. Existing and new neighbourhoods will have a new park fit for the 21st century.

The design of the north of the Park re-establishes a riverine landscape and a rich matrix of wetland habitats set within a sophisticated and highly structured landform. The sculpted topography frames views towards individual venues and buildings including the Velodrome in the north east of the Park.

(continued on page 246)

THE CENTRAL ROLE OF THE CLIENT

Sir John Armitt
Chairman, Olympic Delivery Authority, 2007 onwards

At the outset, one of the most important roles of a client is to establish the entire working culture and structure of a project. If it fails to do this it just won't happen. We wanted to ensure that the project would do more than just deliver the Olympic venues, infrastructure and Park on time and on budget. In investing over 75 pence in the pound for legacy, the additional challenge was to secure many long-term benefits across the whole construction programme. We wanted to make progress and demonstrate real innovation in many areas including health and safety, sustainability, employment and training. This was accomplished in a number of ways, including the process of awarding contracts, and defining how targets were set and progress monitored. Much credit has to be given to David Higgins and his team for the way they set out the wider themes at the beginning of the project.

The outcome is now clear, for example the ODA's safety record is well above the industry average, and over 3,500 training opportunities and more than 450 apprenticeship places were provided though the construction of the Park. We have met around 90 per cent of our sustainability targets across the entire project, including the recycling of waste, and have achieved Level 4 in the Code for Sustainable Homes for the Olympic and Paralympic Village, which was a real stretch for the project. In addition to the formal targets a range of sustainable design and build solutions were delivered including the reuse of steel for the structure of the Olympic Stadium and Velodrome. Many of these achievements are now recorded in good detail in the ODA's learning legacy papers that are available on the web. I think it is fair to say that the first gold medal of the Games should go to the British construction industry for all it achieved; showing the world just what it is capable of doing.

Setting deadlines and keeping to them is another important attribute of a strong client. Many

ODA Chairman John Armitt, on the left, visits Henry Raker at Salix Nurseries in October 2009. Over 300,000 wetland plants were grown in Thetford, Norfolk, for the Park, the largest ever urban river and wetland planting scheme in the UK.

ODA Chairman John Armitt, on the right, viewing the trees with Robert Hillier at Hillier's nursery in Hampshire, the tree supplier for the Park, in June 2009. Around 2,000 semi-mature British grown trees were selected in total.

The wetland bowl and 'Park Live' in the north-west of the Park at the start of the Games in July 2012. The lawns were extremely popular and heavily used by spectators watching the huge TV screen showing events from across the Games. This was one of the most memorable images of the Park during the Games.

organisations set internal deadlines that can often slip, but for the ODA these were set externally, so we couldn't put off difficult decisions. The advantage of the immoveable date of 27 July 2012 for the Opening Ceremony of the Olympic Games was that it forced the decision-making process. As a consequence, we invested a lot in management that focused particularly on programme, risk, budget and performance – it was time and money well spent. We reported monthly and when problems emerged, David and the executive team commissioned small 'deep-dive' teams to carry out reviews and help come up with solutions.

As Chairman, my central role was outward facing. Inevitably, the ODA had numerous stakeholders and we spent a lot of time managing external relationships and particularly those with central Government, our funders and the Mayor of London's office. This included monthly meetings at Westminster for both ministers and shadow teams at which we were equally open about the challenges we were facing and our achievements. Being so transparent with our targets and programme could be seen as making a rod for our own back, but publishing the 10 key Demolish, Dig, Design and Big Build milestones for each year, and then providing quarterly reports on progress

to our stakeholders and the media, helped secure much-needed support from a vast number of external organisations. This was critical to the overall success of the project.

It was a rare opportunity to be able to create such a large park for London – there are not many parks that have the benefit of a river running through them. It is a very mixed landscape and sufficient resources must be allocated to maintain the Park into the future. It was interesting to visit many of the companies and key suppliers around the country, a number of which were relatively small and often family owned. For example, Hilliers of Hampshire supplied the trees for the parklands, Salix of the Gower Peninsula and Norfolk the aquatic plants for the wetlands, and Palmstead Nurseries of Kent the herbaceous plants for the 2012 Gardens. Along with the parklands, the sporting venues, new housing and Orbit we have built the framework for future development and new cultural assets. In creating a total place to work, live, play and learn I think it could become one of the best places in London to live. It may take a further 20 years or more to complete, but in 2030 we will hopefully look back with satisfaction at what we really gained from the Games.

Left: the site for the Park as it was in 2003 with Canary Wharf on the horizon, but the river Lea in the foreground is obscured by dense vegetation. The bus garage on the far side of the river can be seen on the right. **Right: a similar view of the Park in 2012.** Canary Wharf is partially visible on the horizon to the right of the Olympic Stadium. The river has been restored and completely opened up. The bus garage has been replaced by the International Broadcast Centre.

Left: looking south along the Waterworks river close to the junction with Carpenters Road Lock in May 2007.
Right: the Park in 2012. The furthest river wall has been restored and refurbished with the 2012 Gardens behind. The nearest wall has been demolished and realigned to increase the capacity of the river and allow for the addition of marginal aquatic planting, improving the ecological connectivity of the river corridor.

Left: the junction of the Waterworks river with Carpenters Road Lock to the right in May 2007. Right: a similar view of the Park in 2012. The alignment of the old wall on the far side of the river remains the same, the building waste and skip refuse processing premises have been replaced by the northern end of the 2012 Gardens.

Left: the northern end of the City Mill river near its junction with Carpenters Road Lock in May 2007. Right: a similar view of the Park taken in 2012. The power lines have been placed underground, the river has been dredged and its canal-like walls restored and refurbished. New towpaths, planting and seating have been added.

View looking south along the river Lea and across the wetland bowl. Within a year of planting, the reedbeds were already home to a wide variety of birds including warblers, cormorants, mallards and herons.

LESSONS OF THE DEEPER NARRATIVE

The above narratives describe the seen, the experienced and the felt of the Park moving from Games into transformation. Dig a little deeper though, and there is complexity and depth in the hidden narratives of what the Park is, how it came about, its meaning and purpose. Previous chapters have distilled some of those deeper narratives of The Making of the Queen Elizabeth Olympic Park. How it was conceived at the time of the bid, the extraordinary strategic vision that supported the bid, how the Park was planned, designed and then constructed as an exemplar sustainable development. To help raise the bar within the planning, design and construction sector, and act as a showcase for UK plc, the ODA published micro-reports, champion products and peer-reviewed case studies as part of its Learning Legacy.[3] Archaeology, design and engineering innovation, equality and inclusion, health and safety, masterplanning and town planning, procurement, project and programme management, sustainability, systems and technology, and transport. It is an extraordinary compendium and testament to the ODA's work, focusing on programme, management and technical achievements.

Around 50,000 people came together over a seven-year period to deliver the Park. It provided not only a wonderful setting for the Games and the foundations for a lasting legacy, but also changed the way projects will be envisioned, planned, designed and delivered across the world. Existing local communities surrounding the Park, and the new communities arising within the Park, will all benefit from the sports venues for many years to come. They will benefit from a completely new utilities infrastructure, including the Energy Centre working quietly away to produce clean, sustainable, efficient heat, power and cooling, and the waste water recycling treatment plant supplying non-potable, 'grey water' across the Park. The first residents moving into what was the Olympic and Paralympic Village will have a new school, healthcare centre and, for those so inclined, Europe's largest shopping centre right next door with associated commercial and leisure developments. An upgraded and renewed public transport system will connect them to the West End of London, Paris and all points beyond. Together with the parklands and public realm, they will live in a new kind of 21st-century park – common ground for mothers, fathers, grandparents, carers, toddlers, teenagers, senior and solitary citizens of all colours, faiths and backgrounds.

The Olympic and Paralympic ideal promotes a global celebration of all that is good in humanity through sports, arts and culture. By placing 'sport at the service of the harmonious development of humankind' the Games invoke a visceral sense of being part of a global community, reminding us that, as we run out of finite capital resources and feel the impacts of climate change, there is a global context to every human action and endeavour, and that we must act equitably to assure the livelihoods of current and future generations. A compelling vision of the Park after the Games drove the planning, design and delivery of the Park. The Government, with all-party support, along with London's then Mayor Ken Livingstone,

Looking east across a spectator lawn and the river Lea. After the Games the temporary Basketball Arena in the middle of the picture will be removed and reused. The site will then be ready for development: the Village will be extended and transformed into a new neighbourhood.

agreed to underwrite the Games. Some 80 per cent of the British public supported the bid. The social, economic and environmental strands of sustainable development were woven into the vision. But as Jason Prior and Bill Hanway, the masterplanners of the Park, note in their interview for this book, 'it was the idea of the Park and new public open space in the area that attracted the greatest political support from the local communities, mayors and leaders. The Games, and the key element of the Park, then became the structure around which we were able to discuss other issues of social need.'[4]

Independent scrutiny of the ODA by the Commission for a Sustainable London 2012 built the confidence of politicians, press, stakeholders and the general public. The Park set new standards across all of the One Planet Living social, economic and environmental themes, from energy and waste to health and happiness. However, it is acknowledged that the Park is only a step towards One Planet Living. The overarching lesson is that delivering new neighbourhoods, and retrofitting existing ones that enable living within the means of the One Planet, will not be easy. As metrics, the One Planet Living themes supported by ecological footprinting provide a consistent and elegant way to articulate, understand and communicate complex issues. As with the London 2012 bid, all projects should use the

The design of the Park sought to restore the river Lea and create a 'landscape without boundaries', embracing new sports venues as well as existing buildings and neighbourhoods surrounding the Park.

One Planet Living themes as a starting point and means to set sustainability targets to ensure that nothing is missed. The Commission for a Sustainable London 2012 concluded that 'The ODA has met or exceeded nearly every sustainability target that was set for it as part of its planning consent' and that it 'contributed an extraordinary legacy to the construction industry in the UK and worldwide. Through its robust sustainability approach and high targets, it drove innovation, made financial savings, and improved the health and safety outcomes for its workers.'

Spatial planning, design and construction policy were mutually supportive, clearly aimed at sustainable outcomes and were a 'top down' and 'bottom up' process. The UK's unique and robust spatial and planning and building regulation system combined to play a crucial role in the successful delivery of the Park. Planning is a democratic process in the UK so everyone had an opportunity to contribute in some way to the design of the Park. The ODA published what it was going to deliver, how much it would cost, and a programme for delivery very early on. Everyone was aware of what the ODA was doing. Getting the briefs for projects correct at the beginning, informed by strategies, policies, targets and consultations with stakeholders, was essential, as was updating them through all design stages to ensure compliance with more detailed requirements as they emerged. Managing scope and budget enabled value management – 'is it essential or just nice to have?' – and controlled expenditure of contingency funding against the programme and stakeholder requests. Definition and vigilance on scope of works, costs and delivery saved time and money.

Illustrative Legacy Masterplan Framework prepared for the London Development Agency, showing how the Olympic Park might sit within the surrounding urban areas some 20–25 years hence.

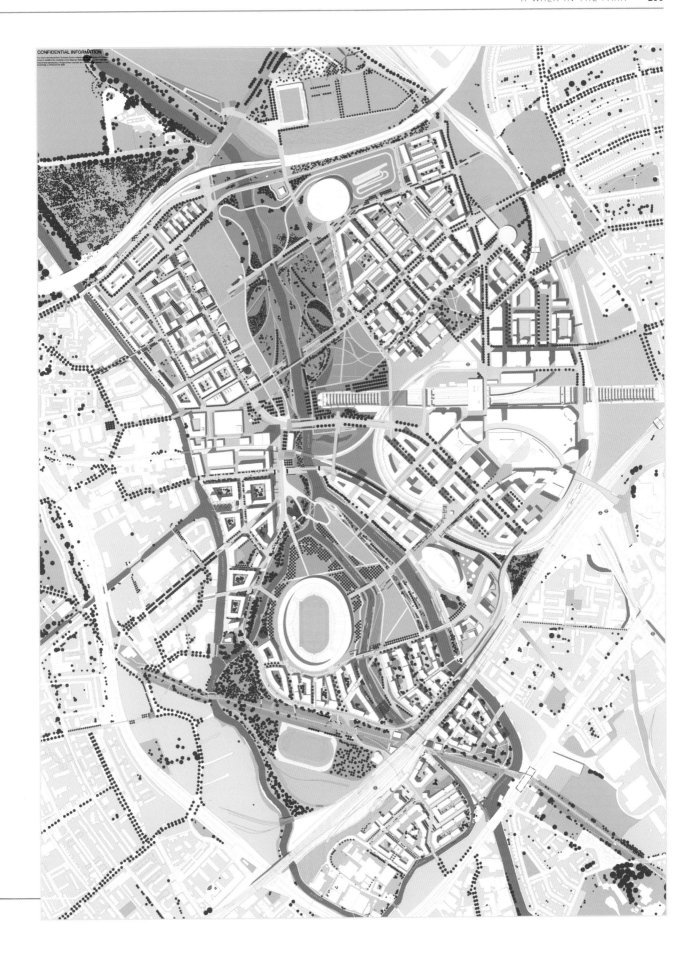

Oxeye daisies lining the edge of a path in the north of the Park. The extensive use of perennial meadows greatly increased the biodiversity of the parklands and was visually stunning.

The Park owes much to the masterplanning, landscape architect, engineering, architect and other design and delivery teams who understood that collaborative planning, design and delivery across professional disciplines, statutory stakeholders, contractors and suppliers was crucial. Professional 'silo' mentalities lead to single-function outcomes. Regular, open and honest consultation, engagement and communication were crucial to achieving consensus and maintaining support. With a multiplicity of stakeholders from the International Olympic Committee (IOC) through all levels of Government to local residents, the ODA had a very sophisticated strategy that was not just about communications or consultations, but genuine engagement and celebration. It was an open organisation and published its programme, policies, budgets, targets and progress on a regular basis. Community consultation is a requirement of the UK's planning system, but the ODA went beyond the narrow requirements and engaged directly with all sectors including faith groups, disability groups and many others. More than 280,000 members of the public were taken on bus tours around the Park throughout construction. Invitations to celebrate the completion of parklands in the north of the Park were extended to many of those who had helped the ODA through the planning and design process. Community engagement was not an 'add-on', it came from the top as can be seen in the reflections of David Higgins in his interview in this book, noting his appreciation of the local community enjoying *their* park at the View Tube.

A frog pond and fish channel carefully integrated within the wet woodland in the north of the Park creating an extraordinarily rich urban landscape.

The Park can be seen as a continuum in Britain's long and distinguished tradition for town, city, landscape and garden planning and design. It is not the 'balanced ecological town' envisioned by Ebenezer Howard's garden cities, but it is perhaps the most complete example yet of ecologically based urban planning and design, certainly at this scale. To ensure that the lessons of history were learned, the ODA studied, visited and documented exemplars very carefully. Previous Olympic and Paralympic Games, large construction projects, venues, sustainability exemplars and parks both in the UK and abroad were all assessed. In the decades to come, the ODA's extraordinary achievement of delivering a £6 billion Park on time, within budget in just seven years will, as recognised in the interview with the landscape engineers, be largely forgotten.[5] What *will* be remembered and continue to be enjoyed is the beautiful Park and parkland setting created for the Games that will double in size when transformed following the Games.

Journalist Simon Barnes has reported on six Olympic Games on four continents for *The Times*. He visited the Park in 2011, noting the difficulty of designing a human-scaled Olympic Park and citing two very strong English traditions that might allow this. 'The first is a spiritual quality: humour, irony, self-deprecation. The second English tradition is a physical one and it has to do with our taste in landscape. We like parks and gardens and wildlife.'[6] He is a naturalist as well as sports writer and spotted several species of bird,

Humour, irony, self-deprecation: a garden gnome secreted clandestinely within the Park.

butterfly, moth and reptile during his visit to the Park. He appreciated the emphasis on wildlife, wetlands and habitats: 'Paradoxically, it makes the place more human: by adding non-human life, we find the better part of humanity – not in generalissimos' boulevards but in wild-edged parkland making the Olympic Games something of a *fête champêtre*, if not a *déjeuner sur l'herb*.'[7] He gave no example of humour, but it is a point well made. Perhaps a final lesson is that in the relentless pursuit of the delivering on time, on budget to everyone's satisfaction, humour is an essential antidote to stress. So maybe it should be no surprise that members of the ODA delivery team clandestinely secreted a garden gnome – that most British of artefacts – within the Park, perhaps symbolising 'humour, irony, self-deprecation'.

In a book exploring the principles of 'cultured landscapes', the co-authors of this book noted that landscape architects 'are becoming increasingly adept at restoring despoiled and polluted landscapes left as a legacy of our manufacturing past, and through this, we are developing new aesthetic and cultural values for these landscapes. Alongside, there is an increasing desire to work with, rather than control, the natural processes and rhythms that have always shaped our environments.'[8] The Olympic Park shows what a 'vast "working landscape" that meets social, economic and environmental imperatives' might look like. Creating our own legacy of 'connected, fully functioning environmental systems on a scale that has never been seen before.'[9]

The ultimate success of the Park lies in legacy. The nascence of that legacy lay in formidable strategic spatial and policy planning underpinning a vision of regeneration and sustainability, and a belief that the power of the Games could accelerate the delivery of that vision. If the regeneration of east London is realised in the coming decades, if people come to settle and dwell in the Park, if the centre of gravity of London shifts eastwards, if the Park is seen as an exemplar of the new post-industrial, ecological age, if One Planet Living and ecological footprinting become the baseline and benchmark for the development of sustainable towns, cities and communities around the world, then yes – the success of the Park will be assured. Only time will tell. With a projected global population of 9.75 billion in 2075 there have to be fundamental changes in the way we shape our environments. The making of the Queen Elizabeth Olympic Park provides some valuable lessons in using and reusing finite resources to help safeguard the future of our One Planet. The next steps require nothing less than a new popular, political and economic vision based on the ecological capacity of the planet to support both current and future global populations, so that they too can celebrate sports, arts and culture at future Olympic and Paralympic Games as we did in London in 2012.

The design of the north of the Park is based around an ecological 'working landscape' providing multiple functions such as managing flood risk, cleaning the air and absorbing carbon within a highly complex urban district.

Looking south across the Queen Elizabeth Olympic Park in April 2012. The new parklands, which will be extended out to the surrounding neighbourhoods during the transformation stage following the Games, are central to the emerging character of this new urban district of east London.

Looking eastwards across the wet woodland towards the Olympic and Paralympic Village in the north of the Park in December 2011.

AFTERWORD

AFTERWORD

Park as Catalyst

Never before has the redevelopment of a site for the Games been so oriented towards what follows them – to the legacy. From Barcelona to Beijing, the aftermath of the Games leaves over-scaled, empty places, bereft of any real connection, relationship or benefit to the surrounding city. The Queen Elizabeth Olympic Park (the Park) is a whole different story, one that is told with great care for detail and completeness by the authors of this book, and one that holds enormous relevance for other cities around the world. At the centre of that story is the creation of a great public park, a rich and varied ecological and social terrain that anchors the sports venues for the Games, while establishing the framework for the development of new mixed neighbourhoods, communities and local economies – a major new piece of *city*.

Paradoxically, the sheer complexity and difficulty of achieving this great transformation will not at all be apparent to future visitors. Landscape after all has the beguiling effect of naturalising, as if has always been there, grown from nature. It will be impossible to imagine just how such a site was actually transformed and delivered – from the brilliant and far-sighted first visions and plans, to the technical re-engineering and re-shaping of the site, to the poetic and artful creation of new landscapes and places for both people and nature, to the democratic process of debate, inclusion, policy, decision-making and delivery within tight timeframes and budgets. This book is absolutely critical for the recording of the impressive human effort exerted to make the Park what is it today. But more than a record, it is also a guide for future efforts of urban regeneration around the world, describing the sort of leadership acumen, planning and design creativity, engineering prowess and clarity of vision necessary to achieve successful outcomes from vastly complex and challenging situations.

Parks are so much more than green passive reserves, naturalising and masking their effects – they are instead hugely significant economic, social and ecological hearts, beating new life, energy and pleasure into the city. And what is particularly brilliant about this Park is that it is less an enclosed or 'room-like' park surrounded by city than it is a web or tissue, reaching out and sending out filaments in multiple directions to connect to and entangle both the existing and subsequent built fabric of the city. Its plan is less figural and discrete than it is extensive and interwoven; and its effect is less focal and scenic than it is irrigational, spreading and active in terms of the potential it yields. The Park rather brilliantly plays on the sense of both industrialisation and the ethics of environmental renewal. The waterways and bridges, in particular, still retain a melancholic sense of past use, and the dramatically shaped landforms by George Hargreaves in the north of the Park echo the industrial wilfulness of engineered form and scale as distinct from a pastoral ruse.

But it is really the ecological function of the Park that resonates the most. This is not simply a scenic park, not a feel-good or deceptive cover-up, but more a working organism, programmed and shaped to renew a place that has been so deeply damaged by both industrialisation and post-industrial decline. Landscape here is not about masking but much more about actively transforming and enabling. The Park is an active agent in renewal, reinvention and remaking. There is neither nostalgia for industrial heritage on the one hand nor scenic pastoralism on the other. Representation here is not the point. Renewal and transformation are the real processes and motors of change, the real industry of landscape systems in reshaping our future cities. This Park inaugurates a new potency for landscape in the city, no longer landscape as compensation or refuge, but landscape as catalyst, engine and living tissue.

Professor James Corner

James Corner is Chair and Professor of Landscape Architecture and Urbanism at the University of Pennsylvania School of Design, and founding director of James Corner Field Operations based in New York City. In addition to designing New York's High Line and Seattle's waterfront, he is also the designer of the legacy park development for the southern part of the Queen Elizabeth Olympic Park on behalf of the London Legacy Development Corporation.

SCHEDULE OF TEAMS INVOLVED IN THE PROJECT

Olympic Delivery Authority (ODA)

- Jack Lemley: Chairman (2006–2007)
- Sir John Armitt CBE: Chairman (2007–ongoing)
- Sir Roy McNulty CBE: Deputy Chairman
- ODA Board: Lorraine Baldry OBE, Tony Ball, Sir Howard Bernstein (until 2008), Stephen Duckworth OBE, Barry Camfield (until January 2012), Neale Coleman, Christopher Garnett, David Fison (from 2009), Sir Peter Mason (until 2009), Kumar Muthalagappan OBE, David Taylor CBE, Baroness Morgan of Huyton, Sir Nicholas Serota.
- Sir David Higgins: Chief Executive (2006–2011)
- Dennis Hone: Chief Executive (2011–ongoing), previously Director of Finance and Corporate Services

Directors

- Wendy Cartwright: Human Resources (2011–ongoing, Head of Human Resources 2006–2011)
- Mike Cornelius: Commercial and Legal (2011–ongoing, Head of Procurement and Commercial 2008–2011)
- Ralph Luck OBE: Property (2006–ongoing)
- Geraldine Murphy: Finance (2011–ongoing)
- Alison Nimmo CBE: Design and Regeneration (2006–2011)
- Vivienne Ramsey OBE: Head of Development Control (2006-2011), Planning Decisions (2011-2012)
- Howard Shiplee CBE: Construction (2006–2011)
- Godric Smith OBE: Communications (2006–2011)
- Hugh Sumner: Transport (2006–2012)
- Simon Wright OBE: Director of Infrastructure and Utilities (2006-2011), Venues and Infrastructure (2011-2012)

Key Staff

- Celia Carlisle: General Counsel (2006–2011)
- Alice Coates: Head of Marketing (2006-2011)
- Stephen Cooper: Head of Security (2006–2012)
- Tom Curry: Head of Media (2006–2011)
- Dan Epstein: Head of Sustainable Development and Regeneration (2007–2011)
- John Evans: Head of Communications (2011–ongoing)
- Jerome Frost OBE: Head of Design (2006–2011)
- Anthony Hollingsworth: Chief Planner, Development Control (2006–2012)
- Richard Jackson: Sustainable Development and Regeneration Manager (2006–2011)
- Julie King: Head of External Relations (2006–2012)

- Kenna Kintrea: Deputy Director of Venues & Infrastructure (2012-ongoing), Head of Programme Assurance (2007-2012)
- David Law: Head of Risk and Audit (2006-ongoing)
- Lorraine Martins MBE: Head of Equality and Inclusion (2007-2011)
- Selina Mason: Deputy Head, Design (2007-2011)
- Niall McNevin: Head of Town Planning Promoter Team (2007-2010)
- Professor Ricky Burdett: Chief Advisor on Architecture and Urbanism
- Steve Shaw: Senior Development Planner (2007-2010), Chief Planner, Town Planning (2010-2012)
- Gordon Shipley: Head of Systems and Technology (2007-ongoing)
- Pieter de Waal: Deputy General Counsel (2007-2011), Head of Legal Services (2011-ongoing)
- Lawrence Waterman OBE: Head of Health and Safety (2006-2012)
- Sarah Weir: Head of Arts and Culture (2008-11)

Project sponsors

- Richard Arnold: Velodrome, Eton Manor, Eton Dorney and RAB Shooting (2006-2012) and IBC/MPC and Handball (2011-ongoing)
- Phil Askew: Parklands and Public Realm (2008-2012)
- David Baird: Structures, Bridges and Highways and Park Services (2006-ongoing)
- Ian Crockford: Olympic Stadium, Water Polo Arena and Aquatics Centre (2006-ongoing)
- Paul Hartman: Olympic and Paralympic Village Property Development and Legacy (2007-ongoing)
- John Hopkins: Parklands and Public Realm (2007-2011)
- Ruari Maybank: Utilities (2008-2012)
- Kevin Moriarty: Utilities (2006-2008)
- Colin Naish: IBC/MPC, Handball, Broxbourne White Water Canoe Centre (2007-2011)
- John Nicholson: Aquatics Centre & IBC/MPC (2006-2010) and Olympic and Paralympic Village (2010-2012)
- Jim Prendergast: Olympic and Paralympic Village Infrastructure and Facilities Management (2008-2012)
- Paul Snoddy: Basketball (2007-2010)
- Jim Woolhouse: Property Development Manager (2007-ongoing)

Delivery Partner (CLM) made up of: CH2MHill/Laing O'Rourke/Mace

- Ian Galloway OBE: Programme Director (2007-2011)
- Jason Millett: Programme Director (2012) previously Director of Venues (2008-2011)

Key members of the CLM Parklands and Public Realm Team

- Jim Avant: Project Manager, South Park (2009-2012)
- Matt Heal: Head of Parklands and Public Realm (2006-2009)

- Peter Keegan: Project Manager, North Park (2011–2012)
- David Lucas: Landscape Manager (2008–2012)
- David Martin: Project Manager, North Park (2009–2011)
- Jackie Roe: Head of Parklands and Public Realm (2011–2012) previously Head of Utilities (2007–2011)
- Adrian Rourke: Design Manager (2007–2011)
- David Stephenson: Operations Manager (2008–2012)
- Sam Stevens: Head of Parklands and Public Realm (2007–2011)
- David Wilson: Commercial Manager (2008–2012)
- Stuart Wilson: Contracts Advisor (2007–2009) and Deputy Project Sponsor for Landscape Management (2011–2012)

Masterplanning

EDAW Consortium comprising EDAW (now AECOM), Allies and Morrison, Foreign Office Architects, Buro Happold, HOK Sport (now Populous)

- AECOM: Jason Prior and Bill Hanway
- Allies and Morrison: Bob Allies, Graham Morrison, Simon Fraser, Eddie Taylor, Greg Holme and Chris Schulte
- Foreign Office Architects: Farshid Moussavi and Alejandro Zaera-Polo
- Buro Happold: Andrew Comer and Bob Tong
- Populous: Rod Sheard, Derek Wilson, Chris Jopson, Philip Johnson and Tom Jones

Landscape architecture

- LDA Design (lead consultant): Neil Mattinson and Andrew Harland
- Hargreaves Associates: George Hargreaves (Design Director), Mary-Margaret Jones, Glen Allen (d 2011) and Gavin McMillan
- LDA Design Ecology: Peter Shepherd
- Buro Four Project Services: Peter Smith
- University of Sheffield (specialist ecology, meadows and horticulture): Professor James Hitchmough and Professor Nigel Dunnett
- Sarah Price Landscapes: Sarah Price (2012 Gardens and Great British Garden)
- Horticultural soils: Tim O'Hare Associates, Tim O'Hare and Tim White
- Irrigation: Waterwise, Richard Owen
- Lighting design: Sutton Vane Associates, Mark Sutton Vane and Mike Grubb
- Tree planting: James Urban and Associates, James Urban
- Landscape management: ETM Associates, Tim Marshall

Landscape engineering

- Atkins: Alison Braham and John Crocker (Landscape Engineering), Martyn Lass MBE (Site Wide Infrastructure), Mike Vaughan (Wetlands Engineering)
- Arup: Bill Grose, Tom Armour, Kate Hall, Stephanos Samaras

CABE Space Enablers

- Coordinator: Peter Neal
- Enablers: Annie Coombs, David Lambert, Land Use Consultants, Tony Leach, Robert Holden, Jeremy Purseglove, Philip Sayers, Ken Worpole, Stuart Wilson

Landscape contractors and suppliers

- Tier One contractors: BAM Nuttall (northern Park), Skanska (southern Park) and Team Stadium
- Tier Two landscape contractors: northern Park – Frosts Landscape Construction, Gavin Jones, Land and Water Group, White Horse Contractors; southern Park – Willerby Landscapes
- Team Stadium landscape contractor: Willerby Landscapes
- Tree supplier: Hillier Nurseries
- Wetland plants supplier: Salix River & Wetland Services
- 2012 Gardens plant supplier: Palmstead Nurseries
- Landscape maintenance contractors: BAM Nuttall/Gavin Jones/Willerby Landscapes (northern Park) and Skanska/Willerby Landscapes (southern Park)

The Greenway

Architect: Adams & Sutherland. Engineering and project management: Arup. Landscape consultant: Jonathon Cook Landscape Architects. Lead Contractor: Volker FitzPatrick. Architect/contractor for the View Tube: Urban Space Management.

Central Bridge

Architect: Heneghan Peng Architects. Structural engineer: Adams Kara Taylor. Lead contractor: Lagan Construction.

Olympic Stadium

Architect: Populous. Lead contractor: Sir Robert McAlpine. Structural and services engineer: Buro Happold. Landscape architect: Hyland Edgar Driver.

Aquatics Centre

Architect: Zaha Hadid Architects. Lead contractor: Balfour Beatty. Sports architect: S+P Architects. Engineering: Arup. Steel roof construction: Rowecord.

Velodrome

Architect: Hopkins Architects. Lead contractor: ISG plc. Structural engineer: Expedition Engineering. Services engineer: BDSP Partnership. Track designer: Ron Webb. Landscape architect: Grant Associates/LDA Design.Hargreaves Associates.

Copper Box (Handball Arena)

Architect: MAKE. Sports architect: PTW. Detailed design: Populous. Engineers: Arup. Structural engineer: Sinclair Knight Merz. Main contractor: Buckingham Group Contracting.

Eton Manor

Architect: Stanton Williams. Engineers: Arup. Main contractors: Mansell Construction Services and PJ Careys, Slick Seating Systems, MITIE Engineering, A&T, Nussli. Landscape architect: LDA Design.Hargreaves Associates.

Basketball Arena

Architect: Wilkinson Eyre Architects. Sports architect: KSS. Engineers: Arup. Structural engineer: Sinclair Knight Merz. Main contractors: Barr Construction plus Slick Seating, Bose, MITIE, Envirowrap, Volker Fitzpatrick and McAvoy.

Water Polo Arena

Architect: David Morley Architects. Structural engineer: Buro Happold. Environmental engineer: Max Fordham. Main contractors: ES Group and Jackson Civil Engineering Group Ltd, Alto Seating Systems Ltd, A&T/Barr & Wray, Byrne Group plc, Balfour Beatty.

International Broadcast Centre/Main Press Centre Complex

Architects for International Broadcast Centre (IBC): Allies and Morrison. RPS: Envelope design.

Architects for Main Press Centre (MPC): Allies and Morrison. Structural and services engineers: Buro Happold. Landscape architects: Townshend Landscape Architects. Lead contractor: Carillion.

Locog key staff

James Bulley, Head of Infrastructure and Venues; Kevin Owens, Design Principal; David Hickey, Project Integration; Helen Ewings, Project Manager.

GLOSSARY

BAP	Biodiversity Action Plan
BioRegional	A social enterprise that works with organisations and businesses to deliver practical solutions for sustainability that demonstrate a sustainable future is attractive and affordable
BOA	British Olympic Association
BREEAM	BRE Environmental Assessment Method is a voluntary measurement rating for green buildings that was established in the UK by the Building Research Establishment (BRE)
CABE	Commission for Architecture and the Built Environment
CEEQUAL	Assessment and Awards Scheme for improving sustainability in civil engineering, infrastructure, landscape and public realm projects, based in the United Kingdom
CPO	Compulsory Purchase Order
CLM	Delivery Partner, a consortium specifically formed for the Games comprising CH2M Hill, Laing O'Rourke and Mace
Commission for a Sustainable London 2012	An independent body which monitored and assured the sustainability of the London 2012 Olympic and Paralympic Games
DCMS	Department for Culture, Media and Sport, the Government department responsible for overseeing the Games
The Games	The 30th Summer Olympic and Paralympic Games held in London in 2012
GLA	Greater London Authority
GOE	Government Olympic Executive. A section within the Department for Culture, Media and Sport (DCMS) that oversees the London 2012 project on behalf of the Government

Host Boroughs	The London Boroughs of Greenwich, Hackney, Newham, Tower Hamlets, Waltham Forest and Barking & Dagenham who will be the primary hosts for the Games
Host Cities	Cities chosen by the IOC to host the Summer and the Winter Olympic and Paralympic Games
IBC	International Broadcast Centre
IOC	International Olympic Committee
IPC	International Paralympic Committee
LDA	The London Development Agency was created in July 2000 to help the Mayor of London support the growth of London's economy. It was abolished on 31 March 2012 and its functions folded into the GLA
LEED	Leadership in Energy and Environmental Design which consists of a suite of rating systems used in the United States for the design, construction and operation of high-performance green buildings, homes and neighbourhoods
LLDC	London Legacy Development Corporation responsible for the transformation and long-term development and management of the Park and its environs and taking over the responsibilities of the OPLC
LOCOG	London Organising Committee of the Olympic Games and Paralympic Games responsible for preparing, staging and hosting the Games
LVRPA	Lee Valley Regional Park Authority
MPC	Main Press Centre
ODA	Olympic Delivery Authority
Olympic masterplan	The masterplan for the Olympic Park site as a whole
Olympic Park	The Olympic site as a whole, including structures, bridges, highways, utilities, buildings, landscape and public realm

Olympic Parklands	The parkland at the heart of the Olympic Park capable of designation as Metropolitan Open Land
Olympic Village	The Olympic and Paralympic Village
OPLC	Olympic Park Legacy Company reconstituted as the LLDC in April 2012
Orbit	The ArcelorMittal Orbit is a sculpture by artist Anish Kapoor and structural engineer Cecil Balmond commissioned by the Mayor of London, Boris Johnson, and funded by ArcelorMittal and the London Development Agency
Public realm	The streets, squares, bridges, gardens and other landscape and townscape infrastructure
Riverside Arena	The name given to the temporary hockey pitches located in the north-west of the Park
TfL	Transport for London
WWF	World Wildlife Fund

REFERENCES

Note: Olympic Delivery Authority weblinks

At the time of going to press the weblinks to the Olympic Delivery Authority's Learning Legacy and other documents provided in the footnotes were in the process of being transferred to the government's Major Projects Authority, part of the Cabinet Office. When the transfer of the London 2012 website is complete readers are recommended to visit learninglegacy.independent.gov.uk or search for individual ODA or Learning Legacy documents using the full name with an appropriate search engine.

INTRODUCTORY ESSAY – THE POWER OF THE GAMES

[1] London 2012 candidate file, *Introduction*, p 7. Letter from Mayor Ken Livingstone to President of the International Olympic Committee, Jacques Rogge, 1 November 2004.

[2] On 2 April 2012, the London Legacy Development Corporation took over responsibility for the ongoing regeneration and development of the Olympic Park and surrounding areas of east London. http://www.londonlegacy.co.uk/development-corporation-takes-on-the-legacy-baton/; accessed April 2012.

[3] One Planet Living is a trademark of WWF and BioRegional.

[4] *The Olympic Games Impact Study* (OGI1) was initiated by the International Olympic Committee to develop an objective and scientific analysis of the impact of each edition of the Games. In June 2007, the IOC issued the first OGI Technical Manual. This is the governing document for the study; it sets out the rationale, scope and technical requirements, and incorporates material from the International Paralympic Committee (IPC).

[5] *London 2012 Sustainable Design – Delivering a Games Legacy* by Hattie Hartman tells the more detailed story of sustainability; *The Architecture of London 2012: Vision, Design and Legacy of the Olympic and Paralympic Games* by Tom Dyckhoff, Claire Barrett and Edmund Sumner (photographer) tells the more detailed story of the architecture; both John Wiley & Sons (Chichester), 2012.

[6] Alexander Garvin, *The American City: what works, what doesn't*, McGraw-Hill (New York), second edition, 2009. Garvin writes: 'Since I do not believe that project success necessarily results in any improvement to the surrounding city (indeed some have made things worse), I also redefine successful city planning as public action that generates a desirable, widespread, and sustained private market reaction.', preface to the first edition, p ix.

[7] Anthony Alexander, *Britain's New Towns*, Routledge (Abingdon), 2009, p 4.

CHAPTER ONE – START WITH THE PARK

[1] David Lambert, http://learninglegacy.london2012.com/documents/pdfs/design-and-engineering-innovation/parklands-and-public-realm-design-brief-part-2-of-4-.pdf; Appendix 1J commissioned through the enabling work of CABE Space and the ODA; accessed March 2012.

[2] Natural England, *Our Natural Health Service: The role of the natural environment in maintaining healthy lives*, 2009, p 4.

[3] Natural England, *Our Natural Health Service: The role of the natural environment in maintaining healthy lives*, 2009, p 9.

[4] Alexander Garvin, Gayle Berens et al, *Urban Parks and Open Space*, ULI – The Urban Land Institute (Washington, DC), 1997.

[5] Lerner and Poole, *The Economic Benefits of Parks and Open Space*, 1999, quoted in *Does Money Grow on Trees?*, CABE Space, 2005, p 13.

[6] Lambert, p 13.

[7] Lambert, p 12.

[8] Lambert, p 39.

[9] Thames Gateway South Essex Green Grid, LDA Design, http://parklands.greengrid.co.uk/index.php/greengrid or http://www.helm.org.uk/upload/pdf/JHopkins2.pdf?1333938968 (John Hopkins, author).

[10] The Thames Estuary Parklands, 2006, http://webarchive.nationalarchives.gov.uk/20110118095356/http://www.cabe.org.uk/files/tg11-full-report.pdf; accessed March 2012. This initial study was commissioned by CABE on behalf of the Department of Communities and Local Government (DCLG) to support the Thames Gateway Strategic Framework. It developed ideas from CABE's Thames Gateway Identity Project. It described the concept, what is happening now, what is planned, and what should happen next. Later, DCLG and Sir Terry Farrell changed the name to the 'Thames Gateway Parklands'.

[11] At the time of the bid, and during the early life of the ODA, there were 5 Host Boroughs: Tower Hamlets, Hackney, Newham, Waltham Forest and Greenwich. Barking and Dagenham was added in November 2010. Facts and figures throughout the book are, therefore, based on the original Host Boroughs.

[12] Olympic Legacy Park Local Context Mapping, prepared by Land Use Consultants on behalf of the Commission for Architecture and the Built Environment, January 2007. The area studied covered two zones: the first, land within 1.2 kilometres of the Park (roughly a 15-minute walk at an average pace); the second, land within 3.2 kilometres of the OLP boundary (roughly a 40-minute walk). These are the recommended maximum distances of households from a District or Metropolitan Park (which the Olympic Park at approximately 100 hectares would be) in the London Plan's Public Open Space Hierarchy.

[13] Health Profile of England, Department of Health 2006.

[14] http://www.independent.co.uk/news/business/news/canary-wharf-workers-take-home-an-average-of-163100000-514835.html; accessed 29 December 2011.

[15] http://www.payscale.com/research/UK/Location=Stratford-England%3A-London/Salary; accessed 29 December 2011.

[16] http://www.planningportal.gov.uk/planning/; accessed 29 December 2011.

[17] The new National Planning Policy Framework was published on 27 March 2012 by the coalition government, replacing all previous policies.

[18] http://www.21stcenturychallenges.org/focus/the-thames-gateway/; accessed 29 December 2011.

[19] Department for Communities and Local Government, Thames Gateway Parklands Vision, October 2008.

[20] Civic Trust, *A Lea Valley Regional Park: an essay in the use of neglected land for recreation and leisure*, 1964, p 21.

[21] London 2012 Candidate File, Volume 1–Theme 1 Olympic Games Concept and Legacy, p 23.

[22] Lower Lea Valley Opportunity Area Planning Framework, Greater London Authority, January 2007.

[23] Donella H Meadows, Dennis L Meadows, Jørgen Randers and William W Behrens III, *The Limits to Growth: a report for the Club of Rome's project on the predicament of mankind*, Universe Books, 1972.

[24] Gro Harlem Brundtland, *Our Common Future*, United Nations World Commission on Environment and Development, 1987.

[25] See Introductory Essay; pp19–22.

[26] International Olympic Committee, Olympic Charter, July 2011.

[27] *Towards a One Planet Olympics*, http://assets.panda.org/downloads/opl_olympics_brochure.pdf; accessed 30 December 2011.

[28] London 2012 candidate file bid documents http://www.london2012.com/about-us/publications/?pubType=&sort=date&keyword=candidate+file&pubcode=&x=0&y=0; accessed 14th October 2011.

[29] The Olympic Park Legacy Company (now the LLDC) subsequently decided not to reduce the Olympic Stadium's capacity in 2010.

[30] This was subsequently reduced to 2,800, see Chapter 3, p 74 for an explanation.

[31] London 2012 candidate file bid document, *Theme 1: Olympic Games concept and legacy*, p 25.

CHAPTER TWO – DELIVERING THE PARK

[1] http://webarchive.nationalarchives.gov.uk/20120326141511/http://www.lda.gov.uk/our-work/2012-games/site-preparation/lower-lea-valley-cpo.aspx

[2] 'Compulsory purchase powers are provided to enable acquiring authorities to compulsorily purchase land to carry out a function which Parliament has decided is in the public interest. Anyone who has land acquired is generally entitled to compensation', Compulsory Purchase and Compensation – Compulsory Purchase Procedure, Department for Communities and Local Government, 2004.

[3] http://www.guardian.co.uk/society/2007/mar/12/communities.olympics2012; accessed 4 January 2012.

[4] Manor Gardening Society Allotments, http://www.lifeisland.org; accessed 4 January 2012.

[5] Cleve West, 'Track and field', *Independent*, 27 August 2005.

[6] http://www.london2012.com/publications/programme-baseline-report-summary.php; accessed April 2012.

[7] *Observer*, 20 November 2005.

[9] *Guardian*, 1 December 2006.

[8] Notes:

[1] The Base Cost and Gross Cost columns show figures net of contributions receivable totalling £589m, which includes amounts related to Enabling Works, Utilities and Village.

[2] Projects that are not disaggregated (eg: Other Olympic Park Venues), or that are combined (eg: IBC / MPC and Village) are still subject to contract and individual details are commercially sensitive at this stage.

[3] Programme delivery includes a provision for performance-related payments to CLM, the ODA Delivery Partner.

[4] Contingency as announced on 15 March 2007 totalled £2,247m. This comprises £2,009m as shown above and £238m identified as Security Contingency within the Non-ODA Budget. The Security Contingency of £238m was announced to Parliament on 17 October 2007 (Hansard 17 October 2007 Column 1133W).

[5] Whilst a cost to the Games, all tax paid by the ODA will be a receipt to the Exchequer and accordingly will not be an additional cost to the public sector.

KEY ASSUMPTIONS

The key assumptions on which the scope and budget have been prepared are as follows:

[1] Legacy Planning will transition to the LDA over the 2008 calendar year.

[2] VAT has been applied at 17.5 per cent on appropriate costs (including inflation and contingency).

[3] Corporation tax is payable at 30 per cent on interest received and any profit share from the Village.

[4] No further allowance will need to be made for significant adverse ground conditions and/or existing services diversions beyond those already known.

[5] Any design and construction team contractor incentivisation measures are self-funding.

[6] Compliance with all codes as at December 2007 relating to fire and safety in sports grounds requirements.

[7] Inflation has been built into the programme budget at a rate of 6 per cent pa for capital expenditure.

KEY EXCLUSIONS

The key exclusions from the ODA budget and scope are as follows:

[1] Overlay and other works to venues, transport and security that are to be delivered by LOCOG.

[2] Crossrail scope and interface is the responsibility of the Department of Transport.

[3] Costs for additional security that may be required in future.

[4] Changes to the Green Guide (Guide to Safety at Sports Grounds, published by DCMS) from the current version for design parameters.

[5] Landfill and aggregates tax.

[10] ODA Programme Delivery Baseline Report, January 2008, p 9.

[11] http://www.london2012.com/documents/oda-publications/olympic-park-programme.pdf; accessed April 2012.

[12] http://www.london2012.com/documents/oda-publications/oda-sustainable-development-strategy-full-version.pdf; accessed April 2012.

[13] http://www.london2012.com/about-us/publications/publication=london-2012-sustainability-policy/; accessed July 2012; and http://www.London2012.com/documents/Locog-publications/London-2012-sustainability-plan.pdf; accessed April 2012.

[14] http://www.london2012.com/publications/carbon-footprint-study.php; accessed April 2012.

[15] Leadership in Energy and Environmental Design (LEED) is a suite of rating systems for the design, construction and operation of high-performance green buildings, homes and neighbourhoods developed by the US Green Building Council (USGBC).

[16] Section 106 (S106) of the Town and Country Planning Act 1990 allows a local planning authority (LPA) to enter into a legally binding agreement or planning

obligation with a landowner in association with the granting of planning permission. The obligation is termed a Section 106 Agreement. These agreements are a way of delivering or addressing matters that are necessary to make a development acceptable in planning terms. They are used to support the provision of services and infrastructure, such as highways, recreational facilities, education, health and affordable housing. The scope of such agreements is laid out in the Government's Circular 05/2005.

[17] http://www.london2012.com/documents/oda-publications/hse-standard.pdf; accessed 10 January 2012; p 12.

[18] http://www.wrap.org.uk/construction/halving_waste_to_landfill; WRAP (Waste & Resources Action Programme); and http://www.london2012.com/documents/oda-health-and-safety/code-of-construction-practice-final-low-res.pdf; accessed 10 January 2012.

[19] http://www.bre.co.uk/greenguide/page.jsp?id=2069; accessed 10 January 2012.

[20] Shaun McCarthy, Chair of the Commission for a Sustainable London 2012; *Blueprint for Change*, Foreword, July 2011, p 6.

[21] Commission for a Sustainable London 2012, *Legacy Review*, March 2012, p 38.

[22] http://www.number10.gov.uk/news/london-2012s-olympics-legacy/; accessed April 2012.

CHAPTER THREE – PLANNING AND DESIGNING THE PARK

[1] http://news.bbc.co.uk/sport2/hi/other_sports/olympics_2012/4335216.stm; accessed 24 January 2012.

[2] http://www.london2012.com/press/media-releases/2006/01/top-team-chosen-to-design-olympic-park.php; accessed 24 January 2012.

[3] http://learninglegacy.london2012.com/documents/pdfs/masterplanning-and-town-planning/157-effective-management-mptp.pdf; accessed 26 January 2012.

[4] This was achieved by an amendment to the 2007 section 106 legal agreement that accompanied the original planning approval.

[5] http://www.london2012.com/press/media-releases/2006/01/london-2012-organisers-update-olympic-park-plans.php; accessed 24 January 2012.

[6] http://www.london2012.com/news/2006/05/lower-lea-valley-regeneration-strategy-launched.php; accessed 23 January 2012.

[7] http://leariverpark.org/node/7; accessed 24 January 2012.

[8] http://webarchive.nationalarchives.gov.uk/20110118095356/http:/www.cabe.org.uk/news/london-2012-masterplan-praised; accessed 29 January 2012.

[9] Personal conversation Grayson Perry/John Hopkins; 2009.

[10] http://learninglegacy.london2012.com/documents/pdfs/masterplanning-and-town-planning/425009-350-arts-and-culture-aw.pdf; accessed July 2012.

[11] http://www.london.gov.uk/media/press_releases_mayoral/zaha-hadid-chosen-design-first-olympic-venue; accessed 18 February 2012.

[12] http://www.london2012.com/press/media-releases/2007/11/new-era-of-stadium-design-begins-with-olympic-stadium.php; accessed 28 January 2012.

[13] http://www.london2012.com/press/media-releases/2011/10/london-2012-velodrome-rides-off-with-prime-minister-s-be.php; accessed 28 January 2012.

[14] http://www.london2012.com/press/media-releases/2007/11/design-team-appointed-for-handball-arena-with-multi-sports-legacy.php; accessed 28 January 2012.

[15] http://news.bbc.co.uk/2/hi/entertainment/3257370.stm; accessed 29 January 2012.

[16] http://www.london2012.com/ibc-mpc; accessed 18 June 2012.

[17] http://www.london2012.com/news/2010/06/statement-on-olympic-park-wind-turbine.php

[18] http://www.london2012.com/press/media-releases/2007/11/design-shortlist-unveiled-for-sporting-hub-in-north-of-the-olympic-park.php; accessed 29 January 2012.

[19] http://www.london2012.com/news/2007/11/winning-team-announced-to-design-basketball-arena.php; accessed 29 January 2012.

[20] http://www.london2012.com/news/2008/09/pump-it-up.php; accessed 29 January 2012.

[21] http://www.london2012.com/news/2008/02/sustainable-substation-designs-released.php; accessed 29 January 2012.

[22] George Hargreaves, 'Large Parks: A Designer's Perspective', Chapter 4, p 121 in Julia Czerniak, George Hargreaves, John Beardsley, *Large Parks*, Princeton Architectural Press (New York), 2007.

[23] http://www.legacycompany.co.uk/winning-designers-chosen-to-create-new-public-spaces-for-london/; accessed 2 February 2012.

24 http://www.london2012.com/press/media-releases/2009/02/london-2012-parklands-get-planning-green-light.php; accessed 2 February 2012.

CHAPTER FOUR – CONSTRUCTING THE PARK

1 http://www.london2012.com/press/media-releases/2006/12/public-support-for-london-2012-higher-than-ever.php; accessed February 2012.

2 Denis Campbell, 'Revealed: the true cost of Olympics', *Observer*, 19 November 2006.

3 http://www.builderandengineer.co.uk/news/london-2012/london-olympics-faces-industrial-relations-disaster-1170.html; accessed February 2012.

4 http://www.london2012.com/press/media-releases/2007/09/partnership-agreed-on-employment-standards.php; accessed 24 February 2012.

5 http://www.bbc.co.uk/news/uk-17200835; accessed April 2012.

6 http://learninglegacy.london2012.com/themes/procurement/index.php; accessed February 2012.

7 http://www.london2012.com/press/media-releases/2006/07/oda-announces-its-procurement-policy-at-leeds-business-s.php; accessed February 2012.

8 Jackson and Bonnard, 'Delivering London 2012: environmental management', *Proceedings of Institution of Civil Engineers*, Volume 1, May 2011.

9 http://learninglegacy.london2012.com/themes/archaeology/index.php; accessed February 2012.

10 http://learninglegacy.london2012.com/publications/eradicating-invasive-weeds-during-the-construction-of-th.php'; and http://learninglegacy.london2012.com/publications/treating-japanese-knotweed-on-the-olympic-park.php; both accessed February 2012.

11 http://learninglegacy.london2012.com/publications/translocation-of-habitats-and-species-within-the-olympic.php; accessed February 2012.

12 The full story of the architecture of the Olympic Park can be found in Tom Dyckhoff, Claire Barrett, Edmund Sumner (Photographer), *The Architecture of London 2012: Vision, Design and Legacy of the Olympic and Paralympic Games*, John Wiley & Sons (Chichester), 2012.

13 http://learninglegacy.london2012.com/publications/olympic-parklands-green-infrastructure.php; accessed February 2012.

14 http://learninglegacy.london2012.com/publications/olympic-park-soil-strategy.php; accessed February 2012.

15 http://learninglegacy.london2012.com/documents/pdfs/design-and-engineering-innovation/159-soil-strategy-dei.pdf; accessed March 2012.

16 http://learninglegacy.london2012.com/documents/pdfs/design-and-engineering-innovation/279-river-edges-dei.pdf; accessed February 2012.

17 http://learninglegacy.london2012.com/publications/designing-river-edges-in-the-olympic-park.php; accessed February 2012.

18 http://learninglegacy.london2012.com/publications/the-olympic-park-bridge-abutments-and-retaining-wall-fac.php; accessed February 2012.

19 Brownfield habitat is a general term used to describe self-established vegetation that has grown up on previously developed sites.

20 http://learninglegacy.london2012.com/documents/pdfs/design-and-engineering-innovation/176-outfall-design-optimisation-dei.pdf; accessed February 2012.

21 http://learninglegacy.london2012.com/publications/the-planting-strategy-for-the-olympic-parklands.php; accessed February 2012.

22 http://learninglegacy.london2012.com/publications/promoting-biodiversity-in-the-olympic-parklands.php; February 2012.

23 http://learninglegacy.london2012.com/publications/translocation-of-habitats-and-species-within-the-olympic.php; p 6; accessed March 2012.

24 http://learninglegacy.london2012.com/documents/pdfs/design-and-engineering-innovation/163-integrating-trees-and-utilities-dei.pdf; accessed February 2012.

25 Nigel Dunnett and James Hitchmough, eds, *The Dynamic Landscape: design, ecology and management of naturalistic urban planting*, Spon Press (London and New York), 2004.

26 http://learninglegacy.london2012.com/publications/the-planting-strategy-for-the-olympic-parklands.php; p 7; accessed March 2012.

27 William Robinson, with new chapters and photographs by Rick Darke, *The Wild Garden*, Timber Press Inc. (Portland, Oregon and London), 2009.

28 Tim Richardson, 'The Olympic Park and other top gardening news for 2012', *Telegraph*, 19 December 2011; http://www.telegraph.co.uk/gardening/8966661/The-Olympic-Park-and-other-top-gardening-news-for-2012.html; accessed March 2012.

29 http://learninglegacy.london2012.com/publications/ensuring-quality-construction-for-the-olympic-park.php; accessed March 2012.

30 http://learninglegacy.london2012.com/publications/the-olympic-park-management-and-maintenance-plan.php; accessed February 2012.

31 http://www.london2012.com/publications/building-the-olympic-park-2005-11-part-one.php; accessed February 102.

CHAPTER FIVE – A WALK IN THE PARK

[1] http://www.thisislondon.co.uk/business/westfield-has-23m-visitors-in-first-year-6474240.html

[2] http://greatlengths2012.org.uk/freeze-frame-project/freeze-frame/; accessed March 2012.

[3] http://learninglegacy.london2012.com/; accessed March 2012.

[4] Interview with Jason Prior and Bill Hanway; pp 46–7.

[5] Interview with the landscape engineers; pp 190–3.

[6] Simon Barnes 'Why the Games are a great choice to go wild' *The Times*, 27 August 2011.

[7] Ibid.

[8] Peter Neal and John Hopkins, 'The Search for a Creative Way Forward' in Sheila Harvey, Ken Fieldhouse and John Hopkins, eds, *The Cultured Landscape: Designing the environment in the 21st century*, Routledge (Abingdon and New York), 2005, p 166.

[9] Ibid, p 170.

INDEX

Figures in italics refer to captions.

PICTURE CREDITS

The author and the publisher gratefully acknowledge the people who gave their permission to reproduce material in this book. While every effort has been made to contact copyright holders for their permission to reprint material, the publishers would be grateful to hear from any copyright holder who is not acknowledged here and will undertake to rectify any errors or omissions in future editions.

Front cover image © Peter Neal

Background back cover and flap image © LOCOG/Anthony Charlton

Three back cover inset images © ODA/Anthony Charlton

t – top, b – bottom, l – left, r – right, c- centre

p 2 © ODA/Anthony Charlton
p 6 © Jeff J Mitchell/Getty Images
pp 8-9 © Edward Denison
pp 12-13 © Peter Neal
p 15 © Adrian Dennis/AFP/Getty Images
pp 16, 17 © ODA/AECOM
p 18, 31 Courtesy of London Development Agency
pp 22-23 © Peter Neal
p 25 (l) Hargreaves Associates (r) © Franz-Marc Frei/Corbis
p 26 © Anthony Palmer
p 27 ©Peter Neal
p 29 © Anthony Palmer
p 32 © GLA Planning Decisions Unit
p 34 © Anthony Palmer
p 35 (tl) © ODA, (tr) & (bl) © LDA/AECOM, (br) © Peter Neal
p 36 (l) © Reuters/Darren Whiteside, (c) © ODA/David Cowlard, (r) © ODA/Steve Bates
p 37 © LDA/AECOM
p 38 © GLA Planning Decisions Unit
p 39 © Farrells
p 40 (l & r) © ODA/LDA Design. Hargreaves Associates
p 41 © GLA Planning Decisions Unit
p 42 © GLA Planning Decisions Unit
p 44 © BioRegional
p 45 © London 2012
p 47 © ODA/AECOM
p 48 © ODA/AECOM
p 50 © London 2012
pp 52-53 © London 2012
pp 54-55 © London 2012
p 56 © London 2012
p 57 © London 2012
p 58 © London 2012
pp 60-61 © Peter Neal
p 63 © ODA/David Poultney
p 64 © ODA
p 65 © ODA/David Poultney
p 66 (l) © ODA, (r) © ODA/Anthony Charlton
p 67 © ODA/John Zammit
pp 68-69 © ODA/Anthony Charlton
p 70 © ODA
p 71 Source National Audit Office Report on: Preparations

for the London 2012 Olympic and Paralympic Games - Risk assessment and management HC 252 2006-07.
p 72 © ODA
p 73 © ODA
p 75 © ODA
p 76 (l & r) © ODA
p 77 (l & r) © ODA
p 80 (r) © ODA/David Poultney, (l) © ODA/Steve Bates
p 81 © ODA/Anthony Charlton
p 82 © ODA/Anthony Charlton
p 85 © ODA
p 86 © LOCOG
pp 88-89 © ODA/David Poultney
p 90 © ODA
p 91 © ODA/David Poultney
p 92 © ODA/David Poultney
pp 94-95 © ODA/Anthony Charlton
p 96 © ODA/Anthony Charlton
pp 98-99 (t & b) © ODA/Anthony Charlton
pp 100-101 (t & b) © ODA/Anthony Charlton
pp 102-103 (t & b) © ODA/Anthony Charlton
pp 104-105 © Peter Neal
p 108 © ODA/AECOM
p 109 © ODA/AECOM
p 111 © ODA/LDA Design. Hargreaves Associates
p 113 Courtesy London Legacy Development Corporation/ Allies & Morrison
p 115 © ODA/Steve Bates
p 116 © ODA/LDA Design. Hargreaves Associates
p 117 © ODA/Anthony Charlton
p 118 © ODA/Anthony Charlton
p 119 © ODA/Anthony Charlton
p 120 © ODA
p 121 © ODA/David Poultney
p 122 © ODA/David Poultney
p 123 © ODA/Anthony Charlton
p 124 © ODA/Anthony Charlton
p 126 (t & b) © ODA/Anthony Charlton
p 127 © ODA/Anthony Charlton
p 128 © ODA/Anthony Charlton
p 129 © ODA/Anthony Charlton
p 131 © Phil Askew
p 132 © ODA/Anthony Charlton
p 133 © Anthony Palmer
pp 134-135 © ODA/David Poultney
p 137 © ODA/LDA Design. Hargreaves Associates
p 140 © ODA/LDA Design. Hargreaves Associates
p 141 © Edward Denison
p 142 © Anthony Palmer